Niet

Gudrun von Tevenar (ed.)

Nietzsche and Ethics

PETER LANG

Oxford · Bern · Berlin · Bruxelles · Frankfurt am Main · New York · Wien

Bibliographic information published by Die Deutsche Bibliothek
Die Deutsche Bibliothek lists this publication in the Deutsche
Nationalbibliografie; detailed bibliographic data is available on
the Internet at ‹http://dnb.ddb.de›.

British Library and Library of Congress Cataloguing-in-Publication Data:
A catalogue record for this book is available from The British Library,
Great Britain, and from The Library of Congress, USA

ISBN 978-3-03-911045-2

© Peter Lang AG, International Academic Publishers, Bern 2007
Hochfeldstrasse 32, Postfach 746, CH-3000 Bern 9, Switzerland
info@peterlang.com, www.peterlang.com, www.peterlang.net

Printed in Germany

Contents

GUDRUN VON TEVENAR

Introduction

This anthology is a collection of papers, some revised and extended, originally given at the 'Nietzsche and Ethics' Conference organized by the Friedrich Nietzsche Society, UK, in September 2004 at the University of Sussex in Brighton, UK. It is, I believe, an excellent collection and I would like to take this opportunity to thank all the contributors, the publishers Peter Lang AG, and Daniel Came who initially started this enterprise with me merely extending and completing it.

Most scholars agree that Nietzsche is a moral philosopher of great importance, although some might still complain that he has not as yet received the full recognition and distinction he deserves. But when it comes to agreeing what precisely his moral philosophy consists in, other than its novel and controversial nature, the conclusions of scholars often diverge. Yet in the case of Nietzsche such divergent interpretations are only to be expected, and, as anyone familiar with his thought will readily appreciate, Nietzsche himself would have taken conflicting interpretations as an entirely positive sign of the fact that his thoughts were receiving the kind of attention he deemed appropriate to them. For Nietzsche never intended that the questions and problems he raised, and the solutions, or groups of solutions, he offered, were of a kind suitable for neat and convenient academic pigeonholes. He feared that, once pigeonholed, his thought would inevitably lose its controversial and uncomfortable edge and with it its ability to disturb and to arouse conflict and opposition. For only by way of testing, opposing, conflicting again and again with what is settled, accepted, and comfortable could the kind of progress Nietzsche believed necessary get started. Thus it follows that any enquiry into

Nietzsche's moral philosophy must be open minded if it is to be profitable; indeed, it can only be profitable if it is open minded.

The essays collected in this volume are the result of ongoing debates
about and research into Nietzsche's ethical thought by contemporary
philosophers. Thus they are an excellent reflection of current international scholarship. In what follows a brief introduction will be given
to each essay; not by way of a summary as this would inevitably lead
to oversimplification of the rich argumentative detail of scholarly
works, but rather by selection of representative points or topics.

The first essay is by Ken Gemes. As the title suggests, it investigates
what it is to be an agent by Nietzsche's standards and what value or
otherwise we are to assign to the scientific spirit and its will to truth.
Gemes' paper has a number of interesting and illuminating themes,
one of which is his examination of Nietzsche's intriguing claim, made
in the preface to the *Genealogy of Morals*, that we are 'strangers to
ourselves'. Gemes shows that being strangers to ourselves is not simply just a lack of self-knowledge, since lack of knowledge could easily
be rectified, in theory at least. The problem is, rather, one of self-
estrangement in as much as we fall apart or splinter, so Nietzsche
claims, into a multiplicity of separate and competing drives and
affects that have no coherent connection with each other. We are
therefore unable to achieve the kind of integrated unity by way of
hierarchically ordered drives which, according to Nietzsche, is a
necessary precondition for genuine agency. So the problem is not so
much that we *are strangers to ourselves*, but that we *have strangers
within ourselves*. Hence we are the weak, disconnected, fragmented
beings who are tossed about by our diverse and usually conflicting
drives and affects. And because we have not imposed an organizing
and unifying hierarchical structure on these conflicting drives, we
have, therefore, no genuine selfhood, are without autonomy and are,
hence, unable to pass Nietzsche's ethical test of 'making promises'.
Genuine selves and genuine agents, on the other hand (those who
Nietzsche recognizes as 'sovereign individuals'), have achieved their
selfhood precisely by imposing on themselves the required unifying
hierarchy. Only when thus unified and integrated can agents be

deemed to have free will and autonomy and thus to be able to stand surety for themselves by way of 'making promises'.

The next two essays concern the extremely difficult question what a positive Nietzschean ethics is about. Their authors, Robert Guay and Edward Harcourt, start from very similar basic statements: Guay states that Nietzsche is 'less concerned with establishing the truth or warrant of a theoretical position than with prescribing or possibly even trans-forming how life is to be led'; while Harcourt argues that both Nietzsche (and the neo-Aristotelians) start with the same central ques-tion, which is 'not "what makes an action the morally right one?" but rather "what sort of life would be good for us?"' However, they arrive at utterly different conclusions: Guay argues that while it is difficult to ascertain any substantive ethical position in Nietzsche, his immoral-ism could, possibly, come near to that position, with Harcourt arguing, by contrast, that Nietzsche is an eudaemonist.

After explaining why immoralism is an extension rather than an antithesis to moralism, and thus why it has a rightful place within moral discourse, Guay guides us around various objections Nietzsche lodges against moralism and its alleged normativity by way of its claims to objectivity and universality. For instance, claims to object-ivity are dismissed by Nietzsche as leading to 'un-selfing' and thus to negative consequences for life; while claims to universality are merely attempts to be *wissenschaftlich* (scientific) and thus quite unsuitable for the kinds of practical demands and guidance that are required from an ethical position responsive to how our lives should be lived. Trad-itional moralities should be dislodged, Nietzsche claims, precisely because they tend to be discontinuous and unresponsive to our prac-tical concerns, which usually transcend goodness of character, adher-ence to principle, and general welfare. Thus Guay concludes that the ultimate ethical concerns expressed in Nietzsche's immoralism are neither with truth or falsehood nor with goodness, but with making sense of life, with our engagements in the here and now of life, and with the meaning life has for us.

Harcourt defends his claim for Nietzsche's eudaemonism by drawing attention to the similarity in the respective starting positions of Aristotle (and neo-Aristotelians) and Nietzsche in their seemingly

common concern as to what is conducive to a flourishing human life
given human beings natural capacities and limitations. And to specify
human flourishing as the ultimate ethical goal is precisely to be an
eudaemonist. Nietzsche's well-known disregard for happiness cannot
be accepted as a valid objection to this conclusion, Harcourt argues,
since it all depends what one understands under happiness or flourishing. Thus, while the famous question 'how should I live?' is the same
for virtue ethics and Nietzsche, the answers are different. One of the
differences is best explained by their respective attitudes to internal
conflict: virtue ethics aims for the unity of virtues, where contrary
impulses are rejected or silenced so that the various virtues can co-
operate in perfect harmony. Not so for Nietzsche. Internal conflict
should not be avoided, he claims; to the contrary, it should be man-
aged and even celebrated, since to be subject to competing and conflicting impulses and drives is simply part of our nature, something to
be accepted, not rejected.

Given that, according to Nietzsche, there are no 'moral facts' so that
all so-called moral facts must be reducible to natural facts, how does
this process actually work? How do natural facts become moral
values? Robin Small provides one possible answer in the fourth essay
of this collection where he investigates Nietzsche's evolutionary ethics.
Small distinguishes Nietzsche's evolutionary theory from others current at this time, particularly the theories of Darwin and of Nietzsche's
contemporary and one time friend, Paul Rée. These differences can
best be demonstrated with the example of altruism. Altruism, it is
claimed, evolved because altruistic behaviour between members of a
group benefits that group though it is acknowledged that it can be to
the disadvantage to the altruistic individual. Now, this would obviously not sit well with Nietzsche who champions the individual. Small
shows that one way Nietzsche can discredit the group selection
scheme while yet staying within evolutionary theory is to challenge
one of evolutionary theory's traditional claims, namely, that what
drives natural selection is 'the will to live' and 'the will to reproduce'.
Nietzsche replaced these with 'the will to power'. This replacement
has a great advantage in the eyes of Nietzsche: while will to power is
just as competitive as the will to live and reproduce, it has, in contrast

to these, the highly desirable result of favouring the individual rather than the group. Thus will to power enables Nietzsche to stay within evolutionary theory's claim of selection via competition, yet modifies the evolutionary process to benefit exceptional individuals rather than groups.

Staying within the theme of will to power, Henry Staten takes issue with the view, most forcefully expressed by Leiter, that consciousness is merely a passive observer of the internal conflicts and competitions amongst drives where will to power exemplifies itself in that the strongest drive always wins. Yet if that is indeed the case, if consciousness is really merely epiphenomenal, then what precisely is the point of any conscious striving to affect change such as Nietzsche is engaged in when he urges us to grow, to overcome, to change? Staten proposes a scheme whereby the relation between thought and drives, i.e. between consciousness and unconsciousness, is credited as open to the determinations and historical sedimentations of cultural and sociological forms. And because thought is internally structured by cultural and sociological forms, it has a certain independence from drives, which Staten describes as 'semi-autonomy'. Thought can thus be taken as constitutive of a distinctive kind of causality. Staten develops this theory with the concept of techne. When one understands techne as a set of 'typed pathways' incorporated into the nerves, muscles, and neurons of a person (*not* a mere human organism) by habituation and thereby encoding the know-how of acquired social, cultural, and bodily practices, then one can see how the habitual skills of techne, as products of socially acquired resources engaged with drives, can function in a way as to blur the distinction between consciousness and unconsciousness. Indeed, the inappropriateness of this distinction in some cases comes instantly to mind when observing the performance of a techne in action, such as, for instance, in the playing of an accomplished pianist, where all of a person's drives, muscles, memory, culturally induced values, and so on, are engaged as a seamless whole. Thus, with the concept of techne Staten has expanded our view of drive-systems to include socially and culturally informed thought.

One of Nietzsche's abiding themes throughout his philosophically productive life was the requirement of human beings to 'overcome' their current values and thus to create conditions for the emergence of new values and higher forms of life. In the sixth essay, Herman Siemens claims that the problem of how to overcome old, and therefore perhaps obsolete or decadent, values occupied Nietzsche already in his early work, *The Birth of Tragedy*, with its critical probing of Socrates and Socratic values. Siemens shows that in *BT* the process of 'overcoming values' (a process whereby values are changed not by repression or obliteration but by *transformation* or *transvaluation*), takes place within the context of *agon*. *Agon* is a concept derived form ancient Greek culture where it designates competition, contest, confrontation, struggle. *Agon* is thus a performance of some kind. And a performance is needed, so Siemens argues, if Nietzsche is to break out of a purely theoretical discourse. A purely theoretical discourse is insufficient for 'overcoming', according to Siemens, because genuine transvaluation demands not just new values but also new ways of evaluating. We are guided by Siemens through the very interesting process of an overcoming modelled on *agon* by a close and comparative reading of some key passages of Plato's *Phaedo* and *BT*.

Anyone acquainted with Nietzsche's all too numerous negative outbursts concerning women might be forgiven for believing that Nietzsche has nothing positive to offer to feminists. However, matters are more complicated than that as Carol Diethe amply demonstrates. Diethe reminds us that Nietzsche, in line with his critique of Christian ethics generally, also criticized the guilt and sin heaped on all natural and especially sexual matters. Yet Nietzsche's attitude to sexual ethics is not consistent and remains ambiguous throughout. While he granted women equal rights to sexual enjoyment, he also maintained that the two sexes were fundamentally antagonistic to each other because they love differently. Women, Nietzsche states, are 'given' in their love and, if not directed towards the having of children, should almost be in prison so great is their degeneration! With a wealth of historical detail, Diethe describes how Nietzsche's sexual ethics inspired quite diverse movements. Amongst them are the '*Kosmiker*', founded in 1897, who emphasized the Dionysian aspect of rapturous sexuality and practiced free love with careful avoidance of the misogyny prevalent at that time. Then there is the eugenics movement following, perhaps, Zarathustra's call for the *Übermensch*. And then, of course, there is Lou Salomé. Diethe demonstrates that Salomé, though agreeing with Nietzsche on many points, also maintained her own quite distinctive stance on sexuality in theory and in practice.

In the eighth essay James Wilson takes those of today's Nietzsche scholars to task who are either blind to, or downplay and sidestep, the less palatable or even highly problematic aspects of Nietzsche's ethical philosophy. Wilson urges us to see in Nietzsche an *opponent* in moral matters notwithstanding his acknowledged brilliance as a moral thinker. To bring home his point, Wilson uses the example of equality. It is undisputed that Nietzsche rejected equality amongst human beings and, according to Wilson, he argues for this position in two ways. The first argument is negative and proceeds from resentment which Nietzsche claims underlies all forms of slave morality and thus, arguably, also our own. Here whatever is great, powerful, mighty, is rejected and equality is promoted simply from a resentful denial of the great and outstanding. This is the 'morality of denial' argument. Nietzsche's second, positive, argument holds that 'the pathos of distance' between the higher and the lower is simply a necessary requirement for human greatness. Wilson refutes both arguments and concludes with the claim that Nietzsche's defense of inequality is not a tenable ethical position to hold, not for ordinary agents and not for philosophers either.

The next two essays, by Rebecca Bamford and myself, have the common theme of Nietzsche's attitude towards *Mitleid*, or pity and compassion. Similarly to Wilson above regarding equality, Bamford raises the issue that Nietzsche's highly critical attitude towards *Mitleid* lays him open to the charge of practical cruelty and failure to abhor human suffering, and that he may therefore be considered to be fairly close to moral bankruptcy. But, unlike Wilson, Bamford rejects these charges and defends Nietzsche's position. She takes a multiple approach in this defense, one of which is the episode with the 'Ugliest Man' in the fourth book of *Zarathustra*. Bamford's reading of this episode relies strongly on her thesis that sufferers, when pleading for *Mitleid*, aim to appropriate pitying agents and to render them passive. On meeting the Ugliest Man for the first time, Zarathustra's initial reaction is one of shame which subsequently turns into a temptation to *Mitleid*. He thus becomes vulnerable to slide from activity into passivity. However, Zarathustra is saved by the very strength of his initial shame (which both Bamford and the Ugliest Man claim is preferable to *Mitleid*), and this enables him to proceed from shame to benevolence by advising the Ugliest Man to follow the road upwards to his cave. Bamford concludes that Zarathustra's capacity for honesty, benevolence, and, above all, shame, allows us to admire him and his rejection of *Mitleid* as virtuous.

My own reading of *Mitleid* in the tenth essay is not in conflict with Bamford's conclusion. I emphasize that the single German word '*Mitleid*' tends to obscure the difference in content of the concepts of pity and compassion. Once this difference is clear, one can readily agree with most of Nietzsche's objections to pity and accept them as well-founded, while keeping on open and/or critical attitude towards Nietzsche's objections to compassion which he calls 'great *Mitleid*'. Nietzsche rejects compassion or 'great *Mitleid*' not because of the much rehearsed objections of insincere motivations or because it alienates and humiliates recipients, but because of the detrimental effects compassion is alleged to have on its givers in as much as it tempts them to succumb to deep sadness and, more dangerous still, to an urge to identify with sufferers. But succumbing to these temptations of 'great *Mitleid*' will eventually, Nietzsche claims, undermine the compassionate agent's self-affirmation as well as her affirmation of life. And, considering that Nietzsche's most abiding ethical goal is affirmation of life and self, it follows that for Nietzsche compassion is a far greater danger than pity.

The eleventh and last essay by Thomas Brobjer helps us towards that very difficult to achieve overview of Nietzsche's ethical thinking by providing us with a detailed account of Nietzsche's development in this area using the direct testimony of Nietzsche's letters and notes as well as statements in his published works. Brobjer divides Nietzsche's development into five periods, starting with an early religious period, followed by adherence to *Mitleids-Moral* inspired by Schopenhauer, and finishing with his mature position of immoralism. It is extremely interesting to witness Nietzsche's progression through almost all conceivable ethical positions, due to the fact that Brobjer provides us with a background setting of those of Nietzsche's ethical preoccupations which have remained more or less constant throughout his life. There is, firstly, the constant presence of a more or less explicit amoralism in his ethical thinking, already detectable during the religious period of his youth. Secondly, there is an abiding attachment to Greek antiquity and the heroic stance, and thirdly we have Nietzsche's constant emphasis on overcoming, particularly self-overcoming (*Selbstüberwindung*). It is surely not too daring to suggest that Nietzsche's ethical development is probably best seen as a kind of development fired and sustained by his own call to self-overcoming.

List of Abbreviations

A   The Antichrist / *Der Antichrist*

AOM   Assorted Opinions and Maxims / *Vermischte Meinungen und Sprüche* (HH part II)

BGE   Beyond Good and Evil / *Jenseits von Gut und Böse*

BT   The Birth of Tragedy / *Die Geburt der Tragödie*

CW   The Case of Wagner / *Der Fall Wagner*

D   Daybreak or Dawn / *Morgenröte*

EH   Ecce Homo / *Ecce Homo*

GM   On the Genealogy of Morals / *Zur Genealogie der Moral*

GS   Gay Science or Joyful Wisdom / *Die Fröhliche Wissenschaft*

HH   Human, All Too Human / *Menschliches, Allzumenschliches*

NCW Nietzsche contra Wagner / *Nietzsche contra Wagner*

TI   Twilight of the Idols / *Götzen–Dämmerung*

TL   On Truth and Lie in the Non-Moral Sense / *Über Wahrheit und Lüge im aussermoralischen Sinne*

UM   Untimely Meditations / *Unzeitgemässe Betrachtungen*

WP   The Will to Power / *Der Wille zur Macht*

WS   The Wanderer and his Shadow / *Der Wanderer und sein Schatten* (HH part II)

Z   Thus Spoke Zarathustra / *Also Sprach Zarathustra*

KGW Kritische Gesamtausgabe: Werke

KGB Kritische Gesamtausgabe: Briefe

KSA Kritische Studienausgabe

KEN GEMES

Nietzsche on The Will to Truth, The Scientific Spirit, Free Will, and Genuine Selfhood

Nietzsche's *On the Genealogy of Morals* contains many striking claims. Perhaps most striking is the claim that the scientific spirit's will to truth is the last expression of the ascetic ideal. What could Nietzsche mean by this extraordinary claim? Before answering this question we need to identify the most general aim of the *Genealogy*. It is important to unravel Nietzsche's general aim because the polemical and rhetorical subtlety of the *Genealogy* often allows, indeed deliberately cajoles, the reader into comforting but mistaken notions of Nietzsche's objective. This typically leads to superficial interpretations of such fundamental claims as that the will to truth is an expression of the ascetic ideal. Only when we have recognized his ultimate polemical aim are we properly equipped to interpret the full meaning and force of such claims. However, because Nietzsche employs a strategy of deliberate misdirection, in order to properly understand his aim it is important to analyze his strategy for achieving it. In the first part of this essay (sections 1 and 2 below), after first expounding what I take to be Nietzsche's central strategy and aim in the *Genealogy*, I seek to elucidate some of his central claims about the will to truth. It is my general contention that the real target of Nietzsche's polemic only comes explicitly into view when he comes, in the third essay, to make his extraordinary claims about the will to truth and science. That target is us, his readers. Nietzsche argues that our will to truth actually functions as a tool to repress and split off part of our nature. The second part of the essay (sections 3 and 4 below) deals with Nietzsche's account of the sovereign individual and his related, novel, account of free will. Both these accounts hinge on the notion of the self as an integrated whole. It is argued that, in contrasting the integrated sovereign individual, who has genuine free will, and we splintered moderns, who are the mere playthings of a myriad of disparate influences, Nietzsche aims to unsettle us with uncanny suggestions that we have no genuine selves. For Nietzsche, we are strangers to ourselves not just in the sense that we lack knowledge about our deeper motivations, but in the more profound sense that we are estranged from ourselves in that we contain drives and affects that are split of from each other. Instead of a unified whole we moderns are but a jumbled congery of competing drives. In the third part of this essay (section 5 below) it is shown that the invocation of the uncanny is actually a central strategy Nietzsche uses to bring home to us his disturbing message that we splintered moderns are strangers to ourselves.

Part I

1. A Strategy of Misdirection

In the first section of his preface to the *Genealogy* Nietzsche tells his readers, that we are 'strangers to ourselves'. This beautiful and uncanny phrase is an echo of the very first line of the preface;

> We are unknown to ourselves, we knowers: and for a good reason.

Of course, in his typical elliptical fashion, Nietzsche does not tell us what that good reason is.[1] Indeed, the whole theme of our being strangers to ourselves is quickly and quietly dropped. Nietzsche, in the second section of the preface, brings up what is ostensibly the focus of the *Genealogy*, the question of the origins of our morality – as Nietzsche says, 'that is what this polemic is about' [GM, Preface, 2]. Certainly the first essay, with its main theme of the triumph of Judaeo-Christian slave morality over the Greek/Roman master morality, seems to bear out the claim that his polemic is about the origins of morality.[2] And, to take us further from the opening claim that we are strangers to

ourselves, Nietzsche suggests in the first essay, and explicitly emphasizes in the second, that showing the origins of something tells us little
if anything about its current purpose and value.

But if that is so, then, how can Nietzsche's aim be to show us
that we are strangers to ourselves? How can the *Genealogy* be about
who we are, when it is telling us mainly about our ancestors? To see
the solution to the problem we must realize that the *Genealogy*, like so
many of Nietzsche's texts, divides into a manifest and a latent content.
Nietzsche cannot afford to be too explicit about that latent content because it is challenging and terrifying, striking at the very centre of our
self-conception. Like a clever psychoanalyst, he knows that a direct
approach will merely awaken the patient's/reader's defences and provoke a reflex denial and a refusal to countenance his message. Moreover, Nietzsche believes that mere intellectual knowledge can often
work against deeper forms of realization that are necessary for genuine change. Nietzsche, educated by Schopenhauer, regarded consciousness as being a rather shallow phenomenon, almost to the point
of dismissing it as epiphenomenal. Prefiguring Freud, he claimed that
for ideas to be truly effective they must work on us at a level below
consciousness. Thus, in the *Genealogy*, he chooses to approach his
aim obliquely. He starts at some distance from us, with our ancestors
and even suggests that his examination of them does not have direct
and immediate consequences for us. But, in fact, Nietzsche is talking
about us, first indirectly and later directly. He is telling us deeply disturbing and momentous truth about ourselves, though we may not at
first recognize that we are the subjects who are being damned in his
polemic. That such indirection is the method of the *Genealogy* is
something Nietzsche himself claims in *Ecce Homo*:

> Every time a beginning that is calculated to mislead [...]. Gradually [...] very
> disagreeable truths are heard grumbling in the distance. [EH, *Genealogy of
> Morals* A Polemic]

We are for Nietzsche strangers to ourselves for the very good
reason that to face who we are is a challenge requiring momentous
courage, a challenge which, properly undertaken, should precipitate a
shattering struggle. But, as Nietzsche warns us in the very first section

of the preface of the *Genealogy*, such challenges provoke strong re-
sistances:

> In such matters we are never really 'with it': we just don't have our heart there
> – or even our ear.

Though, he suggests that when his true message is registered,

> we will rub our ears *afterwards* and ask completely amazed, completely dis-
> concerted, 'What did we actually experience just now?' still more: 'who *are* we
> actually?' [Nietzsche's italics]

The italics here are very telling. The emphasis on 'afterwards' is an
indication of Nietzsche's belief that only after his message has slowly
snuck through our defences will we recognize what the *Genealogy* is
really about. The emphasis on 'are' is an indication that the *Genealogy*
is ultimately about who we are and not, as it might first appear, about
who our ancestors were.[3]

2. Truth and the Ascetic Ideal

What then is the kernel of Nietzsche's message that might lead us to
question who we really are? Basically, the *Genealogy* teaches that our
much prized morality, in particular, our evaluations of good and evil
(essay I), our concept of conscience (essay II), and our commitment to
truth (essay III) are all expressions of impotence and sublimated hostility. In order to get his readers to appreciate this message, Nietzsche
engages his readers' interest by using history as a means for creating a
distance between his ostensive subject, the origins of morality, and his
real subject, the sickness in our current morality. It is in section 23 of
the third essay that we find ourselves for the first time more directly
addressed. Having exposed the historical roots of our sense of morality, and sense of conscience, characterizing these as handymen to the
life-denying ascetic ideal, Nietzsche there asks if there is not a new
counter-ideal in the modern ideal of truth, objectivity and science.[4]
Here he is directly engaging his readers who identify themselves as
adhering to this modern ideal, which they take as being fundamentally

opposed to the religiously motivated ascetic ideal. Secular readers, inspired by Enlightenment ideals, have little resistance to recognizing that the religious founders of Judaeo-Christian morality were in fact inspired by hatred and envy. They see themselves as being far removed from that religious mentality. This provides the comforting 'pathos of distance' that allows the first and second essay to do their work on the reader. But in section 23 Nietzsche provides what he hopes will be a moment of self-recognition when he responds to his question about the existence of a counter-ideal by claiming that the will to truth, the will to objectivity, is not the means by which we have escaped the religious world and its associated ascetic ideal. Rather, it is, in fact, the last and most complete expression of that ideal. This is the moment when we are meant to rub our ears! How is it that we who have thrown off the crutches of superstition and religious obscurantism, who have committed ourselves to embrace the truth at any cost, and thus relinquished the comforting myth of a world to come, can be accused of participating in the ascetic ideal? As Nietzsche himself says, it is our very love of truth that has allowed us to realize the falsity behind the ascetic ideal, the hollowness of religious claims [cf. GM III, 27]. Now he relies on our love of truth to force us to recognize the true meaning of that very love. Here Nietzsche is thinking primarily as a psychologist and is looking at the latent meaning of our commitment to truth. That commitment, he maintains, stems from the same motivation that fuelled commitment to religious ascetic values, namely, fear of life and feelings of impotence.

The religious person attempts to remove himself from the torments of this world, a world that largely resists his desires, by telling himself that what happens in this life is ultimately unimportant. He tells himself that what matters is what is in his soul, which will determine his real, eternal, life in the world to come. The modern scholar similarly removes himself from life by telling himself that what is of ultimate value is not acting in this world, not what he does, but in understanding the world, in what he knows. Both the religious ascetic and the ascetic scholar believe 'the truth will set you free'. Nietzsche has realized that here to be free means to be free of the pull of this world, the tumult of earthly passions and desires. Just as the ascetic ideal demands suppression of the passions, so the scholar's emphasis

on objectivity and truth demands 'the emotions cooled' [GM III, 25].
Where the religious take revenge upon the world by denying that it is
of ultimate importance, the scholar revenges himself by saying that
passive understanding is of greater value than 'mere' action. The
Enlightener values reasons and reasonable belief and is suspicious of
passions and unreasoned desire. But life, at least genuine life, ultimately is a world of passions and desires. Thus, claims Nietzsche, (the
pursuit of) science can act as a means of withdrawal from the world:

> Science as a means of self-anaesthetisation: *are you acquainted with that?*
> [*Genealogy* III, 24 – Nietzsche's italics]

Indeed, Nietzsche had in earlier works already claimed that such
repression of passions, as exhibited in the scholar, is part of a death
drive. In *The Gay Science*, in a passage that Nietzsche explicitly dir-
ects us to in section 28 of the third essay of the *Genealogy*, he characterizes the will not to be deceived as something that might be

> a principle hostile to life and destructive – 'Will to truth' – that can be a hidden
> will to death. [GS 344]

In the same place he tell us

> those who are truthful in the audacious and ultimate sense that is presupposed
> by the faith in science *thus affirm another world* than the world of life, nature,
> and history. [Nietzsche's italics]

These thoughts Nietzsche first fully thematized in his early work
the *Untimely Meditations*. There, in the second essay, 'On the Advantages and Disadvantages of History for Life', he characterizes 'the
scholar, the man of science' as one who 'stands aside from life so as
to know it unobstructedly' [UM II, 10]. Focusing on the use of history, Nietzsche contrasts his demand that we use history for 'life and
action' with the scholar's use of history for the ends of 'easy withdrawal from life and action' [UM II, Foreword]. Nietzsche pictures
'the historical virtuoso of the present day' as 'a passive sounding
board' whose tone and message 'lulls us and makes us tame spectators' [UM II, 6]. It is the desire to stand aside from life that links the
scholar and the priest as practitioners of the ascetic ideal. In the

'Advantages and Disadvantages' essay Nietzsche uses metaphors of mirroring, castration and impotence to capture the passivity of the scholar, and, in particular, the historian. These metaphors Nietzsche repeats throughout his corpus in order to emphasize the same point. In the 'Advantages and Disadvantages' essay he ask the rhetorical question

> [o]r is it selflessness when the historical man lets himself be blown into an objective mirror? [UM II, 8, my translation]

In the same essay Nietzsche asserts that the scholar's ideal of pure objectivity would characterise 'a race of eunuchs'. [UM II, 5][5]

In *Beyond Good and Evil* 207 Nietzsche again captures the element of passivity and otherworldliness behind the exorbitant overvaluation of truth and objectivity by referring to 'the objective person [...] the ideal scholar' as

> a mirror: he is accustomed to submitting before whatever wants to be known, without any other pleasure than that found in knowing and 'mirroring'.

Later, in the same section, he refers to the scholar as a 'mirror soul, eternally smoothing itself out'. These are themes that are also repeated in *Thus Spoke Zarathustra* in the sections 'Of Immaculate Perception' and 'Of Scholars'. In the first of these sections Zarathustra characterizes those who seek 'pure knowledge' as hypocrites, on the grounds that while they are men of earthly lusts they have 'been persuaded to contempt of the earthly'. Again, Nietzsche has recourse to the metaphor of passive mirroring, when he expresses the voice of those seekers of pure knowledge as follows:

> For me the highest thing would be to gaze at life without desire [...] I desire nothing of things, except that I may lie down before them like a mirror with a hundred eyes.

He also repeats the metaphors of impotence and castration in that same section when those who seek pure knowledge are told,

> [t]ruly you do not love the earth as creators, begetters [...]. But now your emasculated leering wants to be called 'contemplation'!

The metaphor of the scholar as mirror is also used in the *Genealogy*. There, in describing modern historiography, which he characterizes as being 'to a high degree ascetic' and 'to a still higher degree nihilistic', Nietzsche says modern historiography's '[n]oblest claim is that it is a mirror' [GM III, 26].[6] In the same section there are multiple metaphors of castration and impotence. For instance, Nietzsche, with a side reference to the famous historian Renan, characterizes certain 'objective' 'armchair' 'contemplatives' in terms of their

> cowardly contemplativeness, the lecherous eunuchry, in the face of history, the making eyes as ascetic ideas, the justice-Tartuffery of impotence! [GM III, 26]

The core of Nietzsche's objection to both the ascetic ideal and its last incarnation, the will to truth, as exhibited most extremely in the scholar, is that they both are a symptom of, and caused by, an 'aversion to life' [GM III, 28].

The world is a hostile place that resists most or our desires – this is a thesis Nietzsche shares with Freud and Schopenhauer.[7] Most people, weak people, in the face of this resistance become scared of the world. They seek to turn away from it. The religious turn away by saying this world does not count, what counts is the world to come. The scholars turn away by saying that acting in the world is less valuable than standing back from the world, contemplating, understanding, and knowing it. As Nietzsche's Zarathustra puts it, 'they want to be mere spectators' [Z II, Of Scholars]. Both take, and try to justify, an essentially passive stance towards the world. They are passive because they are weak and scared, but they dress their passivity up as a virtue and a choice. Nietzsche values the (pre-Socratic) Greeks because they understood that life is essentially, and inevitably, painful, but they still had the strength to affirm it and act decisively, even horribly – think of Medea's terrible revenge in the face of Creon's dispossession of her.[8] The Christian and modern men, in particular scholars, still are fundamentally obsessed with escaping the pain of this life, '*the absence of suffering* – this may count as the highest good' for them, hence their valorization of passivity [GM III, 17].[9] Since all doing inevitably involves (the risk of) pain they seek to avoid doing, hence their valorization of being over becoming.[10] Nietzsche repeatedly uses the metaphors of mirroring, castration and impotence to viscerally bring home the degree of this passivity. He is a philosopher who, more than most, uses metaphor as a marker of significance. The repetition is also a clear marker of the importance Nietzsche attaches to this theme.[11]

Does the fact that Nietzsche attacks the will to truth because it is a manifestation of a passive attitude towards life, coupled with the fact that Nietzsche sees himself as the great advocate of life, entail that he condemns the will to truth unconditionally? That would be surprising for a philosopher who so often condemns the unconditional. Perhaps, then, his objection is to the elevation of truth to an end in itself. There is something to this but it misses the focus of Nietzsche's objection. When Nietzsche objects to a thing, for example religion or the will to truth, it is important to place that thing in its relevant context. The point here, one often made by Nietzsche himself, is that something that is dangerous, unhealthy in a given context may well be beneficial in another. Nietzsche is always a local rather than a global thinker. He will not simply condemn, for instance, the will to truth but rather will condemn it within a given context. The point is what ends does it serve in a given context. In the context of Christianity and the modern scholarly spirit he sees the will to truth as serving the purpose of slandering life. But this still leaves room for him to recognize that in other contexts, or for given individuals within a specific context, the will to truth can be a manifestation of a robust health. Thus, he clearly does not regard Goethe's prodigious curiosity and will to truth as a negative phenomenon. And surely in his own case his insight into human nature, though bought at a terrible personal cost, is not something he sees as a negative manifestation of the will to truth. It is a repeated theme in Nietzsche's corpus that the stronger a being is the more truth they can endure. It would be too facile to simply say that what separates Goethe's and Nietzsche's positive manifestation of the will to truth from the Christian's or the scholar's is that they unlike the later, do not regard truth as an end in itself. Would a typical scholar, say a postmodernist of today, who agreed that truth was no ultimate end, be any less a target of Nietzsche's polemic? And would a Goethe like figure who did indeed take truth to be the ultimate value be a fit subject for Nietzsche's attack? The will to truth in itself is not the object of Nietzsche's attack. Rather it is the will to truth in its now prevalent context of the Christian scholar's passive and negative stance towards life that Nietzsche rejects.[12]

To understand the nature of Nietzsche's complaint against the will to truth in the context of its manifestation in modern men of science, and to contrast it with the healthier will to truth exhibited by rare individuals such as Goethe and Nietzsche himself, it is helpful to return to the second of his *Untimely Meditations.*

We saw how in the *Untimely Meditations*, Nietzsche raises the objection that the modern scholar with his emphasis on objectivity becomes a merely passive mirror of the world about him. We further noted that the fact that Nietzsche so often repeats this theme attests to its importance. Another theme that Nietzsche repeats throughout the second of the *Untimely Meditations* is that the scholar, the modern man of science, falls 'wretchedly apart into inner and outer, content and form' [UM II, 4].[13] It is for this reason that 'our modern culture is not a living thing' [ibid.]. But what does this talk of inner and outer, content and form mean? Recall that Nietzsche's central objection to the scholar is that his knowledge is merely a personal, internal affair that does not express itself in outward action. The content of his knowledge does not express itself in outward forms. Inner and content for Nietzsche refers to man's internal world of thought, the outer and form refer to the external world of action. Modern man's unbridled exhortation of the will to truth facilitates his emphasis on inner content to the exclusion of outer forms. Against this splitting Nietzsche recommends that a

> higher unity in the nature of the soul of a people must again be created, that the
> breach between inner and outer must vanish. [ibid.]

Now note, this unity is exactly the characteristic that Nietzsche so often extols in Goethe and claims to have finally arrived at himself. In them the will to truth does not express itself as a stepping back from the world in order to enter an otherworldly realm of ineffectual contemplation. Rather, it is an active part of their engagement with the world. Nietzsche and Goethe possess active rather than passive knowledge. Indeed Nietzsche's 'Advantage and Disadvantages' paper, which is his most sustained attack on knowledge as a means to inactivity, begins with the following quotation from Goethe, which he tells us he fully concurs with:

> In any case I hate everything that merely instructs me without augmenting or directly invigorating my activity. [UM II, Foreword]

The importance of the notion of unity for genuine person is a theme that we will return to shortly.

The notion of knowledge as a means of withdrawal rather than engagement with the world is given a remarkable and fascinating expression in a minor theme touched on, but never fully developed, in the *Genealogy*. There, Nietzsche suggests that language itself, for both the religious ascetic and the ascetic scholar, functions as a substitute passive satisfaction for the inability to achieve direct active possession of reality. The contrast here is with a more active type (the master of the first essay) who merely uses brute force to take possession of what he desires. The more timid priests, slaves, and scholars, make do, not with direct possession of reality, but with possession of the names of things.[14] More importantly, these 'morbid cobweb-spinners', weave such a fanciful linguistic and conceptual framework around things that soon those things are lost sight of completely [TI, Reason in Philosophy, 4]. The world in which they are clearly impotent is eliminated (from view) in favour of a vast conceptual structure over which they exercise great mastery. In the first essay of the *Genealogy* Nietzsche gives a proto-theory of language acquisition that contrasts the crude language of the masters, where words are used merely as tags (we might say, their words carried denotation without connotation), with the sophisticated language of the slaves (where connotation becomes more important than denotation). Thus he characterizes the language of the masters in the following terms:

> The lordly right of giving names extends so far that one should allow oneself to conceive the origin of language itself as an expression of power on the part of the rulers: they say 'this *is* this and this', they seal every thing and event with a sound, as it were, take possession of it. [GM I, 2, Nietzsche's italics]

This notion of sealing with a sound, mere vocables, clearly suggests the emphasis on denotation over connotation, an emphasis that is heightened a few sections later:

> the concepts of ancient man were rather at first incredibly uncouth, coarse, external, narrow straightforward, and all altogether *unsymbolical* in meaning to a degree that we can scarcely conceive. [GM I, 6, Nietzsche's italics]

This 'external', 'unsymbolical', language Nietzsche then contrasts with the language of aristocratic priests which has become 'deepened, sharpened, and internalized', with the conclusion that

> [t]here is from the first something unhealthy in such priestly aristocracies and in the habits ruling them which turn away from action [...] but it is only fair to add that it is on this essentially dangerous form of human existence, the priestly form, that man first became an interesting animal, that only here did the human soul acquire depth and become evil – and these are the two basic respects in which man has hitherto been superior to other beasts! [ibid.]

The idea that language could ever be genuinely unsymbolical, and, in particular, the idea that the ancient Homeric Greeks were masters of a purely referential language is, of course, totally far-fetched. Nietzsche, a knowledgeable admirer of ancient Greece, could in no way be seriously endorsing such a claim.[15] We do better, then, to take this as a typically hyperbolic expression of a very reasonable thought, namely, the thought that the conceptual world is for the passive slave types basically a means for obliterating a reality that they resent, whereas for the active master types it is a means of working with, and celebrating, a reality over which they exercise great mastery.[16] The religious straightforwardly obliterate this world by belittling its importance in contrast to their fantasy construction of a world to come. The scholar belittles this world by valorizing the possession of knowledge and representations of it over acting in it. Both these reactions are for Nietzsche essentially life-denying.

Of course, in the *Genealogy* and elsewhere, Nietzsche's primary example of the life-denier is the Christian. For him Nietzsche reserves his strongest rhetoric;

> this entire fictional world has it roots in *hatred* of the natural (actuality!)...
> *But that explains everything.* Who alone has reason to *lie himself* out of ac-
> tuality? He who *suffers* from it. But to suffer from it means to be an abortive
> reality. [A 15, Nietzsche's italics]

Yet we should recognize here a voice not unrelated to that with which
Nietzsche chastises the scholar in the passages quoted above. This talk
of abortive reality is of a piece with his rhetorical question in the
Untimely Meditations concerning the current age of 'universal education':

> Are there still human beings, one then asks oneself, or perhaps only thinking-
> writing-, and speaking-machines. [UM II, 5]

There are, indeed, vast differences in the way Nietzsche regards
the scholar and the Christian. In the latter he sees only forces inimical
to life. In the former and his objective spirit he sees much that is useful and for which we should be grateful [cf. BGE 207]. After all, it is
the scholar, with his will to truth, who helps us see through the fabri-
cations of religion. But for Nietzsche

> [t]he objective man is an instrument [...] he is no goal, no conclusion and
> sunrise. [BGE 207]

His essential passivity toward the world means that

> [w]hatever still remains in him of a 'person' strikes him as accidental, often
> arbitrary, still more disturbing; to such an extent he has become a passageway
> and reflection of strange forms and events even to himself. [ibid.]

This enigmatic talk of being a passageway to strange forms and
events, of the arbitrary and the accidental, hints at some profound
sense of alienation. But what exactly this involves is not thematized in
Beyond Good and Evil. To get a better understanding of what is at
stake here we do well to return to the *Genealogy*.

Part II

3. Accidental, Arbitrary Moderns vs. The Sovereign Individual

When Nietzsche says in the preface to the *Genealogy* that we are
strangers to ourselves, that we are unknown to ourselves, it is tempting to take this estrangement as merely a matter of our lack of self-
knowledge. But then we must ask the question why exactly this should
be taken as a criticism? Surely it cannot be that we are under some
obligation to know the full truth about ourselves; that kind of imperative looks suspiciously like a manifestation of the very will to truth
that is the object of Nietzsche's critique in the third essay of the *Genealogy*. What is more, Nietzsche has often told of the need for self-
deception. Indeed, Nietzsche in many places tells us that ignorance of
one's deeper drives and motivations can often be a healthy phenomenon. This thought goes hand in hand with his general dismissal of
consciousness as a weak, irrelevant, even disruptive force. How can
Nietzsche extol the virtues of knowledge of the self yet otherwise
praise ignorance of the self? Again, part of the answer is to be found
in the different ends knowledge and ignorance can serve in different
contexts. In the case of Wagner and himself he sees ignorance as
something that helps a deeper unifying drive finally reach its full
active expression.[17] In the case of Christians and scholars, their ignorance merely serves to facilitate their passive attitudes and their splint-
ering into weak fragmented personalities. This brings us to the deeper
sense in which Nietzsche takes us to be strangers to ourselves. As the
Genealogy unfolds, beyond our mere ignorance, a deeper, though
related, estrangement is suggested, namely; that of having parts of
ourselves that are split-off. These parts are split-off, not simply in the
sense that we have no conscious access to them, but in the sense that
we contain within us hidden affects and drives. These are separate
movers that are not part of any integrated whole. Taken to the extreme, this notion of being strangers to ourselves actually threatens the
very notion of a unified self. That is to say, we have strangers *within*
ourselves, so that, in fact, our self is no genuine self. We are nothing
more than a jumble of different voices/drives having no overall

unity.[18] Not wishing to directly threaten his audience with this frightening thought, Nietzsche brings this idea to his readers in very subtle ways.

In the first essay of the *Genealogy* Nietzsche playfully torments his audience with variations on this theme of being subverted from within. For instance, the claim that Christian morality is nothing but the inheritor of a Jewish slave morality based on *ressentiment* hints at the claim that his audience need not be worried about being 'jewified' because, with their current morality, they are already as Jewish as they could be. The worry of being 'jewified' was one that Germans of the 1880s were keenly aware of. Where a typical (liberal) German audience of Nietzsche's time sees 'The Jew' as a foreign external body that somehow needs to be cleansed and brought into the Christian-German world, Nietzsche is telling his audience that they themselves are in fact internally and fundamentally contaminated with Jewishness.[19] This is a direct threat to the Germans' sense of identity. The problem of German identity in the 19th century is hugely complex and not something to be seriously approached in detail in this essay. However, what is worth noting here is that, because there was no unified German state until late into the 19th century, and because the notion of a common German language was a known fiction, one of the main means of forging a German identity was by contrast to those who were clearly not Germans. Jews, in particular, were commonly denominated as the paradigm of the un-German. Nietzsche's claim that the Germans are already 'jewified' brings home to his reader in an uncanny way his theme that they are strangers to themselves. It is presumably his sense of provocative playfulness that leads Nietzsche to suggest that the Jewish elders actually gathered as a cabal and consciously repudiated Christ. This, alleged Nietzsche, they did solely in order to make Christ's destructive Jewish slave message more appealing to the non-Jews:

> Was it not part of the secret black art of truly grand politics of revenge [...] that Israel must deny the real instrument of its revenge before the world as a mortal enemy and nail it to the cross so that 'all the world', namely all the opponents of Israel, could unhesitatingly swallow just this bait?[20] [GM I, 8]

We have seen that in the first essay Nietzsche torments his audience with the thought that they are already infected with a Jewish voice, one that they themselves would take to be thoroughly foreign. In the second essay Nietzsche implicitly raises the question of whether such a thoroughly mixed being can be capable of genuine agency. This he does in a rather subtle way, by introducing a figure, the 'sovereign individual' capable of genuine agency, and then implicitly contrasting this strong commanding figure with the weak will of the wisps of his day.

For Nietzsche genuine agency, including the right to make promises, is the expression of a unified whole. The second essay begins with the question:

> To breed an animal with the right to make promises – is this not the paradoxical task that nature has set itself in the case of man? is this not the real problem regarding man? [GM II, 1]

The text might easily lead the unwary reader to think this is a task already accomplished, again leading the reader into a sense of complacent satisfaction. The sense that Nietzsche is talking of past events is heightened when, having first raised this question of nature's task, he concentrates on the pre-history of man, and man's first acquiring of deep memory – memory burnt in by punishment. The task of acquiring memory is one that has been clearly accomplished; it is something that his audience can proudly lay claim to. Nietzsche, after raising his question, immediately refers to the breeding of an animal with the right to make promises as a problem that 'has been solved to a large extent'. This furthers the sense that the task is largely behind us. However, when a few pages later Nietzsche introduces 'the end of this tremendous process' as the 'sovereign individual', his audience should at least have a suspicion glimmering of whether they themselves are this proud, noble-sounding individual or the 'feeble windbags' he despises. Nietzsche describes the sovereign individual in hyperbolic tones clearly not applicable to ordinary individuals. He describes him as one

> who has his own protracted will and the right to make promises and in him a proud consciousness, quivering in every muscle, of what has at length been

achieved and become flesh in him, a consciousness of his own power and freedom [...] [and who] is bound to reserve a kick for the feeble windbags who promise without the right to do so. [GM II, 2]

It is typical of Nietzsche's deliberate, and deliberately confusing, caginess, that it is not at first clear whether the sovereign individual is a creature already achieved or one yet to come. The very terms Nietzsche uses to describe the sovereign individual – 'proud', 'quivering in every muscle', 'aware of his superiority', 'like only to himself', 'bound to honour his peers'– clearly hark back to the descriptions of the masters of the first essay. Since his audience are meant to identify themselves as the inheritors of slave morality, it is clear that they cannot be identified with this sovereign individual, who, unlike them, has been 'liberated from the morality of custom', and who is 'autonomous and supermoral', a 'lord of the free will'. The implicit message to his audience is that you are not sufficiently whole to have the right to make promises; you have no free will, but are merely tossed about willy-nilly by a jumble of competing drives, and, hence, you cannot stand surety for what you promise. You can give no guarantee that the ascendant drive at the time of your making a promise will be effective when the time comes to honour that promise.

4. Nietzsche on Free Will

In the sections of the second essay of the *Genealogy*, where Nietzsche discusses the figure of the sovereign individual, his use of the Kantian terminology of free will and autonomy is in marked contrast to his generally negative use of that terminology. Nietzsche often disparages the notion of free will and autonomy. Thus he says in *The Antichrist*:

In Christianity [...]. Nothing but imaginary causes ('God', 'soul', 'ego', 'spirit', 'free will' – or 'unfree will'). [A 15]

In *Twilight of the Idols* he simply refers to 'the error of free will' [TI IV, 7]. However, in those passages where he disparages the notion of free will it is clear that what is a stake is the notion of a will autonomous from the causal order, an uncaused cause. It is free will in this 'superlative, metaphysical sense' [BGE 21] that Nietzsche rejects. This still leaves room for a more imminent notion of free will. It is this kind of free will that Nietzsche presumably envisages for his sovereign individual who is

> [...] autonomous [...] the man who has his own independent, protracted will [...] this master of a *free* will. [GM II, 2 – Nietzsche's italics]

One gets a sense of Nietzsche's account of free will, and its relation to the tradition, by contrasting it with that of David Hume. Hume, a compatibilist, famously argued that 'liberty of spontaneity' (free will) is consistent with the denial of 'liberty of indifference' (determinism).[21] On Hume's account, one acts freely where that action stems from one's character. Character for Hume is simply glossed as one's deeper dispositions. Here is not the place to canvass the various problems with Hume's notion of character. What is interesting for us is that Nietzsche may be seen as offering a similar account of free will, with the very important difference that he gives a much more robust account of character. To have a character is to have a stable, unified, and integrated, hierarchy of drives. This is a very demanding condition that most humans fail to meet:

> In the present age human beings have in their bodies the heritage of multiple origins, that is opposite and not merely opposite drives and value standards that fight each other and rarely permit each other any rest. Such human beings of late cultures and refracted lights will on the average be weaker human beings. [BGE 200]

In the *Nachlass* from the period of the *Genealogy* Nietzsche explicitly draws the conclusion that

> one should not at all assume that many humans are 'people' [...] the 'person' is a relatively isolated fact. [KSA 12, 491, my translation]

The sovereign individual, who has a unified, independent, protracted will counts as having a genuine character, being a person. Modern man, who is at the mercy of a menagerie of competing forces, internal and external, has no such character.[22]

Why after so much denigration of the terminology of free will and autonomy does Nietzsche in the *Genealogy* employ it in a positive fashion? Presumably, as a subtle challenge to his readers. Rather than simply arousing his audiences' resistance with flat denials of free will and autonomy in the transcendental sense, Nietzsche uses that terminology in a positive, non-transcendental, manner in describing the sovereign individual. He then seeks to unsettle his audience with the uncanny idea that autonomy and free will are achievements of great difficulty, achievements which they themselves have by no means attained. While the thought that free will does not exist is disturbing, how much more so is the thought that free will does exist but one does not oneself possess it!

While Nietzsche may believe in free will, in a compatibilist sense, he clearly does not mean to endorse the notion that possession of a free will means the one who acts in a particular way could have done otherwise.[23] Now those who take the key issue concerning free will to be the question of moral responsibility, and the viability of appraisals of praise and blame, will claim that this is no genuine notion of free will. For them an action is free only if the agent could have done otherwise. But there is another way of approaching the free will debate. This other way does not see the debate directly through the question of responsibility, but, rather, approaches it from the question of agency. Where one approach begins with the question 'For what acts is one responsible?', the other begins with the arguably profounder question 'What is it to act in the first place, what is it to be a self capable of acting?' Those who take the question of responsibility as paramount to the free will question, tend to write as if we already have a notion of self and action more or less firmly in place and are only raising the question of whether such selves are ever to be held responsible for their actions. The other approach seeks to problematize the very notions of self and action. This is part of the import of the famous dictum from the *Genealogy* that 'the doer is merely a fiction added to the deed' [GM I, 13]. Now Nietzsche does, of course, want to question our practices of praising and blaming, our practices of assigning responsibility. This is part of his ongoing battle against the dominant Judaeo-Christian worldview in which responsibility, and, in particular, blame, are key notions. This aim does indeed account for many of his negative comments about free will. But ultimately the more profound Nietzsche wants to raise the question about what exactly it is to be a genuine self. Indeed his whole attack on the Judaeo-Christian worldview is predicated on his belief that it is fundamentally inimical to the development of genuine selves.

To interpret Nietzsche as an opponent of free will is to emphasize a purely negative aspect, his hostility to Judaeo-Christian notions of responsibility. This undoubtedly is an important and oft repeated theme in Nietzsche's work and hence is a defendable interpretation of Nietzsche. To interpret Nietzsche as giving a positive, albeit arguably, revisionist account of free will is to emphasize a positive and wholly original aspect, his notion that under the right conditions genuine agency, a truly great achievement, is possible. Furthermore, this interpretation helps us to properly appreciate the famous passage in *Gay Science* 125, where Nietzsche's 'madman tells us that we must ourselves become Gods to be worthy of the deed of killing God. To become Gods is to be autonomous, self-legislators who are not subservient to some external authority, be it a God, the *sumum bonum*, or an, allegedly, universal moral law. This interpretation allows us to see a Nietzsche who has come to grips with a central problem of modern philosophy in a way that many of his predecessors, contemporaries, and even successors, have failed to do. If we take part of the central trajectory of modern philosophy to be the move from a religious to a secular worldview, we (should) see that giving up the metaphysics of God and soul raises a crucial problem about exactly what we are. The modern tradition offers a number of answers; we are in essence reasoners (Descartes, Kant),[24] we are bundles of sensations (Hume). None of these answers are particularly satisfactory. Nietzsche offers an interesting and rather original alternative. He claims that in a sense we do not exist.[25] This is not a version of that kind of academic, philosophic, scepticism that brings philosophy into deserved disrepute. The existence of human bodies, like the existence of the so-called external world is not something Nietzsche would ever dream of really denying. What Nietzsche questions is whether there are genuine *selves* inhabiting these bodies. In place of empiricist or rationalist accounts of the self, Nietzsche offers, what might be called, a naturalist-aestheticist account: To have a genuine self is to have an enduring co-ordinated hierarchy of drives. Most humans fail to have such a hierarchy; hence they are not sovereign individuals. Rather they are a jumble of drives with no coherent order. Hence they are not genuine individuals or, we might say, selves.

Nietzsche's various attacks on the Kantian notions of autonomy and free will have two main objectives. The negative objective is to show that the notion of a will that transcends the causal order is intellectually unacceptable – a point that is hardly unique to Nietzsche. The positive, and more profound and original, objective is to offer his readers the challenging notion that genuine autonomy, and hence existence as an individual and self, is possible for some. This challenge should awaken his readers to the profoundly disturbing possibility that they themselves are not fully persons.

Part III

5. Nietzsche and the Uncanny

In section 10 of the third essay of the *Genealogy* Nietzsche again invokes the notion of free will. There he suggests a contrast between philosophers as they have occurred so far, 'world-negating, hostile towards life, not believing in the senses,' with a possible successor who, presumably unlike his predecessors, has sufficient 'will of the spirit, *freedom of will*' [GM III, 10, Nietzsche's italics]. In this passage, like the earlier ones concerning the sovereign individual and free will, Nietzsche leaves the reader in some doubt as to whether he is talking about something already achieved or yet to be achieved. In both these cases Nietzsche creates a kind of uncanny effect on the reader. The uncanny here is operating in Freud's sense of something that is disturbingly both familiar and unfamiliar.[26]

Let us first consider the case of the sovereign individual and then return to that of the philosopher. The sovereign individual is at first seemingly familiar to his readers as modern man, the possessor of memory and the right to make promises. But Nietzsche's text, by characterizing the sovereign individual in terms typically applied to the masters of the first essay, disturbingly suggests a gulf between the sovereign individual and modern man, the inheritor of slave morality. The sense of the uncanny comes not simply through the confusion about who exactly is the sovereign individual, but also by a certain play on temporality. Is Nietzsche talking about who we are in the present or is he talking about some envisaged successor?

The same questions of identity and temporality produce an uncanny effect when Nietzsche describes philosophers in section 10 of the third essay of the *Genealogy*. He begins with 'the earliest philosophers':

> to begin with the philosophic spirit always had to use as a mask and cocoon the *previously established* types of contemplative man [...] a religious type. [Nietzsche's italics]

The reference to the earliest philosophers suggests some distance between modern philosophers of Nietzsche's era and the subjects of his descriptions. This suggestion is furthered when Nietzsche then says,

> the ascetic priest provided *until modern times* the repulsive caterpillar form in which alone the philosopher could live and creep about. [emphasis mine]

Yet when Nietzsche then immediately asks the rhetorical question 'Has this really *altered*?' [Nietzsche's italics], his reader is left with the uneasy feeling that perhaps the repulsive caterpillar form is not really a thing of the past.[27]

These temporal shifts are important for creating an uncanny sense of dislocation in the *Genealogy*; what is far away often turns out to be quite close; and what is apparently already with us turns out to be yet to come. A notable example of such dislocation occurs in his characterisation of the 'counter idealists' in section 24 of the third essay. These he accuses of unknowingly sharing the ideal they explicitly repudiate, the acetic ideal, because 'they still have faith in truth'. Interestingly, amongst these counter idealists he includes 'pale atheists, antichrists, immoralists, nihilists'. Now these terms can be applied to Nietzsche himself, and, moreover, he himself has done so in various places. The rhetorical effect here is striking; Nietzsche by his insinuating conspiratorial tone has suggested that he and his reader have now seen things that others have completely missed, namely, the continued prevalence of the ascetic ideal. But then in implicitly accusing himself of still being involved with the ascetic ideal does that accusation not equally fall on his reader?

A similar uncanny effect marks Nietzsche's claims about the Jews and slaves in the first essay. Jewish slaves would at first seem a very foreign people, especially for a 19th century German audience, a people who had very recently emerged as surprising victors in the Franco-Prussian war. But as the *Genealogy* progresses the distance between the psychological make-up of the Jewish slaves and modern man seems to progressively shrink so that the unfamiliar merges with the familiar, each taking on the traits of the other. The Jewish slave turns out to have conquered the whole Western world (not just France!), and modern European man turns out to have continued the Jewish slave's hostility to the real world.

Nietzsche also has recourse to the notion of the uncanny in the *Genealogy* when characterizing nihilism as 'the uncanniest of monsters' [GM III, 14]. While that particular passage merely heralds nihilism as a possibility, in his notebooks of the same period he is much more explicit,

> Nihilism stands before us: whence comes this most uncanny of all guests? [KSA 12, p. 125 – my translation]

His immediate answer, in keeping with the general tenor of the *Genealogy*, is that it is the will to truth that, having destroyed the metaphysics that underpinned our values, is slowly bringing belated recognition that those values themselves now lack any coherent foundations. Thus we are inevitably being led to a void of values. But why does he call nihilism an uncanny guest and the uncanniest of monsters? I conjecture it is because he realizes that for his audience nihilism is, on first approach, rather distant and unfamiliar, and yet in some deep, perhaps, as yet, unarticulated sense, profoundly close and familiar. It is unfamiliar to his audience because, valuing truth, objectivity, science, education, progress, and other Enlightenment ideals, they would regard themselves as having firm, deeply held values. It is somehow familiar because they would have an inchoate sense that the very demand central to the Enlightenment ideal, the demand that all assumptions must face the test of reason, is a test that consistently applied would put those, indeed, all values, into question. Nietzsche, like David Hume, realised that if we were to take seriously the Enlightenment ideal of making no assumptions and subjecting every belief, every value, to the test of pure reason, we would in fact be left with a total devastation of all beliefs and values. It is just this devastation that he predicts for Europe's future – it is for Nietzsche the first step to a full appreciation of the death of God. A fundamental aim of the *Genealogy* is to allow his audience a possible self-awareness that will inevitably hasten such an appreciation. This is not to say that Nietzsche sees nihilism as a goal in itself. However what he does believe is that Europe must first go through nihilism if it is to reach the possibilities of creating genuinely life-affirming values.[28]

The theme of the uncanny and uncanny themes proliferate throughout the text of the *Genealogy*. In no other text of Nietzsche's is there anywhere near as many occurrences of the term 'uncanny' (*unheimlich*) and its cognates. The importance of this notion for appreciating Nietzsche's text is attested to by Nietzsche himself in the very first lines of the section in *Ecce Homo* dealing with the *Genealogy*. There Nietzsche characterises that work as follows:

> Regarding expression, intention, and the art of surprise, the three inquiries, which constitute this *Genealogy*, are perhaps uncannier than anything else written so far. [EH, *Genealogy of Morals* A Polemic]

Indeed, the uncanny makes its first appearance in the *Genealogy* as early as section 5 of the preface. There Nietzsche gives, what may now, in retrospect, be seen as a hint that his announced theme might not be his real theme. In section 4 of the preface he tells us that in *Human, All Too Human* he had already approached the subject that is, allegedly, central to the *Genealogy*, namely the question of the origins of morality. In section 5 he then tells us that even in that work he was really concerned with the value of our morality, rather than 'my own or anyone else's hypothesizing about the origin of morality'. In particular, he tells us that what he saw as 'the *great* danger to humanity' was

> the will turning against life, the last sickness gently and melancholically announcing itself: I understood the morality of compassion [...] as the most uncanny symptom of our now uncanny European culture.

I would finally add that the concept of the uncanny helps us explain the function of the *Genealogy* as a history that is not really a history. Above, I spoke of various temporal displacements that Nietzsche uses; the ancient Jewish slaves who reappear as modern Christians, even as modern truth loving atheists; the sovereign individual who appears first as something already achieved, then as a possible man of the future; the modern philosopher who has thrown off the mask of the religious type, but then is perhaps not so very distant from this caterpillar form. We also noted, in note 2, that in talking of the nobles in the first essay the text, without any forewarning, shifts from a frame of reference focused on ancient Greece to a frame of reference focused on ancient Rome. We also noted how Nietzsche bates his audience with the ridiculous suggestion of an imaginary ancient Jewish conspiracy. These and other factors, for instance, the absence of all the scholarly apparatus typical of a historical work (references, footnotes and the like), the very sweeping nature of Nietzsche's various historical narratives, their lack of historical specificity, and the very fact that he subtitles his work a polemic, create the unsettling feeling that Nietzsche is, despite his explicit rubric of historical interest, not really, or, at least, primarily, telling us about the historical origins of our morality. Furthermore, the idea of Nietzsche being devoted to getting the history right solely for the sake of getting at the historical truth does not sit well with the central themes of the third essay, with its disparagement of the will to truth. Nor does it sit well with his animadversions about history and the scholars search for truth in his essay *The Advantages and Disadvantages of History for Life*. What he is interested in are certain psychological truths about who we are; he is fundamentally interested in making available to us the true meaning of his initial, seemingly passing, comment that we are strangers to ourselves. Nietzsche's genealogies use, perhaps, at times, fabulous, historical narratives to show the employment of different uses, meanings and interrelationships of various concepts over time. Crucially Nietzsche, following Hegel, believes that only by understanding the temporal layering of meanings can we really grasp the current import of our concepts. The very potted nature of his actual historical narratives and his various games of temporal displacement serve to let us eventually see that his text is not what it first appears, and claims, to be. It is not in fact a simple historical narrative, but rather a narrative of psychological development and discovery, culminating for the reader in section 23 of the third essay. There, after having been exposed to the disgusting nature of the ascetic ideal, the reader is shatteringly brought to see that he himself is the embodiment of that ideal, so that afterward he may 'ask completely amazed, completely disconcerted, 'What did we actually experience just now?'' still more: 'who *are* we actually?'[29]

This interpretation of Nietzsche, as not primarily aiming for historical accuracy, helps explain an often-overlooked conundrum concerning the first essay of the *Genealogy*. In that essay Nietzsche paints a picture of the Greeks as healthy, active, and happy. This is the picture championed by the early romantics, for instance Goethe and Winkelmann. It is the image that captured the popular imagination of Germany throughout the 19th century. Yet Nietzsche, in his first book, *The Birth of Tragedy*, famously rejected this simplistic vision, claiming that the Greeks were profoundly pessimistic, realizing that life is inevitably painful, at least until Socrates, an essentially slavish type, mendaciously convinced the Greeks that reason and the pursuit of truth could alleviate all that is wrong with the world. Why does Nietzsche revert to this more idyllic, conventional picture of the ancient Greeks? To understand this it helps to consider that Nietzsche in the *Genealogy* repeatedly preys upon the conventional characterizations of various historical types, for instance the conventional characterization of the Jews as malicious, subterranean, overly cerebral, schemers. These nods to conventional representations are best understood as devices to draw his audiences in by playing to their prejudices. Of course, Nietzsche merely draws his audience in order to later surprise them with his eventual revelation that they themselves are the Jews (carriers of ascetic ideals) 'even thrice more' [cf. the quotation from *The Antichrist* in endnote 19]. But the point to be noted here is that his wilful, simplistic, mischaracterization of the ancient Greeks makes little sense if we see him as aiming for historical accuracy. It is perfectly understandable if we see him as primarily manipulating his audience to a psychological insight.

In *Ecce Homo* Nietzsche says '[t]hat a psychologist without equal speaks from my writings, is perhaps the first insight reached by a good reader' [Ecce Homo, Why I Write Such Good Books, 5]. This is one of Nietzsche's few self-assessments which I take to be absolutely correct. In reading Nietzsche we should follow the implied advice of looking for psychological, rather than philosophical, or historical, insights. The fundamental insight of the *Genealogy* is that with the change from the religious to the secular worldview we may have changed our beliefs about the nature of this world, we, unlike the religious, accept this as the one and only world, but we have still fundamentally clung to the same hostile attitude towards it. It is because we fail to engage with, in both a cognitive and deeper sense, the nature and the level of our resentment that we remain, so profoundly, strangers to ourselves. We should not simply keep the model of the psychologist in mind when trying to unravel the what of Nietzsche's text but also in unravelling the how of it. By uncannily invoking the pathos of distance, and deliberately confusing the temporal scope of his claims, Nietzsche has found an ingenious, subterranean, method of getting his highly challenging and subversive message to slowly sink into his readers, without immediately provoking the defences a more direct approach would surely arouse.[30]

References

For a general bibliography of Nietzsche's work in German and English see end of volume.

Freud, S., *The Standard Edition of the Complete Psychological Works of Sigmund Freud*, translated by J. Strachey, The Hogarth Press, London, 1955

Galasso, D., *Nietzsche: Asceticism, Philosophy, History*, Birkbeck College, University of London

Gemes, K., 'Post-Modernism's Use and Abuse of Nietzsche,' *Philosophy and Phenomenological Research*, 62:337–60, 2001

Hume, D., *A Treatise on Human Nature*, edited, with an analytical index by L.A. Selby-Bigge, Clarendon Press, Oxford, 1978

Leiter, B., *Nietzsche on Morality*, Routledge, London 2003

Marr, W., *Der Sieg des Judenthums über das Germanenthum*, Costenoble, Bern, 1879

Marx, K., 'On the Jewish Question', in *Karl Marx: Early Texts* (ed.) D. McLellan, Blackwell, Oxford, 1971

Schopenhauer, A., *The World as Will and Representation*, translated by E.F.J. Payne, 2 vols., Falcon's Wing Press: Indian Hills, Colorado, 1958

Wagner, R. 'Judaism in Music', in *Richard Wagner: Stories and Essays*, ed. C. Osborne, Peter Owen, London, 1973

Notes

1   Nietzsche does tell us 'We have never sought ourselves' [GM, Preface, 1]. But this is hardly an answer to the question of why we are unknown to ourselves. Since we are knowers who enquire persistently about practically everything, it merely raises the question of why have we not sought ourselves.

2   Notoriously, the first essay of the *Genealogy* leaves the reader in some confusion about who exactly are the bearers of master morality referred to in the

text. In much of the text, especially the early sections, it seems Nietzsche has the Greeks in mind. His first explicit mention of a particular nobility is that of Greek nobility in section 5, and his characterization in section 10 of the nobles, as self-affirming and merely condescendingly pitying to the slaves, is presented solely with reference to Greek nobility. Section 11, which stresses the reck-lessness and life affirming nature of the nobles, contains references to Pericles, the Athenians, Hesiod, and Homer. Indeed, Romans only get sustained mention in section 16, the penultimate section of the first essay. By contrast, the Jewish slaves of *ressentiment*, who are presumably more connected to the Romans than the Greeks, are given substantial mention as early as section 7. The early juxta-position between Jewish slaves and Greek masters is confusing since, of course, it was the Romans who were eventually, on Nietzsche's account, conquered by the Jews through their conversion to Christianity. This is captured in Nietzsche's phrase, 'Judea against Rome'; Jewish slave morality directly tri-umphed over Roman master morality, not Greek master morality. This un-heralded, confusing displacement of the reference of 'nobles' from Greeks to Romans is deliberate and serves a strategic purpose as argued in section 5 below.

3   The question of how seriously Nietzsche takes the various historical analyses offered in the *Genealogy* is dealt with in greater detail in section 5 below.

4   In this text where Nietzsche talks of *Wissenschaft* I talk of 'science'. However it is important to recall that for the German speakers of the 19th century, and indeed for Germans speakers of today, *Wissenschaft* does not simply refer to what we call the natural sciences (*Naturwissenschaften*) such as physics, chem-istry and biology, but also to the human sciences (*Geisteswissenschaft*) such as philology and philosophy and even formal sciences such as Mathematics and Geometry. We do better, then, to think of the practitioners of *Wissenschaften* as scholars than as scientists.

5   The third essay of *Genealogy*, may, to some degree, be seen as a reprise of 'On the Advantages and Disadvantages of History for Life'. In both essays Nietzsche questions the pursuit of knowledge as an end in itself, and points out that this mentality betrays a fear of life. However a significant difference is that the *Genealogy* contains much greater psychological insight into the motivation and mindset behind this pursuit. Also it is much more sophisticated in the means it employs to get the reader to appreciate this point. It is possible that by the time of the *Genealogy* Nietzsche had come to see that his untimely message of the hollowness at the core of our current culture needed to be delivered in a much more subtle way if it was to make an impression on his complacent, self-satisfied, audience.

6   Chris Janaway has helpfully pointed out that Nietzsche's repeated negative references to passive mirroring when characterizing the will to truth and object-ivity are probably a deliberate reference to, and in contrast with, Schopenhauer who favourably spoke of the intellect 'abolishing all possibility of suffering'

[WWR II, 368] when it renounces all interest and becomes 'the clear mirror of the world' [WWR II, 380]. It is presumably Nietzsche's early struggles with Schopenhauer that first alerted him to the possibility that intellectual contemplation can function as a means for attempting escape from this painful world of becoming.

7   It might be thought that there is a fundamental difference between the resistance suffered by slaves and that faced by Nietzsche's audience. The latter of course belong to a dominant successful society. While there are differences, the key point is that that success is now the success of a herd animal who has still repressed many of his individual desires to pursue an alleged common good. This is not to say that Nietzsche was against all repression. Rather, much like Freud, he favoured sublimation where the repressed desires are allowed to express themselves productively, albeit directed to new ends than those they originally sought. Cf. Gemes (2001)..

8   This is a central theme in *The Birth of Tragedy*, for example, see sections 7–9. In that work, still under the influence of Schopenhauer and Wagner, Nietzsche takes art, in particular tragedy, as providing the Greeks with the means to affirm life despite suffering. As this influence waned art came to play a much less significant part in his account of the life-affirming spirit of the Greeks. Thus in the first essay of the *Genealogy*, where the Greeks are clearly configured as life-affirming, there is no appearance of art as their means of affirmation.

9   In section sections 13–22 of the third essay of the *Genealogy* the ostensible subject is the ascetic ideal as personified by the ascetic priest. In these sections the ascetic priest is characterized as the sick physician to a sick herd. He attempts to combat the 'dominant feeling of listlessness ...first, by means that reduce the general feeling of life to its lowest point. If possible no willing at all, not another wish' [GM III, 17]. However these sections also contain many references that go well beyond priests, including references to anti-Semites, to Nietzsche's contemporary, the philosopher Eugen Dühring, to modern European *Weltschmerz*. These references already indicate that Nietzsche's polemic against those who advocate passivity as a means of combating and avoiding the pains of life has a much wider target than just the priests. However, as argued above, it is only in section 23 that the full scope of his target comes clearly into view.

10   For Nietzsche, the scholar's valuing truth, like the religious person's valuing the world to come, is generally paired with a valorization of being over becoming. Even if the scholar were to take his truth to be truth about the world of appearance this would not abrogate Nietzsche's point. Fundamentally, in Nietzsche's work, the being/becoming dichotomy aligns with the passive/active dichotomy. This explains his rather monotonous emphasis on being over becoming throughout his corpus, which is only broken in the *Gay Science* 370. There he lets on that a valorization of becoming in certain contexts can actually

be manifestation of a rejection of life and a valorization of being can in certain contexts be a manifestation of a healthy attitude to life.

11 An interpretation with a different point of emphasis is advanced in Brian Leiter's generally excellent *Nietzsche on Morality*. Leiter does allow that the unconditional pursuit of truth can be life-denying. However he recognizes this mainly on the limited score that certain truths can be so terrible that the very knowledge of them can be a threat to life. Leiter does not recognize the full import of Nietzsche's claim that the very will to truth is a will to escape this life, and indeed refers to this aspect of the asceticism of science as 'only a minor theme in Nietzsche's discussion' [Leiter, p. 265]. Besides the claim that certain truths 'can be terrible, a threat to life' [ibid., p. 267], Leiter claims the other major objection Nietzsche has to the overestimation of truth is that it supposes falsely, that our knowledge could be 'presuppositionless'. More precisely, the will to truth is a will to non-perspectival truth... [p. 268]. Now a number of things seem to have gone wrong here. First, it seems strange that Nietzsche would get so worked up about a mere cognitive error, the mistake of taking one's truths as absolute, presuppositionless truths. Indeed, Leiter himself elsewhere points out that Nietzsche does not take such intellectual errors to be of great import. Recall Nietzsche's exhortation concerning Christianity's morality that 'it is not error qua error that horrifies me at this sight' [EH, Why I am a Destiny, 7]. For Nietzsche the problem with the ascetic ideal, science, and indeed the will to truth, is not that they presuppose faulty beliefs or metaphysics, but that they manifest an entire attitude and orientation of hatred towards life – 'that one taught men to despise the very first instincts of life' [ibid.]. More generally this kind of abstract intellectual mistake, taking one's truth as being without presuppositions, is not in itself of great concern to Nietzsche. As Leiter himself elsewhere notes, Nietzsche generally thinks our abstract intellectual life is epiphenomenal in the sense that it may reflect and be caused by our deeper motivations and passions but it does not really influence them, or indeed our actions. Second, and relatedly, if the scholar merely suffers from a false belief could he not then simply correct it by changing to the view that his theories do not reflect any absolute, presuppositonless truth? Indeed, surely many scholars would resonate with the claim that truth is perspectival. Note the disparaging remark from Nietzsche's Zarathustra, quoted above, about the scholar's desire to mirror with one hundred eyes – this itself sounds more like perspectival than absolute knowledge. Finally, and ironically enough, given Leiter's hostility to Postmodernism, on Leiter's reading postmodernist scholars would be exempt from Nietzsche's critique of scholars since they clearly do not make the error of taking our knowledge to be without presuppositions.

12 While generally Nietzsche discusses the *vita contemplativa* in the context of its use as a negative life-denying orientation [cf. Daybreak 42–3], *GS* 310 shows that Nietzsche recognizes that the *vita contemplativa* can in fact be the means to the highest form of creativity.

13   The emphasis on the inner/outer distinction though apparent enough in the
      Hollingdale translation of the *Untimely Mediations* is somewhat weakened by
      the fact that the German term *Inneres* is sometimes translated as 'inner', occa-
      sionally as 'interior' and often as 'subjectivity'. These translations though per-
      fectly legitimate, nevertheless, steer the reader away from recognition of the
      centrality of the inner/outer distinction to Nietzsche's thinking of the time.

14   Nietzsche in several places directly canvases the idea that language and thought
      are means of appropriating reality, for example *D* 285, *WP* 423, *WP* 584, *GS*
      355. At other places he talks of language and contemplation as a means of
      creating a substitute reality, for example *D* 43, *HH* I, 11, and *GS* 354.

15   Wilfred Sellars, for one, does in fact endorse the claim that for initiates into
      language, in particular children, language originally functions as non-conceptu-
      al naming – their initial language use consists in the utterance of meaningless
      vocables. However that goes on against a background where those vocables
      have their natural place in a fully functioning conceptual framework wielded by
      their elders.

16   The interesting idea of the origins of the conceptual, as a substitute satisfaction
      for a reality that resists one's desires, is something also suggested by Freud –
      the first entry into the conceptual being the fantasy of the breast, that fantasy
      being a substitute for the breast that at some point has been withheld from the
      baby by the mother. Cf. *S.E.* Vol. I, p. 328 and Vol. V, p. 564. Nietzsche, fol-
      lowing Schopenhauer, is generally suspicious of the (conscious) mind and treats
      it as largely epiphenomenal. What he adds is that the development of mind is a
      fundamentally negative phenomenon, its development being the result of a
      failure to directly and instinctively navigate the world. Nietzsche's thoughts on
      this topic are both profound and presumably erroneous. The chimera of a lan-
      guage affording direct, conceptually unmediated, contact with reality (Nietzsche's
      seeming suggestion about the language of the Masters) is something that is a
      source of perennial confusion in philosophy, including, for instance, Derrida's
      self-acknowledged pointless hand-wringing about the so-called 'logocentric
      predicament'. The idea that the conceptual somehow represents a fall from
      some mythical adamic position of grace of unmediated contact with reality is
      more worthy of psychological diagnosis, perhaps on Freudian lines suggested
      above, than of serious philosophical investigation.

17   In reference to Wagner [cf. *UM* II, 2] and in reference to Nietzsche [cf. *EH*,
      'Why I am So Clever', 9].

18   The Nietzschean theme that modern men are not genuine persons but mere
      jumbles of drives is one explored extensively in Gemes (2001).

19   This subversive theme is repeated in *The Antichrist* where Nietzsche says: 'The
      Christian, that ultima ratio of the lie, is the Jew once more – even thrice more'
      [*A*, 44]. The (despicable) rhetoric of *Verjudung* (Jewification) – overly polite
      scholars often refer to it by the misleadingly benign title 'Judaization' – is
      something that current readers are largely unaware off. The background for this

was the question, raised by the ongoing 19th century Jewish emancipation, of how the Jews were to be integrated into the modern state. Nietzsche belongs to a series of 19th century intellectuals who sought to turn this question on its head, asking, not how the Jews are to be emancipated from their inferior state, but, how we (Christians) are to be emancipated from the Jewishness that has now enslaved us. The claim that we are already thoroughly Jewish is the central claim of Marx's *On the Jewish Question* and Wagner's *Judaism in Music* – the later of which Nietzsche was clearly acquainted with. Both Marx and Wagner generally equate being jewified (*verjudet*) with materialism, Nietzsche equates it with acceptance of the morality of pity (slave morality).

20   Note, this is posed as a question, which may be taken to suggest that Nietzsche himself does not seriously endorse this conspiracy theory. The idea of a Jewish conspiracy against the Christian world is at least as old as the medieval blood libel that each year the elders of Israel convened to decide upon a young Christian child to be slaughtered and drained of blood to be used for making the Passover matzo. In the 19th century, after Napoleon convened the famous Sanhedrin of the Jews in 1806 in order to settle the question of Jewish emancipation and integration into the new Europe, new myths about Jewish conspiracies, including conspiracies of the bourse, arose with alarming regularity. While Nietzsche's little conspiracy joke about the Jews repudiating Christ in order to get the Christians to swallow the bait is perhaps relatively harmless, the contemporaneous publication of Wilhelm Marr's *Der Sieg des Judenthums über das Germanenthum* [The Victory of Jewry over Germandom], and other conspiracy works, culminating in the Russian secret police's infamous conspiracy work *The Protocols of the elders of Zion*, were to have far more devastating effects. It is of no credit to Nietzsche, and indeed displays a knowing recklessness on his part, that he participated in the rhetoric of *Verjudung*. That he intentionally tweaks his audience, giving a subversive twist to this usually wholly negative rhetoric, by configuring the Jewish slave revolt as creative and as making man interesting, giving him depth, hardly mitigates this recklessness.

21   Cf. *Treatise of Human Nature*, Book II, Section 11. Note, I do not mean to suggest here that Nietzsche is best read as explicitly endorsing both the claim that all events are determined by prior events and the claim that free will is possible. Rather, he is a compatibilist in the sense that he does not take determinism to be incompatible with free will. As will become clear below, Nietzsche is best read as one who has implicitly realized that the issues involved in making sense of free will do not have a direct connection with determinism. I do believe Nietzsche is committed to the idea that some rare individuals act freely; as for determinism, I do not think he has any real commitment there. More generally, I think such metaphysical views were not within his philosophical provenance – he occasionally flirted and dabbled with such theses but did not give them sufficient reflection necessary for genuine commitment. More typically, he uses such metaphysical claims as occasional

tools to help dislodge various ideas he takes to be harmful, for instance the moralist's obsessions about guilt and responsibility. Nietzsche is a *Kultur-kritiker* and psychologist, perhaps even a moral philosopher, but a meta-physician he is not, nor did he care to be. The one exception to this claim is perhaps his thought concerning will to power.

22   For more on this see Gemes (2001).

23   In *HH* I, 105 Nietzsche explicitly says of both 'he who is punished' and 'he who is rewarded' that neither punishment nor reward are deserved because 'he could not have acted otherwise'. There are of course forms of compatibilism which allow that one might have done otherwise, but this is not a position evidenced in Nietzsche's text.

24   Of course, Descartes and Kant were theists. Nevertheless, the intellectual tra-jectory of their work, whether intended or not, was inevitably towards a secular worldview.

25   The Hume of the *Appendix* to his *Treatise* came to realize that the account of the self given in the *Treatise* rendered the self non-existent (cf. Hume, 1978, pp. 635–6). However this for Hume was an unintended and unacceptable consequence of his philosophy. For Nietzsche our failure to achieve genuine selfhood, and the possibility, for at least a select few, of overcoming that failure, is the very point of much of his philosophy.

26   In his Essay, *The Uncanny*, Freud characterizes the uncanny as: ' something which is secretly familiar which has undergone repression and then returned from it'. [*S.E.*, p. 245] In that essay Freud notes that psychoanalysis itself can be seen as a case of the uncanny [ibid., p. 243]. In fact, most readers of Freud's essay are struck by its very uncanniness. Given Freud's general attempt to suppress his huge intellectual debt to Nietzsche, and one suspects, especially to the *Genealogy*, one of the uncanniest aspects of Freud's essay is that it, like the first essay of the *Genealogy*, begins with an etymological investigation. The temptation to assume that this is a disguised, perhaps even unconscious, expression of Freud's debt to Nietzsche, and especially the *Genealogy*, where the notion of the uncanny is both used and mentioned more than in any other of Nietzsche's text, is near overwhelming.

27   Dario Galasso in his Ph.D thesis *Nietzsche: Asceticism, Philosophy, History*, argues convincingly that in sections 5–10 of the third essay, where Nietzsche discusses the meaning of the ascetic ideal for philosophers, there are various subtle temporal shifts and identity shifts at work. He notes that Nietzsche at times identifies the philosopher as a successor to the priest, continuing the ascetic ideal's negative valuation of life. At other times Nietzsche identifies the philosopher with a more positive version of asceticism. On the positive account withdrawal is merely the means to allow the philosopher space to form his own creations. Withdrawal here does not embody a rejection of life but a means of adding to life. The solution to this seeming contradictory account is that when Nietzsche is associating philosophy with the ascetic ideal in a negative way he

is referring to philosophy as it has been so far practiced. When he gives the positive account of philosophical asceticism he is giving an account of philosophy as it should, and he hopes will one day be, practiced. That Nietzsche throughout the relevant sections of the third essay moves without much in the way of explicit signaling from reference to past philosophers to reference to philosophers of the future is part of a deliberate strategy of unsettling his readers.

28 Cf. *WP* 2 for his most succinct statement of the inevitability of nihilism.

29 This is not to say that Nietzsche does not think that his historical narratives in their broad outline contain a good deal of truth. It is only to claim that historical truth is not his ultimate aim. He needs at least some initial plausibility to his narrative if it is to have the desired rhetorical effect on his readers, and truth in the broad sense is a suitable way to achieve that plausibility. The note at the end of the first essay of the *Genealogy* suggesting a 'series of academic prize-essays' that might provide the kind of historical and philological detail his essay lacks, I take, to some degree, to be another instance of Nietzschean irony and baiting of his audience. Nietzsche had long since departed the academic world and made well known his general opinion of what he considered the often able but always pathetic *Fachleute* that inhabit that twilight realm. That said it should be noted that Nietzsche's relation to history is indeed more complicated than the above suggests. This is indicated in the preface of volume II of *HH* where Nietzsche says 'what I said against the historical sickness I said as one who had slowly and toilsomely learned to recover from it and was in no way prepared to give up 'history' thereafter because he had once suffered from it'. Nietzsche throughout his career remained a resolutely Hegelian thinker in holding that the meaning, or, better, meanings, of a thing are mediated by its history.

30 This piece has benefited greatly from input from Maudemarie Clark, Dario Galasso, Sebastian Gardner, Dylan Jaggard, Chris Janaway, Brian Leiter and John Richardson.

ROBERT GUAY

How to be an Immoralist

Nietzsche occasionally referred to his substantive ethical position as 'immoralism,'[1] but gave only a vague impression of just what this position amounts to. The strategy of this essay will be to determine how to be an immoralist by identifying what is affirmed in Nietzsche's negation of morality. That is, I wish to consider aspects of the critique of morality not to show that morality is wrong – that is not my goal here – but to identify what Nietzsche's substantive ethical position is. I hope to show two things: that Nietzsche characterizes his immoralist position as an extension of rather than as an antithesis to a moralist one, and that Nietzsche offers a teleological position different from any of the familiar ones.

Nietzsche's thought seems to be fundamentally practical in orientation.[2] That is, he is less concerned with establishing the truth or warrant of a theoretical position than with prescribing or possibly even transforming how life is to be led. Unfortunately it is in no way clear what his substantive ethical position is. This unclarity, further, seems to stem not so much from a lack of specification as from deep commitments. The familiar elements around which an ethical theory might be constructed are cast into doubt: commands *D* 108; rules *GS* 328; principles *GS* 21; happiness *EH*, destiny, 4; welfare *BGE* 228; pleasure *D* 575. So Nietzsche left himself few resources to make sense of any substantive ethical account: although offering something imperatival in character, he nevertheless seems to reject imperatives, and while offering a broadly teleological theory, he nevertheless seems to dismiss the importance of both welfare and the virtues. Nietzsche's entire philosophical enterprise can even seem to be fundamentally critical. He declares, 'I myself do not believe that anyone has ever looked into the world with an equally profound suspicion' [HH, preface, 1], and relates this suspicion specifically to the authority of values.[3] And by referring to himself as a 'posthumous man' [TI, maxims, 15], and identifying the untimeliness of his position,[4] Nietzsche even suggests that *any* normative claim is problematic: it requires a standpoint outside its own time. He, at any rate, can at best offer little 'experiments' or 'attempts' to an audience that might not, and might never, exist.

But this critical stance is intended to contribute to Nietzsche's constructive, or 'affirmative' program. He insists that 'negating *and destroying* is a condition of saying Yes' [EH, destiny, 4; cf. EH, Z, 6], and declares that immoralists dissect 'only to know better, to judge better, to live better; not so that the whole world dissects' [WS 19; cf. GM II, 24]. This suggests that his criticism plays both an instrumental role and a substantive role in the affirmative project. By criticizing morality, the ground is cleared for immoralism; and more substantively, the criticism of morality is what serves to determine the content of immoralism, if not itself part of the substantive content. And Nietzsche's critical commitments themselves require him to offer a constructive program. His understanding of morality as part of the 'ascetic ideal' compels him to offer something non-ascetic in its place; to criticize that which had satisfied a justificatory need without offering anything better in its place would fall within the ascetic tradition that he criticizes. So no kind of value agnosticism or scepticism is available as a default:[5] such a stance would represent not theoretical cautiousness, but a specific and dubious engagement, and one which calls for the same kind of 'suspicion' that a dogmatic assertion of value would.

Out of Morality

Immoralism, whatever it is, must comprise some substantive ethical position. As Nietzsche says, 'we immoralists [...] do not easily negate; we store our honour in being *affirmers*' [TI, morality, 6]. The substantive content of immoralism even seems to hold an unusually intimate relation to its object of criticism. While conceding that this is counterintuitive, Nietzsche represents immoralism as incorporating, just as morality itself does, unconditional duties. In a section entitled 'We immoralists,' Nietzsche claims, 'We are spun into a severe yarn and shirt of duties and *cannot* get out – in this we are 'persons of duty,' we, too' [BGE 226]. And not only does immoralism incorporate this kind of practical necessity, but immoralism is *itself* represented as having a practical necessity that derives from, of all things, fundamental moral commitments. Nietzsche refers to the 'selfovercoming of morality' [BGE 32] and says that 'the trust in morality is cancelled [...] out of morality' [D, preface, 4].[6] Immoralism, although opposed to morality, is arrived at on moral grounds.[7]

So our point of access to immoralism is through Nietzsche's critique of morality, and the critique of morality requires some notion of what morality is. Here Nietzsche provides many – perhaps too many – suggestions. Morality, Nietzsche suggests, is characterized by a superlative notion of free will, unconditional and general obligations, a hatred of contingency, an emphasis on altruism, and so on.[8] These features are certainly the object of Nietzsche's criticism. But they cannot be decisive in resolving what Nietzsche's critique of morality is: none seem to be essential to morality, and therefore an objection to one (or all) does not constitute a critique of morality *per se*. Part of the difficulty here is that what Nietzsche is attacking is not the truth of a theoretical claim, but a historical institution. Just as Nietzsche's objections to socialism or Christianity do not primarily concern an essential core of belief, Nietzsche does not aim to find a false premise and thereby to demonstrate the falsity of morality. Rather, Nietzsche aims to show that the institution, with its concomitant traditions and practices, should be abolished. But as a historical institution, morality can have no precise identity conditions. Rather, there are chains of continuities and discontinuities, in which particular features come and go or take on different meanings:[9] that which calls for genealogy rather than analysis.[10]

Nietzsche's objection to morality is accordingly not with that which the category determinately marks out, but with the use of the category to mark out anything at all. In employing the category of the

moral we make sharp distinctions that turn out to be empty, and mud-
dle distinctions that we would otherwise deem important; morality
promotes a way of classifying our selves and our actions that we have
grounds for dispensing with. We mislead ourselves about, and thereby
alter, our activity insofar as we understand it in moral terms. So 'Morality is not attacked,' insists Nietzsche, 'it is merely no longer considered' [EH, destiny, 1].[11]

There can, in any case, be no univocal critique of morality: there
are too many diverse phenomena to account for, and no prospect of a
fully comprehensive account. Morality must then be criticized as a
kind of institutional failure, and this is why Nietzsche says that "good
and evil' is merely a variation on the problem [of decadence]' [CW
preface]. The shortcomings of morality do not lie in a lack of veri-
dicality, but in the institution failing to sustain itself. But such a
collapse is not incomprehensible. Morality makes sense as a unifying
category because its failings have a common structural explanation.
And what brings together these diverse objections to the moral is
Nietzsche's arguments about the normative.

The unity of Nietzsche's criticism of morality lies in his arguments that it represented a series of mistakes about the normative.
Morality, in all its diversity, is the accumulation of a series of failed
attempts at securing the force of our ethical commitments. In particular, morality represents the attempt to demarcate some kind of special,
unconditional authority that decisively grounds particular values.[12]
This is why Nietzsche refers to morality not only as the 'Circe of
humanity' [EH, books, 5], but specifically as the 'Circe of all thinkers'
[EH, destiny, 6], and even more specifically as the 'Circe of philosophers' [D, preface, 3].[13] It represents a seductively simple philosophical response to a philosophical issue: how to secure the
legitimacy of a way of life. But the philosophical seduction of a conclusive ground proves to be a mistake both in its aim and in its means.

Nietzsche did not claim that morality was wrong because it
incorporated a false belief about special overriding authority, or even
that special authority is ineliminable from morality. Rather, morality
forms a complex whose center is the search for a kind of normative
stability. Worry about the soundness of practical commitments produced a series of ideas that were intended to guarantee the availability

of soundness. Nietzsche identified five broad categories of interrelated features that together represent a bet about what soundness must consist in if it is to exist at all: purity [D, preface, 3], rules [WS 5], conclusiveness [D 59], comprehensiveness [BGE 198], and certainty [WS 16]. But this bet turned out to undermine the security of our practical commitments all the more.

The five categories of features are usually run together in Nietzsche's work, but it is worth, provisionally, considering them as distinct, if only better to examine how they are interconnected. The *purity* of morality is that it '*negates* the world' [CW, epilogue]: morality is conceived as detached from any contingent concerns or features of the world. 'Humanity must have something that it can *obey unconditionally*' [D 207], insists Nietzsche, and this is what preserves the independence and therefore stability of its authority. Because of this purity morality must be represented as '*commanded to one* from somewhere' [D 108]: what morality demands is obedience [D, preface, 3] or even servility [GS 5]. Philosophers, responsible for the mistakes here, conceived of that which demands obedience independent of all contingency as moral *rules:*

> *An original sin of philosophers.* – Philosophers have at all times appropriated the propositions of examiners of humanity (moralists) and *ruined* them by taking these propositions unconditionally and wanting to demonstrate this as necessary [...]. [AOM 5, cf. GS 328, HH 96]

Here rules, or 'unconditional propositions,' are represented as a meta-theoretical mistake. Philosophers formulate (or appropriate) rules because they think that rules are the only form that 'necessary' truths could take. Apodictic rules, furthermore, can offer practical *conclusiveness*: the possibility of a completely and finally adequate ethical judgment of actions. Morality thereby offers not ongoing guidance, but a way out of reflection entirely:[14] a shorter '*shortcut to perfection*' [D 59]. Morality also 'needs to take itself as unconditional and address itself to everyone' [BGE 221]: that which could have secure authority should be *comprehensive* and universal. Morality, finally, is something about which there should be *certainty*: 'In this field absolutely *nothing but certainties*' [WS 16].

These features are mutually supporting in forming a particular picture of ethical authority: one in which it is articulable, fixed, and indubitable. Rules provided a form in which a comprehensive morality could be articulated. The comprehensiveness of morality could be explained in terms of its purity: independence of contingency ensured that no morally relevant differences between persons or suitably similar occasions obtained. Purity allows for fixed and satisfiable criteria, and thereby underwrites the conclusiveness ascribed to morality. Conclusiveness enables there to be certainty. Certainty is best explained in terms of rules, and so on. All this contributed to a picture of ethical authority that not only fulfilled a 'metaphysical need' [WS 16], but could serve as the basis for social regulation.[15] But, according to Nietzsche, such a picture of ethical authority was adopted not because it was truly desirable, could function as action-guiding, or even could plausibly obtain. Instead, this picture was adopted because in it the desire for stability and certainty coincided with the belief that these conditions must be satisfied for a way of life to be legitimate.

Here Nietzsche considers the consequences of such a picture of ethical authority:

> However gratefully one may encounter an *objective* spirit – and who isn't already sick to death of everything subjective and its damned ipsissimosity? – in the end one also has to learn caution against one's gratitude and put a halt to the exaggeration with which the deselfing and depersonalization of the spirit has been celebrated recently, as if it were a goal in itself, redemption, and transfiguration. [BGE 207])

We should be grateful for those seeking objectivity in those things that concern 'the spirit,' because the opposite approach – the insistence that all such matters are left to subjective taste or purely personal determination – sickens us to death. But as desirable as objectivity is, the way in which it is exaggerated is as dangerous as 'ipsissimosity.' Objectivity is turned into the 'goal in itself,' interfering, perhaps, with some other goal, and associated with 'redemption' and 'transfiguration': as if what objectivity provided were some conclusive, certain validation, rather than merely a way out of excessive subjectivity. The cost of such a misguided pursuit is 'deselfing and depersonalization of the spirit.' That is, confusing what sort of objectivity is available in matters of spirit takes away from that which constitutes the spirit as such. Rather than validating commitments, it removes people from the commitments that they did have, thus estranging the self from itself.[16]

Therefore, according to Nietzsche, 'this only morality that has been taught so far, the morality of unselfing [...] fundamentally *negates* life' [EH, destiny, 7]. Nietzsche seems to have three major complaints against the distinctly moral picture of the normative. One is that it makes no sense. 'Only if humanity had a universally recognized goal' [D 108], suggests Nietzsche, could we understand what moral imperatives amount to in terms of that goal. But that is not the case. And all authority that we are familiar with, Nietzsche suggests, is conditional and revisable, so moral authority would have to be something completely different. It would require the 'transposition of morality into the metaphysical' [EH, destiny, 3], or the invention of a 'true world' outside the world of appearance, in which to reside. But, ponders Nietzsche: 'The true world – unattainable? In any case, unattained. And as unattained, also *unknown*. Consequently, not comforting, redeeming, or obligating: what could something unknown obligate us to do?' [TI, true world, 4]. This passage is famously compressed, but one of Nietzsche's points seems to be that distinctly moral authority, to be what it is, must be so far removed from familiar practices as to prevent us from understanding it. But, implies Nietzsche, an incomprehensible authority is inert, and inert authority amounts to nothing at all. Authority is the sort of thing that must be at least potentially recognized as such to obtain.

The second main complaint against the moral picture of the normative is that it mixes up meta-level commitments with substantive ones. As Nietzsche depicts it, the 'hostility to life' involved in morality demands that one's values be detached from that which one actually cares about; otherwise, one's values would be contingent upon the cares that one happens to have. But then commitments about what the normative consists in bleed into first order values. On the one hand, since 'all regulations of action relate only to the gross exterior' [GS 335], everything but the gross exterior is excluded from moral significance. On the other hand, morality crowds out other values by insisting that they meet its standards to count as such. And thus, claims Nietzsche, 'Every morality that affirms itself exclusively kills off too much good strength and is too costly a gain for humanity' [D 164].[17]

The third main complaint against the moral picture of the normative is that it fails to be action-guiding. Morality fails to be action-guiding in part simply because it demands unconditional obedience. Nietzsche seems to think that a call for obedience that is so far removed from our everyday reasons, commitments, and motivations will eventually just 'evaporate' [D 9]. But the deeper reason why morality fails to be action-guiding is that morality's generality of form prevents it from having enough specificity to inform practice. There are three related issues here. One is that insofar as morality takes on an abstracted form, it fails to cover matters of genuine importance; morality is thus an 'incitement to sins of omission' [BGE 221]. The second issue is that morality's generality prevents it from having enough content to know what it means to apply it correctly. What a moral rule, for example, amounts to, depends on a potential infinity of considerations that arise as that rules relates to practice; or, more simply, the import of a rule might vary radically in two different interpretations of it. As a result, 'two persons with the same principles probably aim with them at something fundamentally different' [BGE 77]. The third issue is that morality insists on universality of application, where that is inappropriate:

> All these moralities that address themselves to the individual [...] all of them baroque and unreasonable in form – because they address themselves to 'all' because they generalize where one may not generalize – all of them speaking unconditionally, taking themselves for unconditional [...]. All of it is, measured intellectually, of little worth and very far from 'science,' let alone 'wisdom,' but rather, to say it once more, three times more, prudence, prudence, prudence, mixed with stupidity, stupidity, stupidity. [BGE 198]

This view of Nietzsche's, that standards with universal purport are bad, is familiar: the explanation usually adduced for it is that Nietzsche thought that some people are better than others, and thus that the standards do not apply to everyone equally. That might also be true,[18] but notice here that the basis on which Nietzsche criticizes universal standards is that it is unreasonable and stupid to rely on rules in certain ways. By implication, Nietzsche suggests that the appeal to universal rules is an attempt to be *wissenschaftlich*. But a scientific form is not suitable to the content, so a science of morals only detracts from intellectual content. Nietzsche has nothing against science, and even has nothing against universal standards *per se*. Indeed, he even says that they evince a degree of 'prudence'. I take it this means that they could indeed serve a cognitively useful function. Such standards could play a heuristic or deliberative role. But such standards are stupid if they are supposed to provide a general and decisive ground for ethical judgment. They obscure the particular ways in which ethical concerns might be operative in specific situations, and thus confound practical deliberation.[19]

Nietzsche's criticisms, apart from depending on their own soundness, depend on successfully identifying their target. So one could object that Nietzsche's view of morality as a misguided view of ethical authority misses the mark. Maudemarie Clark, citing Samuel Scheffler, seems to raise such an objection:

> Although many moral theorists defend the overridingness of moral concerns, others now seem willing to dispense with such privilege. For instance, Scheffler argues in *Human Morality* that the loss of overridingness is a problem for moralists only if they assume that morality must have a special source in order to have authority. He then argues that morality has sufficient authority in our life even if it does not have a special source that makes it superior to all else.[20]

This passage combines specialness, overridingness, and superiority into one, but this need not concern us for present purposes, since it suggests that *all* of these features could be discarded without touching morality as such. And this point must be conceded: all that is needed to establish it is for someone to invent a version of morality, familiar enough to deserve its name, that does not have these features.

But this does not affect Nietzsche's critique of morality, for two reasons. One reason is that such a response would mistake Nietzsche's level of criticism. Nietzsche did not claim that morality was wrong because it incorporated a false belief about special overriding authority. Nietzsche, rather, adduced the notion of special authority to explain morality's more basic practical failure. The potential eliminability of special authority does not, therefore, affect the critique; at most it undermines the account of how it was that morality failed in providing normative assurance. The second reason that Nietzsche's critique is unaffected is that he not only concedes that there are no essential features of the historical institution of morality, he even specified the abandonment of special authority as part of his story of asceticism. Morality was itself an ascetic enterprise, and taking away morality's privileged status while leaving behind the empty carapace of norms and obligations was even more ascetic.[21] Holding on to morality as a system of constraints without any special status seems to leave its basic specially-sanctioned character intact, even while denying that it conveys or makes available any distinctive worth that the special sanction would bring.

What Nietzsche's critique of morality clearly does not lead to is an anti-moralism in which something like Milton's Satan is combined with the language of obligation: one then has strict duties to do bad things. The most famous version of this reading is that of Philippa Foot, who interpreted Nietzsche as proposing an 'aesthetic form of evaluation' which antagonizes justice and the common good.[22] Foot developed this reading in part on account of her belief that justice and the common good are conceptually related to morality and that aesthetic values are the main alternative to moral ones: an immoralist position must then be an aesthetic one against justice and the common good. But the basic outlook is shared by others.[23] This reading, however, makes Nietzsche into an inverted moralist who preserves the same picture of ethical authority even as the content is turned upside-down. As the above discussion should make clear, Nietzsche's immoralism does not offer new, especially malevolent injunctions with a special overriding authority that derives from a special source of value. Instead Nietzsche calls for some kind of reappraisal of familiar aspects of moral life:

> I do not deny, as is – assuming that I am no fool – self-evident, that many actions called immoral are to be avoided and resisted; similarly, many actions called moral are to be done and demanded. – But I think that the one should be avoided and the other demanded *for different reasons* than hitherto. We have to *learn anew* [*umlernen*] – in order eventually, perhaps very late, to attain yet more: *to feel anew* [*umfühlen*]. [D 103]

What distinguishes Nietzsche's position here are the reasons, thoughts, and feelings associated with action, and not a radical opposition to morality as such.[24] It seems to be Nietzsche's position that once morality's mistakes about the normative are taken away, the significance of these things will appear in a much different light.

To consider the implications of Nietzsche's criticisms, it would be helpful to consider three alternative interpretations of what Nietzsche's substantive ethics consists in. These three interpretations each react to Nietzsche's critique of morality by offering a teleological theory of some kind, that is, one structured around a *telos*, an end or goal. They plausibly see this as the best way of maintaining some philosophical discourse about ethics while incorporating Nietzsche's claims about morality, and in particular about the mistakenness of morality's picture of distinctive ethical authority. Nevertheless, even they fail to capture the content of immoralism.

There are three main strands of teleological interpretation of Nietzsche: we can call them *aretaic consequentialists*,[25] *criterial aretaists*, and *standard aretaists*. According to the first, 'individual human beings or character' of some kind 'are the ultimate *telos* or value,'[26] and the additional content of ethics is that this *telos* is to be maximized: one is to promote as much greatness or good character or as many excellent human beings as possible.[27] The second interpretation, criterial *aretaism*, reads Nietzsche as arguing that the right course of action is whatever stems from a valuable state of character or motive. For example, on Christine Swanton's reading, an action is right or valuable if and only if it expresses some form of strength in the agent.[28] Strength, that is, is the fundamental *telos*, and thus determines what counts as good and right. Finally, there is standard *aretaism*, or plain old virtue theory. This approach is primarily concerned with presenting an account of human flourishing – what it is to have a valuable or worthwhile life – in which virtue or some set of virtues play an intrinsic role. An account of right action is of incidental and derivative importance. On this approach, Nietzsche is roughly Aristotelian with an alternative, slightly nutty set of virtues to praise.

Aretaic consequentialism, that Nietzsche advocated a single overriding duty 'to maximize the achievement of human excellence,'[29] does respect a genuine concern of Nietzsche's, namely, human excellence. But the reading seems shortsighted because there are other ways to respect human excellence than to invoke an overriding duty to bring about the greatest possible quantity of it. Indeed, what seems to mark off *aretaic* consequentialism is the presumption of just what Nietzsche found problematic with morality. A basic concern is turned into an impersonal good of singular, overriding importance.[30] One considers this good only as represented in an outcome, and it serves as the ground for an unconditional imperative. And this ground is not even potentially affected by any other consideration: the imperative is not authoritative because of its connections to other deliberative elements, but is completely disconnected. This account is substantively defective in that outcomes and imperatives are simply not Nietzsche's fundamental concerns. But more deeply problematic here is the way in which a simple concern is presented as inevitably taking on a distinctly moral character. The consequentialist reading gets it wrong by fitting Nietzsche's concerns into a theoretical framework marked by a rule, purity, conclusiveness, comprehensiveness, and certainty.

According to criterial *aretaism*, Nietzsche is proposing some fundamental account of virtue or human excellence, and all other ethical properties are determined exclusively by reference to virtue or excellence. Thus Michael Slote reads Nietzsche as offering what he calls an 'agent-based' theory:

> If we treat as the sole criterion of ethical admirability or deplorability whether one's actions [...] come from strength or from weakness, we are committed to what I call 'agent-based' virtue ethics. Such ethics treats all ethical characterizations of actions as derivable from fundamental and independent *aretaic* characterizations of the inner states [...] agent-basing makes the moral or ethical quality of actions more completely depend on the excellence or deficiency of the agent's inner states than anything we find, say, in Aristotle.[31]

The ascription of such an approach to Nietzsche derives, I think, from some familiar features of his thought: again the concern for human excellence, and also Nietzsche's resistance to moral rules and his suspicion about a picture of intentions that might otherwise be required for a backward-looking moral theory. Indeed, this approach very effectively conveys the connection that Nietzsche insists on between moral psychology and morality. But the criterial approach seems to replace each objectionable element with a less plausible but equally objectionable element.

Christine Swanton presents this reading in terms of Nietzsche's critique of a certain picture of intentions. She claims, first, 'For Nietzsche, in short, it is the 'origin' of an action that 'decides its value' [BGE 32]'.[32] The central issue of ethics is then what originates action. So along with this criterion of value she supplies Nietzsche's moral psychology: 'What is important then for Nietzsche are not the reasons which the agent rehearses to herself and to others, but the nature of the deeper *desires* expressing strength or weakness which are the springs of her actions.'[33] There can be no doubt, for reasons that Swanton supplies, that Nietzsche rejects a picture of intentions in which they are 'reasons which the agent rehearses to herself.' But this does not lead to the conclusion that deeper desires, rather than intentions, furnish the criterion of value, both because there is no such criterion of value, and because deeper desires are no more transparent than intentions. The two issues turn out to be related: morality sought a decisive measure of moral significance, and therefore encouraged a picture in which there are psychological elements that, because immune to contingency, can function as criterial. So it can hardly have been Nietzsche's aim in criticizing morality simply to replace one perfectly valuable inner state with another one and thereby preserve a unified sense in which all right action is right in a common way.

Consider, thus, what Nietzsche says about the first issue in the passage that Swanton cites:

> In the last ten thousand years, we have nevertheless, step by step, gone so far in a few large areas of the earth that it is no longer the consequences but the origin of an action that is allowed to decide its value [...]. But today shouldn't we have arrived at the necessity of once more concluding upon a reversal and fundamental shift in values, on account of a further self-examination and deepening of the human being? [BGE 32]

Nietzsche is precisely *not* advocating treating the origin of an action as deciding its value; he is advocating the replacement of that idea. And he identifies increasing self-awareness and profundity as the impetus for such a change: our psychology has become too complex to contain items of univocal moral significance. Our psychological features, rather, become meaningful only in relation to the rest of life:

> In itself it, like *every* drive, has neither that moral character nor any moral character at all, and not even a determinate accompanying sensation of pleasure or displeasure: it acquires all this as a second nature only when it enters into relations with drives already baptized good or evil, or is noted as the property of beings that have already been morally ascertained and assessed by the people. [D 38]

The criterial approach thus merely offers a slightly different morality, with a slightly different inner state at its center. And it places a greater strain on our credulity than an intention-based morality: whereas an intention only had to satisfy a moral standard, criterial virtues must be both intrinsically valuable and value-conferring. And this problem will persist through any version of the criterial approach, for the problem is not with a particular kind of inner state, but with an inner state serving that function at all. In fact, the problem does not even seem to be with inner states, but with *anything* serving as a rule for right action. It surely does not matter what is placed at the center: "'virtue,' 'duty,' the 'good in itself' [...] all phantasms in which the decline and final exhaustion of life [...] expresses itself" [A 11]. What Nietzsche opposes is the very idea that *anything* could in itself provide such a decisive ground. When Nietzsche insists that 'everything un-conditional belongs in pathology' [BGE 154], he makes no special exception for states of character or strength-expressing desires. For anything to play the role that virtue plays in the criterial approach, it would have to have a special right-conveying power. And Nietzsche thinks that no sense can be made of such a power.[34]

A standard virtue theory is much closer, I think, to Nietzsche's approach.[35] A standard virtue theory 'requires an acceptable view of the human good which will enable us to show how morality can be explicated in terms of character traits that are indispensable or useful for the attainment of that good.'[36] This approach presents one signifi-cant problem: no one has identified a plausible account of what Nietzsche thinks the virtues are, or the human good is.[37] But it does offer two features that seem to cohere well with Nietzsche's position. One is that it reads Nietzsche as offering an *attractive* theory:[38] one in which an account of what kind of life is valuable or worthwhile is fundamental, and reasons are derived from this. This feature is appealing because it engages with the agent's own perspective in a natural way. The theory prescribes what the agent herself, if she were sufficiently clear-sighted, would want. The virtues, in particular, are desirable as essential constituents of a good life. And this still leaves room for practical necessity or, as Nietzsche calls it, 'inner necessity' [A 11]: the bindingness then stems from one's own commitments to one's practical identity. The other appealing feature is that it can leave open the source and division of ethical authority. Unlike the criterial approach, according to which inner states possess or convey all practical normative properties,[39] the standard theory leaves room for independent moral considerations that the agent recognizes as well as moral considerations about the agent. Not everything needs to be reduced to agent psychology, and yet the gap between virtue characterizations and the particulars of ethical practice can in principle be closed.

So there are two separate reasons why the standard approach is appealing, both as theory and as Nietzsche interpretation: a eudaemonist reason and an intellectualist reason. And Nietzsche does seem to evince a commitment both to the eudaemonist idea that human flourishing is important, and to the intellectualist idea that what sort of person one is affects one's ability to recognize salient considerations. Nevertheless, Nietzsche's treatment of virtues shows, I think, why the standard approach is not the best way to understand Nietzsche's substantive ethics.

Nietzsche's treatment of the virtues is best understood in terms of their place in what he calls 'the great economy of the whole':

> In the great economy of the whole, the terrible aspects of reality (in affects, in desires, in the will to power) are to an incalculable extent more necessary than that form of petty happiness, so-called 'goodness'; one must even be indulgent to allow the latter any place at all, since mendacity about instinct is its precondition. [EH, destiny, 4]

Here Nietzsche leaves open at least two questions: what the economy of the whole is, and what the terrible aspects of reality are necessary for. But eudaemonism is pictured as both expendable and mendacious.

Goodness is a form of happiness, but a petty one: it is so much less essential to our lives than all the terrors that we suffer and impose. Goodness also presupposes mendacity: it requires deception about what it is and what the world is like.

But this presupposition of mendaciousness does not imply that virtue is therefore faulty; Nietzsche only suggests that virtue's provisional and limited importance is inevitably mistaken for something greater. In Nietzsche's metaphor of an economy, virtue is a component in a productive process so comprehensive that it incorporates the mistakenness about virtue, too. Ethical concerns emerge out of our attempts at self-direction which, in aiming at goodness, inevitably go astray. In particular, taking virtue as part of the end of human life generates an 'unspeakable amount of misunderstanding':

> Through *errors* as to its origin, its uniqueness, its destiny, and through *demands* that have been made on the basis of these errors, humanity has raised itself on high and again and again 'surpassed itself': but through these same errors an unspeakable amount of suffering, mutual persecution, suspicion, misunderstanding, and even greater misery of the individual in and for himself, have come into the world. [D 425][40]

Holding ourselves to the demands of virtue, or any moral standards, does not culminate in the perfection of character, and certainly not in happiness. On the contrary, its accomplishment makes us miserable and dissatisfied. The very responsiveness to the requirements of virtue involves a self-transcendence which is 'purchased' at a price. This is the economics of 'raising ourselves on high': virtue arises within a process of expenditure and productiveness, in which we do not arrive at some final accomplishment, but 'surpass ourselves.' To be agents who have pride and see ourselves and our activity as significant, we need to surpass, and not rest with, our virtues.

So virtue is important, but as provisional accomplishments within a more general process of becoming different, more profound creatures through self-estrangement. The exercise of virtue does not bring happiness, and happiness is not the end of the process. Thus, according to Nietzsche, there are two kinds of mistakes that can arise from misunderstanding the limited place of virtue: to take virtue as independently important, and to take virtue as independently determinate.

Regarding the former, Nietzsche did not seem to think that the state of anyone's soul was inherently important. This is apparent in a comment on a mistake of post-Socratic philosophy: 'With [the pre-Socratics] there was not the 'horrible pretension to happiness' as from Socrates on. Not everything revolved around the condition of their souls' [KSA VIII.6 [14]; cf. GM III, 8 & 22]. The latter mistake, about the determinateness of virtue, arises in a statement of disappointment: 'I sought after great human beings; I always found only the *apes* of their ideals' [TI, maxims, 39]. This, I think, is not the report of an epistemic shortcoming – the maxim is titled 'The disappointed one speaks' – but of the mistakenness of looking for human excellence in the fulfillment of ideals. Ideals take their content from significant accomplishments in different contexts, suitably generalized. So even for one's character to live up perfectly to an ideal is potentially deficient. It could be apelike: a superficial imitation of what had been, in another context, significant. Matching one's stability of character to a fixed standard requires something further: the context in which such a match is significant. Ideals of character depend on some horizon of accomplishment beyond having a stable character; the invocation of 'greatness' here suggests what such a horizon could be. But at the same time, Nietzsche indicates that the issue related to greatness is not restricted to exceptional cases. Zarathustra makes the general wish, 'May your virtue be too elevated for the familiarity of names' [Z I, *Von den Freuden- und Leidenschaften*], praising those characters shaped according to a specificity of context that transcends the generality of ideals.

What this suggests is that however important virtue is, that importance is qualified dependent on a realm of considerations that cannot be fully accommodated in terms of character. One way of expressing this point is Nietzsche's epigram 'As long as one has her *why?* of life, she can endure almost any *how?* – The human being does *not* strive for happiness' [TI, maxims, 12]. Eudaemonist considerations depend on a background of purposes and reasons to be significant, and if components of happiness are not available, then the purposes and reasons suffice. The point of Nietzsche's substantive ethics is not to explain how to be good, but to explain something more basic: how to be engaged, capable of going forward, interesting, and even worthy:

> We violate ourselves nowadays, no doubt of it, we nutcrackers of the soul, ever questioning and questionable, as if life were nothing other than nutcracking; and thus we must necessarily become day-by-day always more questionable, *worthier* of asking questions; and thereby perhaps also worthier – of living? [GM III, 9]

This again indicates why Nietzsche rejects the eudaemonist ground: there is, involved even in self-worth, a kind of self-harm that undermines stable virtues. But this also indicates why Nietzsche rejects the intellectualist ground. Answering ethical questions requires asking ourselves questions, which makes *us* questionable. The very process renders us more complex, which renders the potential answers more complex, which provokes more questions. We generate our own ethical complexity, and features of character have no privileged causal, epistemic, or justificatory standing in this process. Virtues can neither resolve nor engage with the full range of considerations that we are open to.

None of these approaches are adequate, then. Each shares in what Maudemarie Clark, following Nietzsche, has identified as morality's misinterpretation of ethical life.[41] Morality takes itself as discontinuous from the rest of life, and therefore as exceptionally stable, conclusive, and determinate. But this claim to separateness mistakes not only its own proper domain, but all of life.

But morality, in its demandingness, points beyond itself. And thus Nietzsche often recognizes multiple senses of 'morality.'[42] In one, it 'makes stupid' [D 19]: it represents obedience to custom [HH 42] and the refusal to be dissatisfied with oneself [D 343].[43] But in another sense, morality is what compels potentially unlimited reflection on practice:

> But there is no doubt that a 'thou shalt' still speaks to us too, that we too still obey a severe law set over us [...] namely, that we do not want to go back to that which we consider outlived and decrepit, to anything 'worthy of disbelief,' be it called God, virtue, truth, justice, altruism; that we do not allow ourselves any bridges of lies to old ideals. [...] [D, preface, 4]

Morality, without its misinterpretations, still remains as the demand for critical scrutiny on how to lead a life in general. This is Nietzsche's modernism: why, among other things, his ethics cannot be assimilated to virtue theory. On Nietzsche's account, the stability that moral theory offers is bad for morality: '*morality must be shot at*' [TI, maxims, 36] or it becomes mere 'fancy dress' [WS 63].[44] Any approach that offers definitive answers or that relies on the fixity of character to provide stability harms its own provision of practical guidance.[45] By thus limiting challenges to itself, it separates itself from the activity of practical deliberation, and thus loses touch with the details of ethical concern.[46] The stability of virtue theory does not accommodate the specificity and heterogeneity that is involved in informing the conduct of life.[47]

Immoralism thus turns out to be what Nietzsche calls '*being philosophically minded*' [HH 618].[48] Nietzsche declared, 'this much mistrust, this much philosophy' [GS 346], and part of what gives 'immoralism' its name is Nietzsche's claim that morality has become an ossified set of imperatives which ward off rather than embody critical scrutiny. So what the rejection of morality leads to is a newly self-correcting enterprise. The implications of this philosophical enterprise remain, of course, unresolved; Nietzsche recommended 'experiments' rather than solutions.[49] But it does suggest a way to proceed. The task of immoralism is better to represent the domain of ultimate practical concern. We have concerns that transcend goodness of character, adherence to principle, or general welfare. But the shortcomings of these conceptualizations of the ethical point to something beyond them all. What immoralism tries to convey is a sense of what ultimately matters, even if principles, virtue, and even happiness only partially do.[50]

The Value of Values

The critical spirit of Nietzsche's immoralism does not produce an anti-moralism, and it does not itself constitute a substantive recommendation for ethical practice. What the critique of morality suggests, rather, is that an immoralist ethics must cohere with a picture of the normative which is not stabilized by any fixed points, but nevertheless offers a replacement for the intellectualism of character as an account of the recognition of the ethical particulars that inform practice and a replacement for *eudaimonia* as the *telos* of ethical life.

Nietzsche's phrase 'the value of values' suggests how he approaches these matters. Nietzsche calls for an assessment of values – that is, of our practical commitments in general – simply by asking the question of what these values are worth. Of course, this makes for a regressive argument: the first-order assessment depends on an unsupported higher-order evaluation, and so on. But Nietzsche, I think, was not only aware of this, he wished to make use of it. Since Nietzsche did not do much to explain what he meant here, we have to look at his example of what it means to ask after the value of values:

> Have [these values] inhibited or promoted human flourishing [*Gedeihen*] so far? Are they a sign of crisis, impoverishment, of the degeneration of life? Or, on the contrary, do they betray the fullness, force, the will of life, its courage, its confidence, its future? [GM, preface, 3]

Here it might seem as if Nietzsche is advocating assessment in terms of very particular values: flourishing versus impoverishment, or courage versus degeneration, and so on. But, viewed in that light, there does not seem to be a coherent whole: the elements on each side do not match up into contraries, and there are competing versions on the apparently positive side. What unifies the discussion, however, is the genitive 'of life'. By invoking 'life', Nietzsche is struggling to articulate a practical issue more basic than any particular expression of it;[51] the apparent inconsistencies stem from trying to articulate a matter of such generality. Nietzsche is committed to offering some kind of immanentist argument: one in which the critical impetus comes from entirely inside the standpoint being criticized.[52] So his strategy is to remain 'inside', but to be as comprehensive as possible. This comprehensiveness consists in treating all of life as a single, basic issue. And thus by being so inclusive, Nietzsche tries to retain his internal standpoint while obviating any consideration that might undermine his whole approach.

Nietzsche's teleology is thus one without any particular *telos*: there is no ultimate standard to appeal to besides a successful teleology. As Nietzsche expresses it, the 'inhibition' or 'promotion' of bare human *'Gedeihen'* – a verb form indicating nothing more than successful directed activity – is that around which his ethics is structured. This is Nietzsche's notion of life: not a reductively biological notion, nor a sequence of discrete subjective states,[53] but something 'lived'.[54] It is too basic to be characterized in terms of anything in particular,[55] but involves engagement with one's commitments and with the ongoing direction of one's future activity. This of course needs to be sustained by particular commitments, such as 'courage', 'fullness', 'force', and the much more specific ones by which one can make sense of one's self-direction. But what distinguishes Nietzsche, he says, is 'freedom from partiality in relation to the total problem of life' [EH, wise, 1]. And the bedrock that remains when any or all the particular commitments have been let go is life.

The teleology of life is what leads to Nietzsche's not entirely helpful specification of his substantive ethics: 'we ourselves, we immoralists are the answer' [TI, morality, 6]. This answer arises in the context of how, although morality is in some sense a failure, it may nevertheless serve to our 'advantage' in the 'economy of the law of life.' What Nietzsche suggests is that moral ideals served a purpose not in their truth or falsity, but in that they contributed to making sense of the 'deliberations, considerations, and intentions of life,' even if only by opposing themselves to them. And so *we ourselves* are the answer. What counts is not this or that ideal, but that we, through the consideration, adoption, and rejection of ideals, are able to conduct life in a way responsive to and guided by our concerns and considerations. What counts is we ourselves and the lives that we lead. And so this is the focus of ethics: we ourselves, as manifested in some concrete lived life.

This characterization of life, incidentally, illuminates Nietzsche's notion of the will to power. In *Beyond Good and Evil*, after claiming that 'life itself is will to power', Nietzsche warns us to 'beware of *superfluous* teleological principles!'[BGE 13], suggesting that will to power is the most basic teleological principle, and any more specific teleology presents some kind of danger.[56] In *The Genealogy of Morals*, after contrasting the will to power idea with 'the mechanistic senselessness of all events', Nietzsche states that on the latter view, 'The essence of life, its *will to power*, is disregarded; one thereby overlooks the fundamental priority of the spontaneous, aggressive, expansive, formgiving forces that lay out new interpretations and set new directions' [GM II, 12]. Life as will to power is a general directedness, or more specifically a giving-direction and giving-form that includes giving oneself a direction: imposing order on a tractable existence by interpreting one's world.[57]

All this leads to Nietzsche offering a teleological ethical theory, but one governed by sustaining purposiveness in general rather than by any 'superfluous' teleological principles. Life as a whole functions where no standard exterior to ethical practice could; the directedness of the whole makes available the reasons and purposes that inform conduct. Thus Nietzsche articulated the interconnectedness of all the theoretical and practical particulars of a way of life in terms of a familiar example of natural teleology:

> We have no right to be *isolated* in any way: we may not make isolated errors nor come across isolated truths. Rather, our ideas, our values, our yes's and no's, our if's and whether's, grow out of us with the necessity with which a tree bears its fruit. [GM, preface, 2][58]

Nature Redux

There is no teleology apart from our practices and our ways of explaining things:[59] there is no '*the way*' [Z III, *Vom Geist der Schwere*, 2], and it is not tenable that 'the brick that falls from the roof' [D 130]

does so for a reason. And yet we cannot do without governing purposes. 'Human nature', says Nietzsche, 'has been changed by the ever
new appearance of [...] teachers of the purpose of existence [and] now
it has one more need – the need for the ever new appearance of such
teachers and teachings of the 'purpose' [GS 1]. Since there is no
teleology from outside, what directedness we have must be somehow
embodied in our lives, and the directedness of the whole of our
activity must be embodied in a concrete way of life. So we need
teachers of the purpose of existence to make sense of life, and we need
to be able to live up to our sense-making in order to sustain our purposiveness. This creates a tension that transforms human nature but
causes every purposiveness to falter,[60] necessitating an ever new invention of purposiveness. It also creates what is perhaps the central
issue in Nietzsche's substantive ethics, the conflict between health and
profundity.

Consider Nietzsche's picture of what it is to be governed by
some overarching purposiveness. To have such a purposiveness is to
give it to ourselves, not as a conscious decision, but to have one's
entire way of life informed by that purposiveness. There is nothing to
this teleology other than it making sense as a way of understanding
what our lives are, in some sense, about, and conversely, our lives can
themselves embody such a purposiveness simply by making sense in a
particular way. And this is why Nietzsche does not need an intellectualism of virtue as that which explains the recognition of salient
ethical considerations. The way of life as a whole embodies its own
rationality:[61] success in sustaining it, with all its practices of sense-
making and revision, would accompany an available authority of
reasons and judgments. This, I think, explains Nietzsche's otherwise
mysterious claim that a different kind of morality would 'make the
world *more rational*' [CW, epilogue]. A more substantial purposiveness would inform our self-understanding in a way that enabled us to
find reasons for things. Our lives would make sense and thus, the
events of these lives would have their purposes, too. The world would
be more rational.

The end of making the world more rational requires that all of
life be subject to philosophical scrutiny. There is no distinct realm of
moral value on Nietzsche's view; our responsibilities and commit-

ments towards others are continuous with the more mundane aspects of daily life. One result of this approach is that very little is changed. The world to be made more rational is the 'world that concerns *us*, in which *we* fear and love, this almost invisible, inaudible world of subtle commanding, subtle obeying, a world of the 'almost' in every regard, intricate, captious, poignant, and tender' [BGE 226]. This world is not regulated by moral imperatives, but by fears and loves, and the almost invisible, almost inaudible considerations of meaning and importance. And these considerations that comprise the world that concerns us, despite preserving the moral language of commanding and obeying, are intricate, captious, poignant, and tender. So for all of his language of transformation and revolution, Nietzsche wishes to emphasize that the effects of a move to immoralism would actually be quite subtle.

A related result of Nietzsche's approach is an intensified focus on 'the closest things' [WS 6 & 16; HH, preface, 5]. 'An unfortunate consequence' of conceiving of moral value as distinctive, says Nietzsche, is that 'one does not make the closest things, for example eating, dwelling, dressing oneself, and social intercourse, the object of continuous uninhibited and *general* reflection and reformation; but rather, because it is considered degrading, it becomes estranged from its artistic and intellectual seriousness' [WS 5]. The heterogeneity of ethical life should be matched by a philosophical discourse about the everyday – as Nietzsche summarizes it, 'the present and neighbourhood and life and oneself' [WS 16]. These closest things make up more of life and the potential for flourishing than moral emergencies involving trolleys and teleportation, and they generate their own realm of considerations. Thus Nietzsche asks 'what food *means*' [BGE 234], 'what houses mean' [Z III, *Von der verkleinernden Tugend*, 1], and what the 'choice of *one's own kind of recreation*' [EH, clever, 3] amounts to. 'The smallest, most everyday matters' [GS 299] not only offer familiar comforts, but take on a greater significance when not crowded out by comparison with moral values.

This attention to the importance of small things is both why Nietzsche calls for a 'return to nature', and why he has reservations about the prospects of any such return. Amid a discussion of Rousseau, Nietzsche says, 'I too speak of a 'return to nature,' although it is really not a going back but a *going up* – up to the high, free, even terrible nature and naturalness, one that plays with great tasks, *may play with them* [...]' [TI, skirmishes, 48]. A renewed attention to the everyday is in a sense a return to nature: affective satisfaction and small comforts rather than self-estranging moral ideals become important. But Nietzsche insists that his naturalism is not one of going back. He is not arguing that nature is fundamentally hospitable to a favoured existence, or that we ought to consider ourselves as exclusively the product of natural determinations, or that nature can somehow serve to resolve ethical worries that we could not otherwise resolve ourselves. Instead, his naturalism is one of an ascent to play and great tasks: the recommendation is not to conduct our behaviour in accordance with a pre-understanding of nature, but to see our mentality – our meanings and norms – as an integral part of the natural world. To *return* to nature is to stop treating the capacities and concerns upon which our aspirations depend as distinct from the rest of our existence. Then, suggests Nietzsche, we could recover for our affective lives the *sui generis* importance represented by our more spiritual or abstract concerns.[62] The result would be not a return to instinct but the mediated spontaneity of a 'second nature'[63] or a 'new' innocence in which the immediate substance of our lives takes on a deeper meaning.

But this nature and naturalness are also 'terrible.' Nature is terrible, on this picture, because it antagonizes itself. The natural phenomena of the ever-new inventions of human purposes changes human nature itself. And with this, affective health changes:

> For there is no health as such, and all attempts to define a thing that way have failed miserably. Determining merely what the meaning of health for your *body* depends on your goal, your horizon, your powers, your impulses, your errors, and especially on the ideals and phantasms of your soul. [GS 120]

But goals, horizons, powers, and ideals are not themselves stable, so there is no stable measure of health. Even affective well-being depends on the availability of ever more spiritual passions and more profound meanings, which is exactly what separates us from our affective well-being. There is no stable equilibrium between health and pro-

fundity: we need to be able to make sense of things in order to flourish, and the meaningfulness of our activity even seems to require
nature's intransigence. So Nietzsche's substantive ethics can offer no
single answer. Instead it suggests a series of risks that at best balance
the preservation of health with the preservation of meaning.

Conclusion: The Meaningfulness of Life

What I have been suggesting is that Nietzsche's substantive ethics
comes to look something like an answer to the old question of the
meaning of life, except without any answer to the question of the meaning of life. For there is no answer. Nothing could possibly both be
meaningful for us in specific, action-guiding ways, and also be independent of all that contingencies that would render it unstable. Productiveness of and responsiveness to meaning arises through an engagement with life, and that is something that takes no single form.[64]
So what remains is something like the meaningfulness of life. There is
no horizon of purpose that lies completely outside of our practices, but
only a reflection on sustaining some meaning in the conduct of life,
and therewith, perhaps, to make sense of what flourishing might
amount to.

   So the resulting ethics is, roughly, Aristotle's, with everything
familiarly Aristotelian stripped away: there is no settled role for
human nature or the virtues, and no fixed *telos*. Instead, Nietzsche
offers an account of how our freedom engages with ethical concern as
a whole, taking up the considerations that condition the resolution of
more particular practical matters. This kind of ethics thus produces
neither an algorithm for action, nor an elucidation of the end of life.
This is, for two reasons, what is attractive about it. One reason is that
the status and application of our ethical categories are sometimes
themselves fundamental matters of concern. For example, if a particular social structure were racist or a leader represented hostility to
Enlightenment, then that could be a genuine focus of ethical concern

independent of how it cashes out in terms of right or welfare. An ethics of meaningfulness allows for historical categories, such as class, gender, *ethnos*, or self, to be directly integrated with ethical discourse, without mediation through an abstract moral framework. The second reason why the openendedness of Nietzsche's account is attractive is that it calls for no stronger generalizations than are available. Meaning offers structure: it sets out the connections among the salient features of the world and, by constraining deliberation, contributes to regulating action.[65] But it presents just as much structure as obtains: it can substantiate claims of practical necessity, but does not need to make universal, or even interpersonal, claims to express its constraints. Not only does this prevent misunderstandings, but gives a wider latitude for treating phenomena as new, original, or unique in some substantial sense.

Two concluding comments. One is that the problem of the meaningfulness of life is what makes Nietzsche declare that he, or philosophy in general, is inadequate to the task before him. Nietzsche offers his legacy to the experimenters and philosophers of the future because, in his view, there can be no setting of answers outside the leading of a life. The substantive content of ethics only arises in relation to the contingencies that one confronts and these cannot be fully anticipated. My second concluding comment is that the meaningfulness of life is resistant to familiar forms of scepticism. There are many ways that one can fail here, but they are all relatively mundane: seeming ridiculous,[66] not finding any purpose in anything one does, having the meaning of one's life upended when one's cause comes to grief, having one's life not mean what one thought it did. There are many ways of getting it wrong, but as long as there are specific ways of getting it wrong, then one need not worry that the whole enterprise is in vain. The specific ways of getting it wrong suggest that there are contrasting ways in which one might succeed, and this potential is all the meaningfulness of life relies on. For such meaningfulness to obtain, there need not be anything beyond its recognition; it makes no difference whether or not 'the world that concerns us' corresponds to or is grounded by something outside of itself. The satisfaction of leading a life whose broad outlines make sense is self-sufficient.[67]

References:
For a general bibliography of Nietzsche's works in German and English see end of volume.

Notes

1   See, for example, the preface of part I of *Human, All Too Human*, section 1. Works by Nietzsche are hereafter cited in the text by fragment or section number; translations are mine and emphasis is original unless otherwise noted. Nietzsche's use of the terms 'immoralism' and 'immoralist,' like his use of most others, is inconsistent. At first it seems to correlate with a fairly typical sense of immoral; by 1886 it seems to designate a distinctive ethical standpoint and is associated with pagans, the renaissance, modernity, and a mysterious 'we'; by the end of his career, Nietzsche insists that he is the first and the only immoralist, and that immoralism is his 'badge of honour' for himself: i.e., it designates what is distinctive about him and his ideas. I am not, however, concerned with sussing out the various uses of the word 'immoralism', but only with clarifying Nietzsche's distinctive ethical account. This account, I believe, corresponds closely with, but is not governed by, post-1886 usage of the word 'immoralism.'

2   I have argued this elsewhere: cf. my 'The Philosophical Function of Genealogy,' in K. Ansell-Pearson ed., *The Blackwell Companion to Nietzsche*, Boston, Blackwell, 2006.

3   Cf. *GS* 1; *GS*, preface, 2; and *GM* I, 14.

4   Cf. also 'philosophers of the future' [BGE, esp. 42 & 44], 'a book for all and none' the subtitle of *Z*, and contrast with what is 'ready to become truths' [BGE 296].

5   Cf. *GS* 114: 'There are absolutely no experiences other than moral ones.'

6   On the self-overcoming of morality, cf. also *WP* 404; *WS* 19; *GS* 153; *WP* 266; *WS* 41; *BGE* 221; *GS* 357; and *GM* III, 27.

7   Cf. my 'Philosophical Function of Genealogy,' in K. Ansell-Pearson ed., *The Blackwell Companion to Nietzsche*, Boston, Blackwell, 2006.

8   Many of these features have become familiar through their adoption in the work of Bernard Williams; cf. *Ethics and the Limits of Philosophy*, Cambridge, MA, Harvard University Press, 1985, esp. chapter 6. The best taxonomy of all the many faults that Nietzsche finds with morality remains Richard Schacht, *Nietzsche*, Boston, Routledge and Kegan Paul, 1983, chapter 7. Cf. also Simon

May, *Nietzsche's Ethics and his War on 'Morality'*, New York, Oxford, 1999, pp. 105ff.

9   Cf. *TI*, improvers, 1, on the semiotic value of morality.

10   Cf. Maudemarie Clark's advice to B. Williams to 'give up his emphasis on the logic of moral obligation' and 'go over to Nietzsche's more genealogical and psychological [...] account,' in 'On the Rejection of Morality: Bernard Williams's Debt to Nietzsche,' in Richard Schacht ed., *Nietzsche's Postmoralism*, New York, Cambridge University Press, 2000, pp. 108 and 111.

11   Cf. *BGE* 23: 'We set off right over morality'

12   An alternate way of putting this point is that morality claims authority for a special kind of 'unconditional' value; cf. Aaron Ridley, 'Nietzsche and the Re-Evaluation of Values,' *Proceedings of the Aristotelian Society* 105:2 (2005), pp. 172ff.

13   Note as well that the earliest of the Circe-claims involves philosophers.

14   Cf. *D*, preface, 3; *D* 19; *KSA* IX, 3 [162]. The last is cited by Tracey Strong, *Nietzsche and the Politics of Transfiguration*, Berkeley, University of California Press, 1975, p. 43.

15   Compare Nietzsche's account of the acceptance of refraining from injury as the '*fundamental principle of society*' [BGE 259] and John Skorupski's invocation of the 'disciplinary forces' that mediate communual life, quoted by Maudemarie Clark, 'On the Rejection of Morality: Bernard Williams's Debt to Nietzsche,' in Richard Schacht ed., *Nietzsche's Postmoralism*, New York, Cambridge University Press, 2000, pp. 104ff.

16   Cf. also *HH* 57: '*Morality as the self-division of humanity.*'

17   Cf. *BT* VS 5 on the relegation of art to the realm of lies, and *TI*, morality, 6.

18   But that would be unlikely, since such an explanation presumes what it denies: namely that there is some universal standard of goodness and badness.

19   Cf. *GS* 76, where the issue is expressed in terms of 'universal binding force': 'precisely the most select spirits bristle at this universal binding force – the explorers of truth above all.'

20   Maudemarie Clark, 'On the Rejection of Morality: Bernard Williams's Debt to Nietzsche,' in Richard Schacht ed., *Nietzsche's Postmoralism*, New York, Cambridge University Press, 2000, p. 114.

21   This is the argument of *GM* III. See also the discussion of 'German free spirits' (i.e., David Strauss) in *EH*, UM, 2.

22   Philippa Foot, 'Nietzsche's Immoralism' in Richard Schacht ed., *Nietzsche, Genealogy, Morality*, Berkeley, University of California Press, 1994, p. 6. Cf. also 'Nietzsche: The Revaluation of Values,' in *Virtue and Vices*, Berkeley, University of California Press, 1978: p. 86. This antagonism is qualified on Foot's reading: only the 'strong' or 'ascending' have such an imperative.

23   See the work of Paul Loeb, for example, 'Zarathustra's Laughing Lions,' in Acampora and Acampora eds., *Nietzsche's Bestiary*, New York, Rowman and Littlefield, 2004, p. 131.

24   Cf. Maudemarie Clark, 'Nietzsche's Immoralism and the Concept of Morality,' in Richard Schacht ed., *Nietzsche, Genealogy, Morality*, Berkeley, University of California Press, 1994, p. 29: what Nietzsche objects to is not the basic components of morality, but to 'the moralization of these ideas and norms.'

25   I borrow the first categorization, but not the exact name, from James Conant, 'Nietzsche's Perfectionism: A reading of *Schopenhauer as Educator*,' in Richard Schacht ed., *Nietzsche's Postmoralism*, New York, Cambridge University Press, 2000, p. 187.

26   Thomas Brobjer, 'Nietzsche's Affirmative Morality: An Ethics of Virtue,' *Journal of Nietzsche Studies* (26) 2003, p. 73. Brobjer occasionally seems to suggest a form of consequentialism, but primarily offers a standard form of aretaism.

27   There are, of course, many aggregation functions that one could insert here, but they are all equivalent for present purposes.

28   Christine Swanton, 'Outline of a Nietzschean Virtue Ethics,' *International Studies in Philosophy* 30:3 (1998), p. 32f.

29   Thomas Hurka, *Perfectionism* (OUP, 1993), pp. 75f, cited by James Conant, 'Nietzsche's Perfectionism: A reading of *Schopenhauer as Educator*,' in Richard Schacht ed., *Nietzsche's Postmoralism*, New York, Cambridge University Press, 2000, p. 242n19. Cf. also Daniel W. Conway, *Nietzsche and the Political*, New York, Routledge, 1997, p. 54.

30   Cf. *GM* II, 11: an ever more impersonal evaluation of the deed.

31   Michael Slote, 'Nietzsche and Virtue Ethics,' *International Studies in Philosophy* 30:3 (1998), p. 24. On 'agent-based' virtue ethics also see Michael Slote, 'Agent-Based Virtue Ethics,' in Slote and Crisp eds., *Virtue Ethics*, New York: Oxford University Press, 1992, pp. 239–62.

32   Christine Swanton, 'Outline of a Nietzschean Virtue Ethics,' *International Studies in Philosophy* 30:3 (1998), p. 31.

33   Christine Swanton, 'Outline of a Nietzschean Virtue Ethics,' *International Studies in Philosophy* 30:3 (1998), p. 32.

34   These issues are significantly complicated in Swanton's own approach, which involves a rejection of eudaemonism, and a highly revisionist account of right; but this does not affect the reading of Nietzsche presented here. Cf. Christine Swanton, *Virtue Ethics: A Pluralistic View*, New York, Oxford University Press, esp. pp. 77 & 227.

35   Cf. Robert C. Solomon, *Living with Nietzsche: What the Great 'Immoralist' Has to Teach Us*, New York: Oxford University Press, 2003, chapter 6. Lester H. Hunt reads Nietzsche as offering a standard virtue theory with two significant departures: virtues are based on passions, and there can be no list of virtues: cf. *Nietzsche and the Origin of Virtue*, New York, Routledge, 1991, esp. chapter 5.

36   Jerome Schneewind, 'Virtue, Narrative, and Community,' *Journal of Philosophy* 79 (1982), p. 653.

37   Robert Solomon even seems to think that there is no such account, all the while presenting one: cf. *Living with Nietzsche: What the Great 'Immoralist' Has to Teach Us*, New York: Oxford University Press, 2003, p. 14.

38   On the idea of an attractive theory, cf. Charles Larmore, *The Morals of Modernity*, New York, Cambridge University Press, 1996, p. 20.

39   Swanton qualifies this to distinguish her position from that of Slote, but not in a way important for present purposes. Cf. Christine Swanton, 'Outline of a Nietzschean Virtue Ethics,' *International Studies in Philosophy* 30:3 (1998), p. 31.

40   This coincides with Conant's Emersonian obervation that Nietzsche denies that the task of self-perfection culminates in the '*telos* of a perfected self.' James Conant, 'Nietzsche's Perfectionism: A reading of *Schopenhauer as Educator*,' in Richard Schacht ed., *Nietzsche's Postmoralism*, New York, Cambridge University Press, 2000, p. 234.

41   Maudemarie Clark, 'On the Rejection of Morality: Bernard Williams's Debt to Nietzsche,' in Richard Schacht ed., *Nietzsche's Postmoralism*, New York, Cambridge University Press, 2000, p. 111. Clark cites *TI* 'improvers' 1, but Nietzsche's identification of morality with misinterpretation of something or another is pervasive: e.g., *BGE* 108; *BGE* 230; *BT* VS 5; *HH* 135 & 143; *GS*, preface, 2; *GM* III, 20 & 23.

42   Cf. e.g. *BGE* 32; *TI*, morality, 4.

43   Cf. also *D* 107; *WS* 48; *D*, preface, 5; etc.

44   I borrow the translation of '*Charaktermasken*' as 'fancy dress' from R.J. Hollingdale's translation of *Human, All Too Human*, New York, Cambridge University Press, 1986.

45   Cf. Simon May, *Nietzsche's Ethics and His War on 'Morality'*, New York: Oxford University Press, 1999, p. 109.

46   Cf. *AOM* 90: 'The good conscience has as its preliminary stage the bad conscience.'

47   On heterogeneity cf. Charles Larmore, *Patterns of Moral Complexity*, New York: Cambridge University Press, 1987, chapter 6.

48   Cf. James Conant, 'Nietzsche's Perfectionism: A reading of *Schopenhauer as Educator*,' in Richard Schacht ed., *Nietzssche's Postmoralism*, New York, Cambridge University Press, 2000, p. 182: 'one cannot grasp the sense in which his philosophy *is* perfectionist apart from an understanding of why he thinks there is a problem about how philosophy, as he seeks to practice it, should be written and read.'

49   Cf. Volker Gerhardt, ''Experimental-Philosophie': Versuch einer Rekonstruktion,' in Mihailo Djuric and Josef Simon eds., *Kunst und Wissenschaft bei Nietzsche*, Würzburg, Königshausen und Neumann, 1986.

50   Cf. Raymond Geuss, 'Outside Ethics,' *European Journal of Philosophy* 11 (2003), p. 29.

51   Cf. Robert B. Pippin, *Idealism as Modernism*, New York: Cambridge University Press, 1997, p. 368: 'seeing 'life'' in *any* particular terms 'is already to have proposed one possibility among others, not to have reached bedrock.'

52   In spite of my competing efforts, the best account of this aspect of Nietzsche's immoralism is Aaron Ridley, 'Nietzsche and the Re-Evaluation of Values,' *Proceedings of the Aristotelian Society* 105:2 (2005), pp. 171–91.

53   Cf. John Cottingham, *On the Meaning of Life*, New York, Routledge, 2003, p. 32: 'We want there to be a sense of direction; we would like our lives to constitute an intelligible journey rather than being an aimless drift.'

54   Or even 'whipped': cf. Robert Pippin, *Idealism as Modernism*, New York: Cambridge University Press, 1997, p. 322.

55   This is perhaps why Nietzsche seems to be giving 'moral advice,' yet at the same time, seems to offering no specific advice. Cf. Robert Solomon, 'Nietzsche's Virtues,' in Richard Schacht ed., *Nietzsche's Postmoralism*, New York, Cambridge University Press, 2000, p. 125.

56   On the teleology of the will to power, see Peter Poellner, *Nietzsche and Metaphysics*, New York, Oxford University Press, pp. 165–6.

57   Cf. the notion of will to power as 'self-constitution' in Mark Warren, *Nietzsche and Political Thought*, Cambridge, MA, MIT Press, 1988, pp. 137ff.

58   Cf. Brian Leiter, *Routledge Philosophical GuideBook to Nietzsche on Morality*, New York: Routledge, 2002, p. 95. Leiter quotes the same passage and identifies the necessity as being that of a mechanical causation of type facts. Cf. also Nietzsche's frequent metaphors of 'fruitfulness' and 'ripeness,' e.g. *WS* 189; *GS* 289; *Z* IV, *Das Nachtwandler Lied*, 9; *GM* II, 2; *TI*, Morality as Anti-Nature, 3.

59   On Nietzsche's critique of teleology, cf. Christa Davis Acampora, 'Between Mechanism and Teleology: Will to Power and Nietzsche's Gay 'Science,'' in G. Moore and T.H. Brobjer eds., *Nietzsche and Science*, Burlington, VT, Ashgate Publishing, 2004, and Henry Staten, 'The Will to Power: A Socio-historical Critique,' in K. Ansell-Pearson ed., *The Blackwell Companion to Nietzsche*, Boston, MA, Blackwell, 2006.

60   On why such purposes falter, cf. Robert Guay, 'Nietzsche on Freedom,' *European Journal of Philosophy*, 10 (2002), p. 316.

61   Cf. David Wiggins, *Needs, Values, Truth*, New York, Oxford University Press, 1998, p. 128.

62   Cf. the 'emphasis' on 'new meaning' in Christa Davis Acampora, 'Between Mechanism and Teleology: Will to Power and Nietzsche's Gay "Science,"' in G. Moore and T.H. Brobjer eds., *Nietzsche and Science*, Burlington, VT, Ashgate Publishing, 2004, p. 181.

63   On 'second nature,' cf. Sabina Lovibond, *Ethical Formation*, Cambridge, MA, Harvard University Press, 2002, pp. 25f & 63.

64 Cf. Susan Wolf, 'Meaning and Morality,' *Proceedings of the Aristotelian Society* 97 (1997), p. 305, and 'Happiness and Meaning: Two Aspects of the Good Life,' *Social Philosophy and Policy* 14:1 (1997), p. 212.

65 On the relation between meaning and normative commitments, see David E. Cooper, *Meaning*, Ithaca, NY, McGill-Queen's University Press, 2003, pp. 89–94.

66 For one version of what could happen here, cf. Thomas Nagel, *Mortal Questions*, New York, Cambridge University Press 1979, p. 15.

67 I am grateful to all those with whom I discussed the subject-matter of this essay, especially to audiences in Sussex and New York.

EDWARD HARCOURT

Nietzsche and Eudaemonism

[T]here is a great deal in [Nietzsche] that must be dismissed as merely megalomaniac. [...] He condemns Christian love because he thinks it is an outcome of fear [...] It does not occur to [him] as possible that a man should genuinely feel universal love, obviously because he himself feels almost universal hatred and fear, which he would fain disguise as lordly indifference. His 'noble' man – who is himself in day-dreams – is a being wholly devoid of sympathy, ruthless, cunning, cruel, concerned only with his own power. King Lear, on the verge of madness, says:

I will do such things –
What they are yet I know not – but they shall be
The terror of the earth.

This is Nietzsche's philosophy in a nutshell.[1]

Thus, notoriously, Bertrand Russell in his *History of Western Philosophy*, and for a long time mainstream analytic philosophy had little more to say for Nietzsche as a moral philosopher than Russell did. More recently, however, Nietzsche's ethics has begun to be rehabilitated, an effect due in no small measure to the neo-Aristotelian movement. For both Nietzsche and the neo-Aristotelians call not only for a rejection of a Judaeo-Christian (or crypto-Judaeo-Christian) 'law conception' of ethics but also for a new approach to ethical issues in which the central question is not 'what makes an action the morally right one?' but rather 'what sort of life would be good for us, given the sorts of creatures that we are?' – an approach, that is, in which the idea of the good life for man occupies centre-stage. The identification of this common ground between Nietzsche and the neo-Aristotelians may, however, come at a price. If Nietzsche just says the same things as the neo-Aristotelians, as certain recent readings have suggested, this is an interesting exegetical observation but with so many neo-Aristotelians already on the philosophical curriculum, why is there any special need to read Nietzsche? Domesticating Nietzsche as a neo-Aristotelian rescues him from the dustbin to which he was consigned by earlier interpretations portraying him as a megalomaniac or champion of evil, but carries the danger that his distinctive voice in the history of ethics will not be heard. This essay attempts to tread a path between an optimistic neo-Aristotelian reading, which makes Nietzsche sound sensible but in no way distinctive, and 'immoralistic' readings (as in Russell's History and, more recently, in Philippa Foot)[2] which make him genuinely radical but at the same time worthy only of dismissal.

[1]

My strategy will be to compare Nietzsche's critique of the value of the 'morality of pity' with neo-Aristotelian critiques of the 'law conception' of ethics (Anscombe), 'morality in the narrow sense' (Wollheim), or the 'morality system' (Williams),[3] both with respect to what they oppose and with respect to what they aim to put in its place.

   First of all, terminology. I don't want to suggest that these four terms – the 'morality of pity', 'morality in the narrow sense' etc. – all pick out precisely the same sets of ideas, but a bit of imprecision here will, I think, do no harm.[4] Anscombe, Wollheim and Williams all have in mind, at the very least, a conception of practical thought in which a privileged position is occupied by concepts of moral requirement, prohibition and (perhaps) permission. Simple act-utilitarianism is an example: not only are questions about rights, for example, or about particular virtues, resolvable into questions about moral rightness and wrongness (as decided by an act-utilitarian test), but because there is always a single utility-maximizing course of action (unless there's a tie), the only practical question an agent can ever be faced with is the question of what he is morally required to do. So there's no room here even for permission: every practical question is a question about one's moral duty. We need a word for this version of practical thought, so let's call it 'morality in the narrow sense' – Wollheim's term,[5] though I do not by this choice intend to give any special favour to Wollheim's characterization of it.

I want to draw attention, for the moment, to just two neo-Aristotelian objections to morality in the narrow sense. The first is that it has the structure of a legal system and without an accepted supreme legislator this structure is empty: what appear to be laws in fact make no genuine claims on us. Michael Tanner nicely illustrates the Nietzschean credentials of this first objection when commenting on the many points of contact between Nietzsche's call for a 'critique of moral values'[6] in the light of the decline of Christian faith – 'When one gives up the Christian faith, one pulls the right to Christian morality from under one's feet' – and Anscombe's 'Modern Moral Philosophy':

> The concepts of obligation, and duty – moral obligation and moral duty, that is to say – and of what is morally right and wrong, and of the moral sense of 'ought', ought to be jettisoned if this is psychologically possible; because they are survivals, or derivatives from survivals, from an earlier conception of ethics [i.e. the law conception] which no longer generally survives, and are only harmful without it. [...] To have a law conception of ethics is to hold that what is needed [...] is required by divine law [...] Naturally it is not possible to have such a conception unless you believe in God as a law-giver like Jews, Stoics, and Christians [...] It is as if the notion 'criminal' were to remain when criminal law and criminal courts had been abolished and forgotten.

As Tanner says, 'one is amazed again and again by the Nietzschean tone of this unwitting disciple'.[7]

The second, quite different, objection is that a human life governed by morality in the narrow sense will, given the sorts of creatures we are, be less good for the person leading it than it might otherwise be – if we need a slogan here, it would be 'morality in the narrow sense is bad for you'. Of the three broadly neo-Aristotelian writers I have cited so far, perhaps it is Wollheim who articulates this objection most clearly. Morality, he says,

> faces a challenge of remarkable gravity, [that it is] [...] in its origins and throughout our lives, simply a price that we pay [...] for relief from external fear. We are frightened in childhood, we interiorize the fear by substituting an internal [object, i.e. the superego] for an external object, we placate the internal representative of the fear by the sacrifice of instinctual gratification, the gain in tranquillity outweighs even the crippling loss of satisfaction, but the sacrifice has nothing independently to recommend it. Morality is an internalized Danegeld.[8]

And though Wollheim thinks this challenge can in part be answered –
the superego which governs by fear comes gradually to be replaced by
something else – this something else is the Ego-Ideal, the internal
representative not of morality in the narrow sense but of what Wollheim calls, in explicit contrast to it, 'value'. So while our mature
practical thought evolves beyond morality in the narrow sense and
beyond the punitive superego, the challenge as addressed to morality
in the narrow sense itself goes unanswered.

There are really several claims here that need to be disentangled.
First there is the negative claim that morality in the narrow sense is
bad for one. Secondly there is the positive claim that some modes of
life in which morality in the narrow sense does not feature are better
for one, and better for one because morality in the narrow sense does
not feature there. And thirdly there is the further, implied positive
claim that the central question in evaluating types of practical thought
is the question under which type or types does humanity fare best. All
have strong echoes in Nietzsche. [9]

As regards the first, negative claim, there is Nietzsche's claim
that man, or 'life', fares worse under a morality of pity than it did
before that morality took hold.[10] Here he is (from the Preface to *On
the Genealogy of Morals*):

> What was especially at stake was the value of the 'unegoistic', the instincts of
> pity, self-abnegation, self-sacrifice, which [...] became for [Schopenhauer]
> 'value-in-itself', on the basis of which he *said No* to life and to himself. But it
> was against precisely *these* instincts that there spoke from me an ever more
> fundamental mistrust, an ever more corrosive scepticism! It was precisely here
> that I saw the *great* danger to mankind, its sublimest enticement and seduction
> – but to what? to nothingness? – it was precisely here that I saw the beginning
> of the end, [...] the will turning *against* life [...]: I understood the ever
> spreading morality of pity that had seized even on philosophers and made them
> ill, as the most sinister symptom of a European culture that had itself become
> sinister, perhaps as its by-pass to a new Buddhism? to a Buddhism for Euro-
> peans? *to – nihilism?*

Or again, there is the following passage from *Daybreak:*

> Has morality not [...] opened up such an abundance of sources of displeasure
> that one could say [...] that with every refinement of morals mankind has

hitherto become *more discontented* with himself, with his neighbour and the lot of his existence? Did the hitherto most moral man not entertain the belief that the only justified condition of mankind in the face of morality was the *profoundest misery*?[11]

As regards the second claim, there is Nietzsche's portrait of the life led by ruling class men before the 'slave revolt' in morality took place:

> The knightly-aristocratic value-judgments presupposed a powerful physicality, a flourishing, abundant, even overflowing health, together with that which serves to preserve it: war, adventure, hunting, dancing, war games, and in general all that involves vigorous, free, joyful activity.

This is evidently intended as a portrait of human beings (or a sub-group of them) flourishing or doing well: according to the 'aristocratic value-equation', 'good = noble = powerful = beautiful = happy'.[12] Conversely the inventors of slave-morality are, among other things, ill. Nietzsche's critique of morality should be seen therefore as grounded not solely in the first objection (the emptiness of a law conception in the absence of belief in a lawgiver) but also in the second: human beings flourish to the extent that their natural capacities are given the greatest possible room for expression, and 'slave morality' narrows this room disastrously. This brings me to the third claim, the more abstract of the two positive ones: 'We [...] having opened our eyes and conscience to the question where and how the plant "man" has so far grown most vigorously to a height' is just one phrase which betrays Nietzsche's subscription to it,[13] but his work is littered with evidence of it.[14] But to hold that human beings flourish to the extent that their natural capacities are given the greatest possible room for expression is to be a eudaemonist.[15] Nietzsche, therefore, is to be seen as a eudaemonist.

It is important to notice that these two lines of objection to morality in the narrow sense are independent of one another. Philosophers have certainly tried to combine support for morality in the narrow sense with what I'm calling eudaemonism, thus placing themselves in opposition to the second objection: Kant and Mill were, I take it, both (in different ways) supporters of morality in the narrow sense, and I read them both also as eudaemonists. (I think this is obvious in Mill's case,[16] and it should be obvious in Kant's too, to anyone who reads Kant beyond the *Groundwork*, or indeed who reads section 1 of the *Groundwork* with their eyes open.)[17] And if that combination of views is possible, there is no reason why to rejection of the second objection (thus motivated) one should not add acceptance of the first: acceptance, that is, that though a life governed by morality in the narrow sense would in fact be the life in which man flourishes the most were it un-problematically available, such a life could only be led at the cost of great insincerity and bad faith. What rejection of the second objection marks out as the best life for us acceptance of the first places beyond our reach. This position would make one a pessimist, but not obviously inconsistent. Conversely one might hold that a life governed by morality in the narrow sense was bad for man (thus accepting the second objection) while finding no fault per se with Kant's or Mill's attempts to keep the 'law' structure together in the absence of a lawgiver (thus rejecting the first).[18]

Having established, pro tanto, the Nietzschean credentials of both these neo-Aristotelian objections to morality in the narrow sense – and without wishing to suggest that these are the only ones – I want for the rest of this essay to set the first objection aside in order to concentrate on the second. To some readers of Nietzsche, however, the very suggestion that Nietzsche was a eudaemonist may seem preposterous, and we need to say something in reply to this before going further.

One objection to the suggestion rests on Nietzsche's frequent dismissive remarks about the value of 'happiness':

> Whether it is hedonism or pessimism, utilitarianism or eudaemonism – all these ways of thinking that measure the value of things in accordance with *pleasure* and *pain*, […] are ways of thinking […] on which everyone conscious of *creative* powers and an artistic conscience will look down upon not without derision […] Well-being as you understand it – that is no goal, that seems to us an *end*, a state that makes man ridiculous and contemptible – that makes his destruction *desirable*.[19]

But passages like this, central as they are to an understanding of Nietzsche, are no reason for dismissing the claim that he was a eudaemonist; and the passage itself, indeed, shows us why. To say that the extent of human flourishing is not to be measured in terms of pleasure or freedom from suffering – the 'universal green-pasture happiness of the herd, with security, lack of danger, comfort, and an easier life for everyone'[20] – is simply to make a point about what flourishing or eudaemonia is, not to say that the promotion of flourishing, when correctly understood, is the wrong standard by which to evaluate types of practical thought. It would be a mere quibble to observe that 'happiness' often translates 'eudaemonia': Nietzsche's hostility to the ideal of a life free of suffering shows not that he dismisses flourishing (or well-being or eudaemonia) as a value, but that he thinks 'well-being as you understand it' is not well-being.

Another objection is put by Simon May who, though agreeing that 'flourishing is, for Nietzsche, the only unconditioned end in relation to which the worth of all values, ends, practices, and concepts is to be judged',[21] argues that this is 'not Aristotelian' because (1) 'the class over which 'potentiality' ranges [in Aristotle] is the human species [...] whereas for Nietzsche it is the individual', and (2) 'for Nietzsche [...] the perfect and final actualisation of a clear and fixed potential is neither possible, nor knowable, nor should be sought'. As regards (2), I have no quarrel with this either as an interpretation of Nietzsche or as a genuine point of difference between Nietzsche and Aristotle. But its truth does not interfere with the classification of Nietzsche as a eudaemonist as I have explained the term. The reverse would be true, however, of (1) if (1) were correct. However, to read Nietzsche as denying that the relevant potentiality is species-specific renders problematic the great many passages in his work in which the good of the 'species "man"' is under discussion, such as e.g. (in *Beyond Good and Evil* alone) 'the plant "man"'; '[religion] keeps the type "man" on a lower rung by preserving too much of what ought to perish'; 'the moral imperative of nature which [...] is addressed [not] to the individual [...] but to peoples, races, ages, classes – but above all to the whole human animal, to man'; the 'enhancement of the type "man"'; and so on.[22] This is not to say that May is wrong to emphasize the importance of individual potentiality in Nietzsche, but rather that (1) embodies a false opposition between individual and species potentiality: realizing the former, for any individual, is just one of countless different ways of realizing the latter, and unsurprisingly, there is no suggestion in Aristotle that every good life need be led in exactly the same way: even if every good life exemplifies the same virtues, it won't consist – indeed could not possibly consist – of the same exemplifications of these virtues.[23]

If Nietzsche is a eudaemonist, however, it is still very much an open question how close his version of eudaemonism was to that of Aristotle or his followers. The right way to measure the distance (if any) between Nietzsche and neo-Aristotelian critics of morality in the narrow sense is to ask which version of practical thought, according to each of them, is the one under which humanity does best.

[2]

How much space is there, then, between Nietzsche's answers to the question which version of practical thought is the best one for us and the neo-Aristotelian one? The first thing to say, of course, is that there is no such thing as the neo-Aristotelian answer to that question: even if every neo-Aristotelian is, by definition, a eudaemonist in the sense I have explained, it is evident that neo-Aristotelian eudaemonism comes in a variety of different versions with different answers to that question to match.

Granted the independence of the two neo-Aristotelian objections to morality in the narrow sense which I sketched in the last section – that it is based on an empty 'law conception' of ethics, and that it is bad for human beings – it is at least possible for reflection on the version of practical thought under which man does best to lead us straight back to a life in which the only practical question is 'which action is morally the right one?' or, slightly more complicatedly, in which the only virtue is the capacity to master impulse in the service of moral duty.[24] That is, one can be a eudaemonist and subscribe to the 'law conception'. There's evidently no need to invoke Nietzsche's supposed immoralism to demonstrate his distance from that subvariety of neo-Aristotelian eudaemonism.

However, one-virtue virtue theories are probably the minority in contemporary virtue ethics. And once we move beyond those, the difference between Nietzsche and the neo-Aristotelians may be harder to discern without appealing to Nietzsche's 'immoralism'. It has been suggested, for example, that in order to see that Nietzsche was not delivering 'a sermon in praise of ruthlessness' we need only see him as substituting for the narrow question 'what ought I morally to do?' the more broadly based question 'how should I live?'[25] But this is the question of modern 'virtue ethics' par excellence.[26] If Nietzsche's alternative to morality in the narrow sense coincides with this neo-Aristotelian one, the charge of immoralism is avoided at the cost of a disappointing familiarity.

It's an open question, I think, how far acknowledgement of a plurality of virtues really takes one from the primacy of questions of moral duty or therefore from the 'law conception': the various virtues might just be regarded as dispositions needed to enable us to discern and carry out our moral duty in different types of situation.[27] But even supposing that it takes us quite far, the fact that Nietzsche and the pluralistic neo-Aristotelians both ask the same question does not imply that they both give it the same answer. The latter maintain, with Aristotle, that the supreme good for man is a certain kind of life in which the capacities with which we are distinctively endowed by nature are most fully developed. This I take to be part of the lesson of the 'harpist' (or 'flautist') analogy in Book I of the *Nicomachean Ethics*. But of course Aristotle's most famous – and independent – claim there is that 'the good for man is an activity of soul in accordance with virtue'.[28] To claim that the best life for us is the life in which our natures are perfected is one thing (what I've called eudaemonism); to claim that the life in which our natures are perfected is also the life of virtue is another. (For the pluralist neo-Aristotelian this won't typically mean resistance to contrary inclination, but something which could be said to express all the more completely the supremacy of moral over other considerations, viz. the idea that the mark of the virtuous disposition is the silencing of countervailing considerations.)[29] This stance is compatible with upholding the second objection to morality in the narrow sense: the reason morality in the narrow sense is bad for us is just that it is narrow, but once moral righteousness is supplanted by a sufficiently rich catalogue of virtues, the point is reversed – our ultimate satisfaction consists in leading the life of virtue. The 'immoralistic' passages alone would seem to make it clear that the (many-virtued) life of the pluralistic neo-Aristotelian can't straightforwardly be Nietzsche's answer to their common question. There is more than one way of expanding the catalogue of (supposed) human excellences which go with different conceptions of how one should live. However, merely identifying a logical gap between Nietzsche and pluralistic neo-Aristotelians doesn't advance our overall project of helping Nietzsche to tread a path between (familiar) neo-Aristotelianism and (crazy) immoralism: it could still be that, even if Nietzsche doesn't say the same as the neo-Aristotelians, the only reason he doesn't is that he recommends badness instead of goodness.

In pursuit of that project I now want to make the two-cornered discussion between Nietzsche and the neo-Aristotelians explicitly three-cornered by introducing Aristotle himself as an independent voice. For there is the suspicion that the dominance of moral considerations in the good life as envisaged by both monistic and pluralistic neo-Aristotelians is due not to whatever they may share with Aristotle but to their post-Christian inheritance. Correspondingly, it may be that in Aristotle himself we will find the familiar equation of the good life for man with the life of virtue, but in combination with a sufficiently different catalogue of virtues to capture Nietzsche's own version of eudaemonism.

[3]

An unpublished fragment of Nietzsche's repeats, in an explicitly Aristotelian connection, the dismissive attitude we have already noted to 'happiness' as an end of life:

> Happiness as the final goal of the individual life. Aristotle and everyone! Thus it is the dominance of the concept of purpose which has been the ruination of all previous moralities.[30]

But direct references in Nietzsche to Aristotle's moral philosophy are few and far between, and it would be a mistake to infer from a passage such as this – even if it is not a one-off – that Nietzsche and Aristotle are poles apart.[31] On the contrary, the reply to that inference is along the same lines as the reply to the other passages dismissing happiness: Nietzsche makes the mistake in interpreting Aristotle's eudaemonism of assuming 'eudaemonia' means something like being contented or leading an enjoyable life.[32] This would, in the context of Nietzsche's conception of the good life for man, justify the dismissal; but an alternative reading of Aristotle in which eudaemonia is a formal, superordinate goal – the name of what you've got when the substantive goals of life are attained – is also available.[33]

As regards the substance of Aristotle's conception of the good life for man, his un-Christian conception of at least some virtues has often been noted. There's no Aristotelian virtue corresponding to the Christian virtue of modesty (that is, modesty with respect to one's own achievements etc., as opposed to sexual modesty): the vice of boastfulness is contrasted in Aristotle with the virtue of truthfulness and the opposing vice of understatement.[34] Again in Christian or post-Christian accounts of friendship, selflessness tends to be to the fore, whereas Aristotle's true friend may 'sacrifice his own interest' but in doing so he 'assigns *to himself* what is most honourable and most truly good', i.e. the honour in so doing.[35] Aristotle regards 'lack of proper ambition' (*aphilotimia*) as a vice. And his virtues of magnificence (*megaloprepeia*) – as manifested for example in 'objects of public-spirited ambition, e.g. [...] [making] a fine show by the provision of a chorus, or the maintenance of a warship, or even by entertaining the whole city at a banquet'[36] – and magnanimity (*megalopsuchia*), which is 'concerned with honour on a grand scale',[37] may be thought to have a distinctly Nietzschean ring to them.[38]

Might one not argue, then, that there is so much that is 'knightly-aristocratic' about Aristotle's catalogue of virtues that there is after all no space between Aristotle and Nietzsche here? If this were right, it would open up a significant gap between Aristotle and the neo-Aristotelians, and so between the latter and Nietzsche too. For public spirit, benevolence, consideration, industriousness, moderation, modesty, forbearance, pity, qualities which, according to Nietzsche, the 'herd man' glorifies as 'the real human virtues' and through which he is 'tame, peaceable and useful to the herd'[39] – certainly figure in various versions of the neo-Aristotelian catalogue, even if not in Aristotle's own. But it would hardly help establish the uniqueness of Nietzsche's voice in the history of ethics. Nor would it necessarily rescue Nietzsche from the contrasting accusation of simply recommending badness, since I take it that public spirit, benevolence etc. really are virtues: it would simply give him, in the shape of the historical Aristotle, an unexpected partner in crime.

However, matters are, I think, more complicated than this. First of all there is Nietzsche's own verdict on the idea that 'the virtuous man is the happiest man', though the occasion of the verdict is (as it happens) Socrates rather than Aristotle. When Socrates went so far as to say this, the Greeks, according to Nietzsche

> did not believe their ears and fancied they heard something insane. For when he pictures the happiest man, every man of noble origin included in the picture the perfect ruthlessness and devilry of the tyrant who sacrifices everyone and everything to his arrogance and pleasure.[40]

Though Nietzsche might be said to be campaigning against 'morality in the narrow sense' in the name of values he derives from the Greeks, these values are not – in his own estimation at least – to be credited to Aristotle, since Aristotle is such an untypical Greek: '[The Greeks'] myths and tragedies are a great deal wiser than the ethics of Plato and Aristotle'.[41] Now it's possible, of course, that Nietzsche's claim that Aristotle's ethics are an anomaly relative to Greek culture as a whole is based on the same misunderstanding of Aristotle as we identified in relation to Nietzsche's (ill-grounded) dismissal of eudaemonia as an end. It's in any case not the place to adjudicate that claim, as it is irrelevant to the matter in hand. The most we can say is that even if Aristotle wasn't untypically Greek, Nietzsche thought he was, and the reasons for his finding him so are reasons which, if genuine, would place Aristotle and his contemporary followers closer to each other than either is to Nietzsche.[42]

One or two other considerations give some substance to this idea. First there is the question of Aristotle's own attitude towards magnanimity. What perhaps makes this virtue sound especially Nietzschean is the suggestion that it is open only to the rich and well-born: 'people of high birth or great power are felt to deserve honour, because they are in a position of superiority'[43] and (deservingly) claiming honour in large quantities is a requirement of magnanimity. However Aristotle says that 'in real truth only the good man ought to be honoured, but the possessor of both qualities [sc. goodness and high birth, wealth etc.] is felt to deserve additional honour'.[44] Some commentators have taken this to show that Aristotle has his tongue in his cheek when reporting the conventional portrait of the 'great-souled' man.[45] Secondly, even if the strong presence of 'self' in Aristotle's virtues may bring him close to Nietzsche on the negative side – if Nietzsche were a follower of Aristotle it would explain why 'these feelings of "for others", "*not* for myself" [...] the whole morality of self-denial must be questioned and taken to court'[46] – it does not get us very far with, for example, the issue of justice, unarguably an Aristotelian virtue and which includes among other things law-abidingness (enjoining e.g. temperate and patient conduct, or 'anything which tends to produce or conserve the happiness [...] of a political association')[47] and distributive justice, involving the notion of equal shares.[48] This seems in sharp contrast to Nietzsche's 'we hold it by no means desirable that a realm of justice and concord should be established on earth'.[49]

These considerations are, however, somewhat indecisive. But there is a far more decisive ground for setting Nietzsche apart from both Aristotle himself and from the neo-Aristotelians, namely their respective attitudes to internal conflict. Moreover it is Nietzsche's attitude to internal conflict which gives us the best hope of 'placing' his most stubbornly 'immoralistic' passages in such a way as to free him from the dismissive readings such as Russell's with which I began. It is to the subject of internal conflict that I turn in the next and final section.

[4]
The unity of the virtues is a theme in some, if not all, neo-Aristotelian writing. This is unarguably so in the 'one virtue' versions of this outlook, in which the materials for conflict are absent from the start;[50] but it is also the case in some pluralistic versions – as tentatively, for example, Foot in *Virtues and Vices*.[51] Beyond (and independently of) the idea that the virtues cannot conflict, there is also the idea that if moral and non-moral considerations come into conflict then, in a fully virtuous person, it is the virtues that win out – and indeed win out without residue. I take this to be implicit in the 'silencing' idea – that

perfect virtue manifests itself in the silencing of contrary impulses. Now of course Aristotle himself might be argued to include some things in his catalogue of the virtues that, relative to a Christian or post-Christian perspective, would count as non-moral (friendship perhaps, or proper ambition). So his emphasis on the unity of the virtues yields a different content to the good life than is yielded by either monistic or pluralistic neo-Aristotelianism, and thanks to the inclusion of non-moral goods within his catalogue of excellences, he could be said to leave more room for non-moral goods in the good life for man than his contemporary followers. Nonetheless, allowing for these differences in content, the idea that the good life for man – eudaemonia – consists in the harmonious integration of a person's ends is present in Aristotle and neo-Aristotelians alike.

The idea that the good life for man consists in the harmonization of ends – either moral ends at the expense of all others, or of moral and non-moral ones – is notably absent, however, from Nietzsche's thought: conflict both among moral ends and between moral and non-moral ones is not only envisaged but indeed celebrated. The following passage is worth quoting at some length:

> In an age of disintegration [...] human beings have in their bodies the heritage of multiple origins, that is, opposite, and often not merely opposite, drives and value standards that fight each other and rarely permit each other any rest. Such human beings [...] will on the average be weaker human beings: their most profound desire is that the war they *are* should come to an end. Happiness appears to them [...] pre-eminently as the happiness of resting, of not being disturbed, of satiety, of finally attained unity [...]. But when the opposition and war in such a nature have the effect of one more charm and incentive of life – and if, moreover, in addition to his powerful and irreconcilable drives, a real mastery and subtlety in waging war against oneself, in other words, self-control, self-outwitting, has been inherited or cultivated, too – then those magical, incomprehensible, and unfathomable ones arise, those enigmatic men pre-destined for victory and seduction, whose most beautiful expression is found in Alcibiades and Caesar [...].[52]

Here the theme of Nietzsche's familiar opposition to 'happiness' as an ideal is recapitulated but also developed: at the core of Nietzsche's disdain for it is not, or not only, the fact that happiness involves the abolition of suffering, but the fact that it involves the abolition of

internal conflict. Unlike suffering, which is (for Nietzsche) a necessary condition of the 'enhancement of the species "man"', internal
conflict – as the 'Alcibiades' passage reveals – is constitutive of it, a
component rather than a mere enabler. However many 'selfish' or
non-moral excellences of character one adds to the Aristotelian
catalogue of virtues, the contrast between Nietzsche's and Aristotle's
conception of the good life, and therefore between their versions of
eudaemonism, is not going to go away, since the harmonization of
ends is an integral feature of Aristotelian eudaemonia.

Before bringing this picture of Nietzsche's conception of the
good life into connection with his alleged 'immoralism', I want briefly
to defend this statement of the contrast between Nietzsche and both
Aristotle and the neo-Aristotelians against some remarks of Nehamas's about Nietzsche, which may be thought to place the contrast
in jeopardy. Developing Nietzsche's ideal of 'becoming who one is',
Nehamas claims that 'the process of dominating (or creating) the
individual [...] is a matter of incorporating more and more char-
actertraits', a 'continual process of greater integration of one's char-
actertraits, habits and patterns of interaction with the world' which
'maximizes diversity and minimizes discord'.[53] Now clearly the
maximization of diversity fits the high status accorded by Nietzsche,
in the 'Alcibiades' passage, to 'those magical, incomprehensible, and
unfathomable ones' who 'wage war against' themselves. But the
'minimization of discord' does not fit at all, and the fact that
Nietzschean 'becoming who one is' is, correctly, said by Nehamas to
be a process and 'not a final state of being'[54] doesn't make the
problem disappear: if someone is admirable partly insofar as they are
at war with themselves, a process by which discord is minimized can
only make them less admirable, not more so.

One way of pinpointing what has gone wrong is that Nehamas
has, I think, run together two different senses of 'integration': the integration of a person's ends (commitments, desires, passions, ideals,
ambitions) *to their character*, and the integration of a person's ends
(commitments etc.) *with one another*. Orestes' dilemma in the *Eumen-
ides* will serve to illustrate the distinction. He is simultaneously obligated to kill his mother (because one is obligated to avenge one's
father's murder and his mother murdered his father) and not to kill his

mother (because one is obligated not to kill one's mother). Evidently in the second sense of 'integration', these commitments are not integrated with one another: on the contrary, one can be honoured only by betraying the other. But in the first sense they *are* integrated: he is as closely identified with one as with the other, and that is just what makes his situation so difficult. (It is not like a reasoned desire to abstain from something and a persistent desire to do it, which one as it were disowns.) This first sense of 'integration' is well captured by Nehamas's claim that self-creation (or becoming what one is) is 'the development of the ability or the willingness to accept responsibility for everything that one has done and to admit [...] that everything that one has done actually constitutes what one is'.[55] But it almost instantly disappears from view again when he adds 'and in the ideal case its harmonization into a coherent whole',[56] since there are two ways, not clearly distinguished, for such a whole to be 'coherent': for all its constituents to be such that the individual has accepted responsibility for them (integration in the first sense), and for all its constituents to be such that they do not conflict with one another (integration in the second sense). Of course it may be much easier to accept responsibility for all one has done (etc.) if the commitments thereby embodied don't conflict; but just what's admirable about the characters Nietzsche describes in the 'Alcibiades' passage is that they have achieved integration in the first of my two senses even when their commitments do conflict. Failure to distinguish the two senses makes it impossible to express what's admirable about these Nietzschean paragons. Once we have got hold of it, on the other hand, we can agree with Nehamas that integration in the first sense is a crucial component of Nietzsche's conception of human flourishing while at the same time acknowledging the gulf between Nietzsche's and Aristotle's conceptions of it which is created by the contrast between living with unresolved conflict and happiness as 'finally attained unity'. Of course one might try to use this conclusion to rule that Nietzsche cannot possibly be a eudaemonist, on the grounds that inner harmony is part of the definition of 'eudaemonia'. But it's hard to see what the point of this stipulation would be: far better to say that 'eudaemonia' means human flourishing and that, as a believer in the 'enhancement of the species "man"', Nietzsche is a eudaemonist but of a variety distinct either from the neo-Aristotelians we have considered or from Aristotle himself.[57]

We are now in a position finally to comment on the passages in Nietzsche which have led him to be dismissed as an 'immoralist'. The following may serve as an example:

> Everything evil, terrible, tyrannical in man, everything in him that is kin to beasts of prey and serpents, serves the enhancement of the species 'man' as much as its opposite does.[58]

Notice that even here, Nietzsche is not claiming that everything evil (etc.) serves the enhancement of the species *more* than their opposites. The point is rather that

> hatred, envy, covetousness and the lust to rule are conditions of life, [...] factors which (fundamentally and essentially) must be present in the general economy of life.[59]

Nonetheless since Nietzsche is a firm believer in the enhancement of life, or of man,[60] simply to dismiss passages like these seems out of the question. Whatever else he is doing, sometimes he is just recommending evil. I want in conclusion to offer some suggestions as to why he might be doing so.

One explanation of Nietzsche's hostility, in some contexts at least,[61] to the virtues of slave morality – in part, of our morality – is that he was a kind of non-standard consequentialist.[62] On this reading, the goal in the light of which the rightness or wrongness of all acts is to be assessed – corresponding to, though differing from, the Benthamite criteria Nietzsche condemns – is their tendency to promote, or alternatively to promote the reverse of, the flourishing of the species, interpreted along Nietzschean lines.[63] This interpretation is suggested not only by the passage just quoted but also by the following:

> One has hitherto never doubted or hesitated in the slightest degree in supposing 'the good man' to be of greater value than 'the evil man', of greater value in the sense of furthering the advancement and prosperity of man in general (the future of man included). But what if the reverse were true? What if a symptom of regression were inherent in the 'good', likewise a danger, a seduction, a

poison, a narcotic, through which the present was possibly living at the expense
of the future?

It's not, I think, a ridiculous interpretation despite the huge differences
between Nietzsche and standard consequentialisms. Consequentialism
is after all a familiar way of 'valuing values', i.e. of assigning value to
whole modes of valuing particular acts, traits of character and so on; it
also seems to have been a natural place for philosophers to come to
rest in the nineteenth century and turns up in unexpected places.
(Think, for example, of Michael Rosen's non-standard consequentialist interpretation of Marx.)[64] And it makes good sense of the recom-
mendations of evil: Nietzsche would not be the first consequentialist
to face the point that the doctrine is objectionable precisely because it
is liable to redraw the boundaries of the permissible in impermissible
places.[65]

The real difficulty with relying on a consequentialist interpretation to 'place' Nietzsche's immoralism is that consequentialism
relies on a picture of value (be it moral or non-moral) according to
which values can always in principle be balanced against one another
in order to yield a final overall valuation. It is not a wild oversimplification to say that, on this view, a year in which nothing much
happens might come out as equivalent in value to a year in which a
lifetime's research is crowned with the Nobel Prize and one's wife of
forty years is killed in an accident: in either case, a year that is *comme
ci, comme ça*. This picture of value, however, is very much at odds
with Nietzsche's remarks on the role of conflict in the life of some
admirable individuals: if balancing is an available option, it's not clear
what the source of the conflict would be. But these same remarks are
the clue to a better interpretation of the immoralistic passages, which
has the added advantage of placing further distance than the somewhat
indecisive considerations of the last section between Nietzsche and
both Aristotle and (many) neo-Aristotelians.

Alongside the claim that the life of happiness coincides with the
life of virtue, perhaps the most salient feature of Aristotle's view of
the good life for man is the idea that genuine goods fit together into a
harmonious whole: this is just the point of the constitutive conception
of the relation between eudaemonia and other ends in themselves to

which I have already referred.[66] One way to read Nietzsche's immoralism is to see him as arguing for the (often non-moral) costs of moral goodness, and for the (often moral) costs of non-moral goodness.[67] This reading places him in contrast to Aristotle on the issue of the harmony of all goods, but also gives a point to his sympathy with the 'terrible in man' which enables us to see it otherwise than as an angry, reactive heterodoxy. Nietzsche believed, for example – rightly or wrongly, but the truth of the claim is not what is at issue here – that both music and tragedy appeal above all to 'warlike souls':

> Men whose disposition is fundamentally warlike, as for example the Greeks in the age of Aeschylus, are *hard to move*, and when pity does for once overbear their severity it seizes them like a frenzy [...]. But of what use is tragedy to those who are as open to the 'sympathetic emotions' as sails to the winds?[68]

The Athenians in the age of Plato were already softer than in Aeschylus's time, 'but how far they were still from the emotionality of our urban dwellers!' The softer we become, that is, the less use we will have for tragedy (or for music). Now there is no reason to see Nietzsche here as making a taste for tragedy into the sole touchstone of the goodness or badness of a civilization. He could be read as saying that the substitution of a propensity to feel the 'sympathetic emotions' for a 'warlike disposition' is a gain but, since tragedy too is a good, a gain that carries with it a corresponding loss: in contrast to Aristotle, the eligibility of both as ends does not guarantee their compatibility. Other examples illustrating the same point are not hard to find. A great many things that we value now – some of the enduring effects of the Roman or of the British empires, for example – might not have been achieved without measures which now, on moral grounds, we would shrink from. To pretend that we don't really value them because they have simply fallen into our laps through the actions of previous generations is a kind of moral whitewashing of ourselves – a denial of the complexity of our own sensibility – which Nietzsche is precisely campaigning against. Debates about the propriety of competitive games for schoolchildren illustrate, at a microscopic level, the same complexity. For competition not only rewards undeserved characteristics such as height and strength but goes with pride in faring better than others as a result of them (and simply pride in them)[69] – all modes of thought which are anathema to 'morality in the narrow sense'.[70] No race was ever won by saying 'you go first', but this is precisely what the virtue of forbearance[71] enjoins. The point, one might say, of Nietzsche's attack on slave morality is not, as on the reading which relies on the immoralistic passages simply to dismiss him, to get us to throw over pity, forbearance and the rest in favour of a 'knightly-aristocratic' outlook (if this were even possible for us). It is rather to get us to acknowledge, and to integrate into our conception of ourselves, abiding and irreconcilable aspects of our own sensibility – some of which may be heirs to the 'knightly-aristocratic', but the historical claim is not essential – which, once acknowledged, would show that slave morality has after all been only partially victorious.

References

For a general bibliography of Nietzsche's work in German and English see end of volume.

Ackrill, J.L., 'Aristotle on Eudaemonia', in A.O. Rorty (ed.), *Essays on Aristotle's Ethics*, Berkeley/London: University of California Press, 1980.

Anscombe, G.E.M., 'Modern Moral Philosophy', in her Collected Philosophical Papers vol. III: *Ethics, Religion and Politics*, Oxford: Blackwell, 1980.

Aristotle, *Ethics,* tr. J.A.K. Thomson, Harmondsworth: Penguin, 1976.

Bergmann, Frithjof, 'Nietzsche's Critique of Morality' in R. Solomon and K. Higgins (eds.), *Reading Nietzsche*, New York: Oxford University Press, 1988.

Conant, James, 'Nietzsche's Perfectionism', in R. Schacht (ed.), *Nietzsche's Postmoralism*, Cambridge: Cambridge University Press, 2001.

Crisp, Roger, (ed.), *How Should One Live?*, Oxford: Clarendon Press, 1996.

Fontane, Theodor, *Frau Jenny Treibel*, ed. H.B. Garland, London: Macmillan, 1968.

Foot, Philippa, 'Nietzsche's Immoralism', in her *Moral Dilemmas*, Oxford: Clarendon Press, 2002.

Foot, Philippa, 'Virtues and Vices', in her *Virtues and Vices and Other Essays in Moral Philosophy*, Oxford: Blackwell, 1978.

Geuss, Raymond, 'Nietzsche and Genealogy', in his *Morality, Culture, and History*, Cambridge: Cambridge University Press, 1999.

Geuss, Raymond, 'Nietzsche and Morality', European Journal of Philosophy 5:1 (1997).

Hurka, Thomas, *Perfectionism*, New York/Oxford: Oxford University Press, 1993.

Kant, Immanuel, *The Metaphysics of Morals*, tr. Mary Gregor, Cambridge: Cambridge University Press, 1991.

Leiter, Brian, 'Nietzsche and the Morality Critics', in John Richardson and Brian Leiter (eds.), *Nietzsche*, Oxford: Oxford University Press, 2001.

Leiter, Brian, *Nietzsche on Morality*, London: Routledge, 2002.

Lloyd-Jones, Hugh, 'Nietzsche and the study of the ancient world', in J.C. O'Flaherty, T.F. Sellner and R.M. Helm (eds.), *Studies in Nietzsche and the Classical Tradition*, Chapel Hill: University of North Carolina Press, 1979.

Mackie, J.L., *Ethics: Inventing Right and Wrong*, Harmondsworth: Penguin, 1977.

May, Simon, *Nietzsche's Ethics and His War on 'Morality'*, Oxford: Oxford University Press, 1999.

Mill, J.S., *Utilitarianism*, ed. Mary Warnock, London: Fontana, 1962.

Nehamas, Alexander, '"How One Becomes What One Is"', in John Richardson and Brian Leiter (eds.), *Nietzsche*, Oxford: Oxford University Press, 2001.

Nietzsche, Friedrich, *'Wissenschaft und Weisheit im Kampfe'*, in Karl Schlechta (ed.), *Nietzsches Werke in Drei Bänden* (Munich 1954–6; 1966).

Nietzsche, Friedrich, *Werke*: Grossoktavausgabe, ed. Elisabeth Förster-Nietzsche (Leipzig: Naumann, 1894–1904), 15 vols.

Rawls, John, *A Theory of Justice*, Oxford: Oxford University Press, 1973.

Richardson, John, 'Introduction' to John Richardson and Brian Leiter (eds.), *Nietzsche*, Oxford: Oxford University Press, 2001.

Rosen, Michael, 'The Marxist Critique of Morality and the Theory of Ideology', in Edward Harcourt (ed.), *Morality, Reflection, and Ideology*, Oxford: Oxford University Press, 2000.

Russell, Bertrand, *A History of Western Philosophy*, New York: Simon and Schuster, 1945.

Sandys, Sir John (ed.), *The Odes of Pindar*, London: Heinemann/New York: Macmillan, 1915.

Stratton-Lake, Philip, *Kant, Duty and Moral Worth*, London: Routledge, 2000.

Tanner, Michael, *Nietzsche*, Oxford/New York: Oxford University Press, 1994.

Williams, Bernard, *Ethics and the Limits of Philosophy*, London: Fontana, 1985

Williams, Bernard, *Shame and Necessity*, Berkeley/Los Angeles/ Oxford: University of California Press, 1993.

Wingler, Hedwig, 'Aristotle in the thought of Nietzsche and Thomas Aquinas', in J.C. O'Flaherty, T.F. Sellner and R.M. Helm (eds.), *Studies in Nietzsche and the Classical Tradition*, Chapel Hill: University of North Carolina Press, 1979.

Wollheim, Richard, *The Thread of Life*, New Haven/London: Yale University Press, 1999.

Notes

1   Bertrand Russell, *A History of Western Philosophy,* New York: Simon and Schuster, 1945, p. 767.

2   See Philippa Foot, 'Nietzsche's Immoralism', in her *Moral Dilemmas,* Oxford: Clarendon Press, 2002. Foot is patient with Nietzsche where Russell is dismissive, but her aim is nonetheless to steer us away from his 'sadly seductive' philosophy, her central objection to it being that it is 'inimical to justice' [p. 158].

3   See G.E.M. Anscombe, 'Modern Moral Philosophy', in her *Collected Philosophical Papers vol. III: Ethics, Religion and Politics*, p. 30; Richard Woll-

heim, *The Thread of Life,* New Haven/London: Yale University Press, 1999, p. 216; Bernard Williams, *Ethics and the Limits of Philosophy*, London: Fontana, 1985, esp. ch. 10.

4   Cp. Raymond Geuss ('Nietzsche and Morality', *European Journal of Philosophy* 5:1, 1997, p. 1), who remarks that there is no one thing Nietzsche himself meant by 'morality'.

5   The term also appears in J.L. Mackie, *Ethics: Inventing Right and Wrong* Harmondsworth: Penguin, 1977, p. 106, but in a different sense, and not as a special object of criticism.

6   *On the Genealogy of Morals* [henceforth *GM*], tr. Walter Kaufmann, New York: Vintage Books, 1967, Preface 6: '[W]hoever sticks with [the problem of the *value* of pity and of the morality of pity] and *learns how* to ask questions here will experience what I experienced […]. [H]is belief in morality, in all morality, falters - finally a new demand becomes audible. Let us articulate this *new demand:* we need a *critique* of moral values, *the value of these values themselves must first be called in question.*'

7   Michael Tanner, *Nietzsche,* Oxford/New York: Oxford University Press, 1994, pp. 33–4, quoting Nietzsche, *Twilight of the Idols* 5, and Anscombe, *op. cit.*, pp. 30 & 26.

8   Wollheim, *The Thread of Life*, pp. 204–5. Wollheim also raises, roughly, the first objection to morality in the narrow sense, *op. cit.*, p. 197 ('one of the means morality uses to expand its frontiers is to claim total sovereignty over words in which it has only a part share. 'Duty', 'ought', 'virtue', 'good', spring to mind as examples').

9   Of which Wollheim is of course aware: *ibid.*, p. 205.

10   Cp. Brian Leiter, 'Nietzsche and the Morality Critics', in John Richardson and Brian Leiter (eds.), *Nietzsche,* Oxford: Oxford University Press, 2001, p. 235: ('His critique of morality is […] driven by the realization that the *moral* life is essentially inhospitable to the truly creative life') and p. 237 ('a culture in which [morality in the narrow sense] prevails […] will be a culture that eliminates the conditions for the realization of human excellence'); B. Leiter, *Nietzsche on Morality*, London: Routledge, 2002, pp. 128–9; and R. Geuss, 'Nietzsche and Genealogy' (in his *Morality, Culture, and History*, Cambridge: Cambridge University Press, 1999, p. 18): 'The answer to [Nietzsche's question 'what is the value of (our) morality?] […] is that at the moment (our) morality has overwhelmingly negative value as a major hindrance to the enhancement of life'.

11   F. Nietzsche, *Daybreak* [henceforth *D*], tr. R.J. Hollingdale, Cambridge: Cambridge University Press, 1982, 106.

12   Both passages are from *GM* I, 7.

13   F. Nietzsche, *Beyond Good and Evil* [henceforth *BGE*], tr. Walter Kaufmann, New York: Vintage Books: 1966, 44.

14   See on this point Geuss, 'Nietzsche and Morality', p. 9: 'traditional morality
      [according to Nietzsche] is contrary to nature', though Geuss goes on to argue
      that exemplification of will-to-power is a still more important criterion of
      evaluation of moralities for Nietzsche.

15   I might perhaps, following Rawls and Hurka, have used the word 'perfectionist'
      here (see John Rawls, *A Theory of Justice*, Oxford: Oxford University Press,
      1973, p. 325 ff and Thomas Hurka, *Perfectionism*, New York/Oxford: Oxford
      University Press, 1993, *passim*). I choose not to, however, partly in order to
      emphasize a link with Aristotle and partly in order to avoid several implications
      which I fear the term 'perfectionism' – albeit perhaps unnecessarily – has come
      to carry. First, perfectionism is billed as an 'elitist' or inegalitarian teleological
      alternative to consequentialism. But this seems mistaken: as long as the welfare
      realized in a life in which one's natural capacities are fully developed out-
      weighs the welfare realized in other sorts of life *by enough*, there is plenty of
      room for justifying inegalitarian outcomes even within a straight (welfarist)
      consequentialist framework. More seriously, even if the latter contrast between
      perfectionism and consequentialism were well-founded, perfectionism appears
      to share with consequentialism a maximizing conception of the good. In order
      to bring Nietzsche into the eudaemonist fold, it is important that the idea that
      goods can invariably be maximized be an optional, rather than a defining, fea-
      ture of eudaemonism. For more on this, see below, section 4. From a different
      direction, James Conant questions whether the commitment to the perfection
      of human nature *is* inegalitarian, on the grounds that everybody's nature is at
      least capable of the same sort of development ('Nietzsche's Perfectionism', in
      R. Schacht (ed.), *Nietzsche's Postmoralism*, Cambridge: Cambridge University
      Press, 2001, p. 203). I am open-minded about this, though I think Nietzsche's
      frequent references to 'higher types' probably make Conant's Emersonian read-
      ing of Nietzsche something of a long shot.

16   E.g. 'I know not what [...] more beautiful or exalted developments of human
      nature any other ethical system can be supposed to foster', J.S. Mill, *Utili-
      tarianism*, ed. Mary Warnock, London: Fontana, 1962, p. 269.

17   See Kant, *The Metaphysics of Morals*, tr. Mary Gregor, Cambridge: Cambridge
      University Press, 1991, e.g. p. 191: ('Man has a duty to raise himself from the
      crude state of his nature [...] more and more toward humanity [...]; morally
      practical reason commands it absolutely and makes this end his duty, so that he
      may be worthy of the humanity that dwells within him'); and p. 273: ('Who
      should have more reason for being of a cheerful spirit [...] than one who is
      aware of no intentional transgression in himself and is secured [by the culti-
      vation of virtue] against falling into any?').

18   A third Nietzschean objection, that the 'morality of pity' has hidden motives
      which are themselves bad, has no echo in neo-Aristotelianism.

19   *BGE* 225.

20   *BGE* 44.

21 *Nietzsche's Ethics and His War on 'Morality'*, Oxford: Oxford University Press, 1999, p. 4. May explains Nietzschean 'flourishing' as 'becoming what one is', *op. cit.*, p. 108 and ch. 6 *passim.* Cf. Nietzsche, *Ecce Homo*, subtitle and II, 9, tr. Walter Kaufmann, New York: Vintage Books, 1967, pp. 215 & 253; and *The Gay Science*, 335, tr. Walter Kaufmann, New York: Vintage Books, 1974, p. 266. Nietzsche is roughly quoting Pindar, Pythian Odes II, 172; see Sir John Sandys (ed.), *The Odes of Pindar,* London: Heinemann/New York: Macmillan, 1915, pp. 178–9. Incidentally the same form of rough quotation appears in Theodor Fontane's *Frau Jenny Treibel*, published three years after *Ecce Homo*, in which a father explains to his daughter that *'das Klassische, das hat Sprüche wie Bibelsprüche. Mitunter beinah noch etwas drüber. Da haben wir zum Beispiel den Spruch: "Werde, der du bist", ein Wort, das nur ein Grieche sprechen könnte'* (ed. H.B. Garland, London: Macmillan, 1968, p. 175).

22 Quotations are from *BGE* 44, 62, 188, and 262.

23 A similar sort of reply is available to the objection Alexander Nehamas ("'How One Becomes What One Is'", in B. Leiter and J. Richardson (eds.), *op. cit.*, p. 261) makes to classifying Nietzsche as a (to this extent) Aristotelian eudaemonist. Noting (as does May) the importance of the dictum *'werde, der du bist'* as a summary of Nietzsche's conception of human flourishing, Nehamas comments that the self (according to Nietzsche) is something (at its best) which is created. This 'blocks another obvious interpretation of [the] aphorism. This interpretation would hold that to become what one is would be to actualise all the capacities for which one is inherently suited', and would be mistaken because it implies, falsely, that 'becoming who one is' is – as the Aristotelian realization of species-specific potentiality undoubtedly is – a matter of 'uncovering what is already there'. But once again, the opposition between the open-endedness of Nietzschean 'becoming what one is' and the Aristotelian actualisation of one's natural potentialities is false, simply on account of the very general character of the potentialities in the actualization of which flourishing, according to Aristotle, consists. A central example of such a potentiality is rationality, and the potential for this just *does* seem to be 'already there' as part of our natures. But a potentiality like this leaves the nature of any particular life which actualizes it radically underdetermined, so there is room for a great deal of open-endedness in the way a life in which one 'becomes what one is' might actually go *compatibly* with such a life – whatever form it takes – also actualising our distinctive natural endowments.

24 Kant's view: 'virtue signifies a moral strength of the will', *The Metaphysics of Morals*, p. 206.

25 Both quotations are from Frithjof Bergmann, 'Nietzsche's Critique of Morality' in R. Solomon and K. Higgins (eds.), *Reading Nietzsche*, New York: Oxford University Press, 1988, p. 44; cf. also *ibid.*, p. 34, where Nietzsche is said to recommend that practical thought be governed by 'a great diversity of other action-guiding or person-judging codes that are *not* moralities [in the narrow

sense]'. Compare also Leiter's contrast ('Nietzsche and the Morality Critics', p. 230) between the 'good life' and the 'moral life': if we expand our conception of the moral life along more or less neo-Aristotelian lines, perhaps the tension between it and the good life will disappear.

26   See for example Roger Crisp (ed.), *How Should One Live?* Oxford: Clarendon Press, 1996.

27   See e.g. J.S. Mill, *Utilitarianism*, pp. 291–2; also Philip Stratton-Lake, *Kant, Duty and Moral Worth,* London: Routledge, 2000, esp. ch. 4, which makes play with the distinction between primary motives (particular considerations responsiveness to which is characteristic of this or that virtue) and secondary ones (moral duty) in order to harmonize the Kantian claim that right action is action 'solely from duty' (p. 63) with an apparently pluralistic picture of the virtues.

28   Aristotle, *Ethics*, tr. J.A.K. Thomson, Harmondsworth: Penguin, 1976, p. 76.

29   Emphasized by, for example, John McDowell and Jonathan Dancy.

30   Nietzsche, *Werke: Kritische Gesamtausgabe*, ed. G. Colli and M. Montinari, vol. VII–1, Berlin: De Gruyter, 1977, p. 315; cited by Hedwig Wingler, 'Aristotle in the thought of Nietzsche and Thomas Aquinas', in J. C. O'Flaherty, T.F. Sellner and R.M. Helm (eds.), *Studies in Nietzsche and the Classical Tradition*, Chapel Hill: University of North Carolina Press, 1979, p. 43.

31   There is another negative reference at *BGE* 198: 'that tuning down of the affects to a harmless mean according to which they may be satisfied, the Aristotelianism of morals', which latter is a subspecies of 'moralities that address themselves to the individual, for the sake of his "happiness"' and provide 'recipes against his passions'. The swipe is therefore another aspect of Nietzsche's misreading of Aristotle's eudaemonism as simply recommending contentment. On the other hand Nietzsche also pays Aristotle the compliment not only of being a brighter and broader intellect than Plato, but also of a self-comparison: Aristotle stands to Plato as Nietzsche to Schopenhauer, in Nietzsche, *Werke: Kritische Gesamtausgabe*, ed. G. Colli and M. Montinari, vol. V–1, Berlin: De Gruyter, 1971, p. 417; cited by Wingler, op. cit., p. 43.

32   Cp. Kant's mistake in which eudaemonism is interpreted, along quasi-Benthamite lines, as the doctrine that pleasure is what is ultimately aimed at in human action: see *The Metaphysics of Morals*, p. 183.

33   I take this to be the lesson of Aristotle, *Ethics*, tr. Thomson, pp. 73–4: happiness is the end such that all other supreme ends are chosen for the sake of it but such that it is not chosen for the sake of anything else. To avoid contradiction in the first conjunct here, 'for the sake of' must be read (as Ackrill reads it, 'Aristotle on *Eudaemonia*', in A.O. Rorty (ed.), *Essays on Aristotle's Ethics,* Berkeley/London: University of California Press, 1980, in a constitutive rather than an instrumental sense.

34   *Ethics*, tr. Thomson, Book II, pp. 104 & 106.

35   *Ibid.*, Book IX, p. 301; my italics.

36   *Ibid.*, Book IV, pp. 150–1.

37   *Ibid.*, Book IV, p. 159.

38   Hugh Lloyd-Jones, for example, takes it as obvious that there are important affinities here: '[Nietzsche's] superman is no more overbearing than Aristotle's *megalopsych'*, 'Nietzsche and the study of the ancient world', in O'Flaherty *et al* (eds.), p. 3. The point would perhaps have been better made had Lloyd-Jones referred to Nietzsche's 'higher types' rather than to his 'superman'. Kaufmann also claims a strong affinity between the two thinkers on just this point, see *BGE*, p. 138, n 35. Rawls compares Nietzsche and Aristotle in respect of their alleged perfectionism (see above n 15) at *A Theory of Justice*, p. 25.

39   Both quotations are from *BGE* 199.

40   *D* 199.

41   From Nietzsche, *'Wissenschaft und Weisheit im Kampfe'*, in Karl Schlechta (ed.) *Nietzsches Werke in Drei Bänden*, Munich 1954–6; 1966, vol. 3, p. 339, cited by Wingler, *op. cit.*, p. 44. Cf. also Nietzsche, *Werke: Grossoktavausgabe*, ed. Elisabeth Förster-Nietzsche, Leipzig: Naumann, 1894–1904, vol. XVII p. 351f, where Nietzsche says that Aristotle is 'untypically Greek' on the grounds that in treating understanding as a goal in itself 'he sets himself apart from the culture of the Hellenes'; cited by Wingler, *ibid.*

42   In claiming that Aristotle was not a typical Greek, Nietzsche is at least *raising* a question which seems otherwise to be absent – wrongly – from the reflections of (many) contemporary neo-Aristotelians. Fighting under the banner 'back to the Greeks' is unlikely to yield anything spectacularly new if, unwittingly perhaps, the Greek to whom it is envisaged that we return is the one who has untypically much in common with ourselves.

43   *Ethics*, tr. Thomson, p. 155.

44   *Ibid.*, p. 156.

45   E.g. Aristotle, *Ethics*, tr. Thomson, p. 153 n.1. Cf. the related speculation by Nietzsche himself at *BGE* 212, referring to the 'conservatives of ancient Athens who let themselves go – "toward happiness," as they said; toward pleasure, as they acted – and who all the while mouthed the ancient pompous words to which their lives no longer gave them any right': if we can assume that Nietzsche counted Aristotle among these 'conservatives', his remark is at least consistent with the view that Aristotle's account of *megalopsychia* represents a piece of ossifying conventional wisdom to which he no longer wholly subscribed.

46   *BGE* 33, cp. also *BGE* 265, 'egoism belongs to the nature of a noble soul'.

47   *Ethics*, tr. Thomson, Book V, p. 173.

48   *Ibid.*, pp. 176–7: distributive justice 'is shown in the distribution of honour or money or such other assets as are divisible among the members of the community (for in these cases it is possible for one person to have either an equal or an unequal share with another)'.

49   *Ecce Homo* I, 4, cited by John Richardson, Introduction to Richardson and Leiter (eds.), *Nietzsche*, p. 28 n 75.

50   That is, conflict among ends endorsed by the agent: of course conflict between ends he endorses (acting morally rightly) and those he disowns (any countervailing passion) are an integral part of the picture.

51   Philippa Foot, 'Virtues and Vices', in her *Virtues and Vices and Other Essays in Moral Philosophy*, Oxford: Blackwell, 1978, pp. 14–15.

52   *BGE* 200. For related passages, cp. the following: '*master morality* and *slave morality* ... at times occur directly alongside each other – even in the same human being, within a *single* soul' (*BGE* 260); being a battleground for these two systems of morality is 'today [...] perhaps [the most] decisive mark of a "*higher nature*"' (*GM* I, 16). 'where the plant "man" shows himself strongest one finds instincts that conflict powerfully [...] but are controlled' (*Werke*, ed. G. Colli and M. Montinari, vol. VII–2, p. 289); or in Nietzsche's idealization of Goethe who 'bore all the conflicting tendencies of his century within him' (*Werke*, ed. G. Colli and M. Montinari, vol. VI–3, p. 145).

53   The quotations are from Nehamas, '"How One Becomes What One Is"', pp. 269, 270, 272.

54   *Ibid.*, p. 270.

55   *Ibid.*, p. 272, my italics.

56   *Ibid.*; cp. also '[to become what one is] is to identify oneself with all one's actions', and 'to fit all this into a coherent whole' (p. 275), which makes just the same slide again.

57   'Neo-Aristotelian' here is, of course, only a convenient label: I do not want to claim that there is no sense in which a philosopher who held Nietzsche's view of eudaemonia could be described as neo-Aristotelian.

58   *BGE* 44.

59   *BGE* 23.

60   Cf. *GM* I, 12: 'Here precisely is what has become a fatality for Europe – together with the fear of man we have also lost our love of him, our reverence for him, our hopes for him, even the will to him. The sight of man now makes us weary – what is nihilism today if it is not *that*? – We are weary *of man*.'

61   *BGE* 201 makes it clear that Nietzsche does not hold that acts of pity are *always* bad.

62   On some apparent affinities, but also differences, between Nietzsche and Railton's 'objective' act-consequentialism, see Leiter, 'Nietzsche and the Morality Critics'.

63   Of course there's a question as to what exactly it means for a species to flourish. Suppose that a species can be said to flourish if members with certain characteristics exist, however few they are in number and whatever their existence costs the other members (either in terms of exploitation of actual members or in terms of the non-existence of possible future ones). It seems there are at least two ways this idea could be captured within the range of consequentialist options. On one formulation, the goodness of species flourishing wouldn't be arrived at by balancing the welfare of its 'best' members against the welfare of

the rest (actual or possible), so this would rank as a form of 'ideal', i.e. non-welfarist, consequentialism. But the position could also be spelled out in welfarist terms: the good *for each human being* of living the life of a 'strong' (or whatever) member of the species would be argued to be so great that the welfare of these few (if few they are) would be recommendable simply on the grounds of balancing goods and harms, interpreted in a welfarist way.

64   Michael Rosen, 'The Marxist Critique of Morality and the Theory of Ideology', in Edward Harcourt (ed.), *Morality, Reflection, and Ideology,* Oxford: Oxford University Press, 2000.

65   This is an important strand of Anscombe's attack on consequentialism in 'Modern Moral Philosophy'.

66   See above n 33.

67   Cf. Tanner on the contrast between 'greatness' and 'goodness', *op. cit.,* e.g. p. 37.

68   *D* 172.

69   Cf. Williams's discussion in *Shame and Necessity,* Berkeley/Los Angeles/ Oxford: University of California Press, 1993, of the primitiveness, from the perspective of morality in the narrow sense, of a sensibility which admits shame at things for which we are not responsible.

70   Just in case the moral credentials of competitive sport might nowadays be thought to be beyond question, I submit the following anecdote (with thanks to Jane Fior). At a cross-country skiing 'race' in north Norway earlier this year (2006), the first prize was awarded to the participant whose time for completing the course came *closest to the average time,* on the grounds that to reward someone who had tried to distinguish themselves from the rest would be to reward a moral failing.

71   See again *BGE* 199.

ROBIN SMALL

Nietzsche's Evolutionary Ethics

In his autobiographical work *Ecce Homo*, Nietzsche complained that he had been 'suspected of Darwinism' by what he called 'scholarly oxen'.[1] Who these were, I have not been able to find out. The puzzle is why he was so annoyed at being associated with Darwinism. Certainly in later years there were misinterpretations of his ideas which paralleled misinterpretations of Darwinism and took him to be advocating some program of breeding a supposedly superior race, but I doubt that he had these in mind, despite having used the expressions that gave them a foothold. In any case, such misrepresentations of his ideas have long since been exposed, and replaced by careful and accurate accounts of his actual engagements with Darwinism, which tell a different story.[2]

One thing I want to do here is place Nietzsche in the context of today's evolutionary ethics, and see to what extent he can be regarded as a contributor to its debates. On the face of things that seems unlikely, given the many developments in evolutionary theory in the century and a half since the appearance of *The Origin of Species*. Whatever Nietzsche thought Darwinism was, times have changed. For instance, Darwin's own credence in the Lamarckian doctrine of heritability of acquired characteristics (quite pronounced in his later works) was ruthlessly cast aside by his followers, from Thomas Huxley to the so called 'neo-Darwinists'. On the other hand, an evolutionary ethics remained almost completely unrealised for most of that time. Anyone who needs convincing of this should look at A.G.N. Flew's book *Evolutionary Ethics*, which appeared in 1967 – not so long ago, but before the recent controversies over the origins of co-operation and altruism. Flew's discussion has nothing in common with the work of evolutionary theorists like William Hamilton, George Price and Robert Trivers. Instead, most of his book is devoted to two problems.

The first is whether the principle of natural selection (or 'the survival of the fittest') qualifies as a genuinely scientific theory by the criteria of logical empiricism. Flew concludes that it does not. The second is whether an evolutionary ethics is necessarily guilty of committing the 'naturalistic fallacy', or failing to observe the logical distinction between 'is' and 'ought'. On that point he gives a 'not proven' verdict.

Flew in fact does not take evolutionary ethics very seriously as a credible theory: he regards its problems as considerable, and any advantages as doubtful. This is where opinions have changed in more recent times. The re-emergence of an evolutionary ethics arose out of events within evolutionary theory: that is, attempts to solve the problem of unselfish behaviour or, as it is commonly called, 'altruism'. The account put forward by Darwin in *The Descent of Man* (1871) and repeated by Paul Rée in *The Origin of the Moral Sensations* (1877) and Herbert Spencer in *The Data of Ethics* (1879) is that individual unselfishness is an asset to groups, since it enables them to practice co-operation in competing with other groups and so win the struggle for existence. The problem with this model is that unselfishness seems to be a severe disadvantage to the individual, so that natural selection *within* any group would be expected to lead to the elimination of members with that trait.

Rightly or wrongly, later debates over evolutionary ethics have set aside the issues that occupied Flew. Instead, they are about whether there is such a thing as unselfish behaviour, and how it could have developed, given the premises of evolutionary theory. According to the evolutionary theorist Robert Trivers: 'Models that attempt to explain altruistic behaviour in terms of natural selection are models designed to take the altruism out of altruism.'[3] One can see what he is getting at in some versions of the evolutionary approach, such as the one that essentially treats altruism as a sort of insurance policy that a prudent individual might take out, calculating that helping others is likely to pay off in the long run, even if it brings no benefits in the short term, provided that it establishes an expectation of reciprocity, so that the others might be counted on to come to one's assistance when and if that becomes necessary in the future. That is not to say that the benevolent person is not really benevolent, though, as Trivers seems to be claiming. But it does bring the discussion back to an emphasis on the individual rather than the group, the focus of earlier evolutionary ethics.

There is another moral sentiment that one could identify as a puzzle. Why is it that people sometimes harm others, or at least take satisfaction in harm occurring to others, even where there is no benefit to themselves? This is what in German is called *Schadenfreude*. Joseph Butler called it 'disinterested cruelty'.[4] Philosophers have never had much to say about this trait, possibly because not many people admit having it, whereas many people are quite happy to be described as benevolent.[5] Or if it is not denied, it is explained away, as when Lucretius described the satisfaction of someone who observes a shipwreck. He says we feel pleasure at that sight, not because we want anyone to come to grief, but because it reminds us of our own safety and we feel thankful for that.[6] (St Thomas Aquinas made a similar observation about those in paradise who contemplate with satisfaction the sufferings of the sinners condemned to eternal punishment).[7] An evolutionary explanation might be that just as mutual loyalty within a group gives it an advantage over competing groups, so too an instinctive hostility towards those outside the group is an advantage.[8] Like sympathy, malice might thus be innate – even though the tension between the two tendencies is evident.

This is where I think Nietzsche comes in. Central to his thinking about morality is the question of altruism, and characteristic of his approach is its insistence on assessing the value of altruism by its place in an evolutionary model of human life. Nietzsche is a naturalist's naturalist. That is, it is not just moral sentiments but moral values that become naturalised in his model. In that regard he differs from his friend Paul Rée, who simply accepted an identification of morality with benevolence without question. Rée adopted Schopenhauer's account of the basis of morality (in his essay of that name) while rejecting his further metaphysical explanation of the nature of sympathy. Nietzsche is distinctive in not separating a meta-ethics from an evaluation or re-evaluation of moral values themselves, or rather a *trans*-valuation, an expression implying an inversion of the valuation of altruism and selfishness.

Nietzsche's Attitude towards Darwinism

That Nietzsche was not well informed about Darwin's theories is generally recognised. In fact it is signalled by his own practice of referring broadly to 'the school of Darwin', a phrase that takes in various writers who set out to modify or extend Darwin's ideas in ways that have not always stood the test of time.[9] What is more, two philosophical writers who made use of Darwin's ideas are important here: Paul Rée and Herbert Spencer. Nietzsche's relation to the Darwinism of his time is largely a dialogue with these two writers.

As far as one can tell, there is only one piece of writing by Darwin that Nietzsche actually read. This was due not to any particular interest on his part, but simply a result of circumstances. In August 1877 Nietzsche was travelling in Switzerland, having been on leave from his university for a year, suffering from an assortment of health problems. The previous winter had been spent in Sorrento with a group of friends including Paul Rée, important here not so much as a philosopher but as a Darwinist, that is, someone who was trying to apply Darwin's ideas – both those of *The Origin of Species* and the more recent *The Descent of Man* – to issues of ethics.

Rée thought that natural selection could account not only for feelings such as benevolence and sympathy but also for the specifically moral sentiment of remorse or guilt. This is just the theory put forward by Darwin, who had argued that the social instincts have been favoured by natural selection because they provide an advantage for tribes or groups in their competition with other groups, and that our moral ideas are based upon this class of instincts. On his view, the pain of regret or guilt is really just the frustration of a social instinct of sympathy. What makes human beings prone to this feeling in a way that, as far as we know, other species are not is just their greater power of memory and reflection. Thus, if a dog who has disobeyed his master could reflect on his past behaviour and identify himself with it, he would feel guilty over his disloyal act. Rée disagreed with this aspect of Darwin's account, objecting that it left out the influence of upbringing, habit and moral discourse. These themes had no doubt been prominent in the daily discussions of Nietzsche and Rée in Sorrento.

On the way back to Basel with his health not much improved, Nietzsche stayed at Rosenlaui, a health resort in Switzerland. There he met an English philosopher who knew a good deal about Darwin. This was George Croom Robertson, professor of philosophy at University College, London and the editor of the new philosophy journal *Mind,* in its second year of publication and at that time ranging beyond philosophy into neighbouring areas of psychology and ethnology. Croom Robertson showed Nietzsche the latest issue, which included an article by Darwin entitled 'Biographical Sketch of an Infant'. Darwin argued, amongst other things, for evidence of conscience or feeling of guilt in a two-year old child. This not very well known piece is a footnote to *The Expression of the Emotions in Man and Animals,* in which Darwin argued for the presence of instincts and innate responses in human beings as in other animals – one aspect of his doctrine that Nietzsche could readily endorse.

On the other hand, Nietzsche was more ready to accept the Lamarckian aspect of Rée's account of the moral sense than the strictly Darwinian side. That is, he accepted that habits and associations of ideas became independent of the experiences that originally gave rise to them and could be passed on to offspring, and so become stronger through successive generations. This is what accounts for morality as Rée explains it, a judging of actions as good and bad in their own right, rather than as good or bad *for* something. Herbert Spencer was already proposing a similar model, and Darwin had become more sympathetic to the principle of use and disuse, mainly because natural selection alone seemed too slow a process to produce evolutionary change in the time available. Nietzsche too had postulated processes of forgetting in the formation of concepts in his early unpublished outlines of epistemology, so the attraction of that side of Rée's theory is not surprising.[10]

Natural Selection and Altruism

Central to Nietzsche's disagreement with Darwinism is the question of natural selection. His most fundamental objection is that he regards the concept, in the form of group selection, as a rationalisation of the altruistic perspective. It seems that this view comes from his encounter with Paul Rée's version of Darwinism (though he displaces his attack on to Herbert Spencer, accusing him, incorrectly, of advocating 'the triumph of altruism'.)[11] Earlier in his career Nietzsche seems to have understood Darwinian selection as a completely individualistic struggle for survival. There may be some support for that view if one's attention is restricted to *The Origin of Species*, but the later *Descent of Man*, on which Rée relies in his theory of the moral sense, tells a different story. There Darwin points to the advantages of sympathy and co-operation for groups competing with other groups, and argues that these traits will be selected and passed on for that reason.[12]

There are problems with this model. Willingness to subordinate one's interests to others may be an advantage for the group but is not for the self-sacrificing individual. Later evolutionary theorists have puzzled over how altruism can exist as a continuing trait, that is, how it can be favoured by natural selection. Darwin first touches on this issue in his chapter on instinct in *The Origin of Species* when he asks how the co-operation of bees in hive construction could have arisen, since the individual bee seems to get no benefit from its own activity, taken by itself.[13] He acknowledges that it presents a difficulty for the individualistic model of natural selection. In his later treatment of the social instinct, it is clearly assumed that the benefit of co-operation for the group outweighs any disadvantages for the individual to such an extent that when the groups containing altruistic individuals prevail over others, the proportion of altruists in the overall population increases, even if – apparently paradoxically – it does not increase *within* any one group.[14]

We need to be clear that Nietzsche is not questioning the existence of group selection. On the contrary, he describes how it occurs when he characterizes the anti-individualistic 'herd' and its psychology. The 'last men' of the Prologue to *Thus Spoke Zarathustra* are the longest lived, that is, the most successful in the struggle for survival. He thinks that the Darwinians have overlooked the effectiveness of the herd virtues of conformity and use of numbers in bringing this about.[15] The theoretical problem about group selection is not Nietzsche's reason for opposing it. In fact, he allows that co-operation may in fact be favoured above individualism. What he objects to is the identification of this with morality. The theory of the 'herd instinct' is strangely absent from *On the Genealogy of Morals*, but this is just because that work is essentially an unfinished one – a point overlooked by many commentators.[16] It remains one strong reason for Nietzsche's identification of group selection with altruism.

In *The Gay Science* Nietzsche rejects as 'profoundly erroneous' an idea that he says is especially popular in England: the doctrine that 'what is called good preserves the species, while what is called evil harms the species.'[17] His counter argument is that 'the evil instincts are advantageous, species preserving and indispensable to as high a degree as the good ones; their function is merely different.' This is apparently an *ad hominem* argument. That is, Nietzsche does not accept that criterion of moral worth, but wants to argue that it does not lead to the conclusions its supporters imagine. It is not unlike the well known 'private vices, public benefits' argument of the British political economist Mandeville (though Mandeville restricted his argument to the traditional deadly sins such as greed, envy and pride).

Nietzsche's position about evolution and values is explained most clearly in *On the Genealogy of Morals*, where he is asking about the value of values themselves.

> Something, for example, that possessed obvious value in relation to the longest possible survival of a race (or to the enhancement of its power of adaptation to a particular climate or to the preservation of the greatest number) would by no means possess the same value if it were a question, for instance, of producing a stronger type. The well-being of the majority and the well-being of the few are opposite viewpoints of value: to consider the former *a priori* of higher value may be left to the naïveté of English biologists.[18]

This question is especially directed towards Rée and Spencer, for whom 'good' always means good *for* something, until we arrive at a final intrinsic good – which for Spencer is pleasure, and for Rée utility which, following Darwin, he does not identify with the happiness of the greatest number. For Nietzsche, as it turns out, the final good is power.

> Indeed, life itself has been defined as a more and more efficient inner adaptation to external conditions (Herbert Spencer). This definition misjudges the essence of life, its *will to power*; it overlooks the essential priority of the spontaneous, aggressive, expansive, reinterpreting, redirecting and form-giving forces, although 'adaptation' follows only after their influence; it denies the dominant role of the highest functionaries within the organism itself, in which the will to life appears active and form-giving.'[19]

My argument is that this claim arises out of Nietzsche's rejection of the view that he attributes to mainstream evolutionary thought, that natural selection is driven by two things, a will to live and a will to reproduce. Let us look at what he says about those.

The Will to Live and Will to Reproduce

The closest Nietzsche came to accepting a Darwinian concept of natural selection was when he was in the company of his friend Paul Rée throughout the winter of 1876–77. At that point he followed Rée in accepting natural selection in its most rigorous and economical formulation.

> Why accept a *drive to self-preservation* at all? Amongst countless accidental forms arose some capable of life, capable of *ongoing* life; millions of years of adaptations of the particular human organs were necessary until finally the regular emergence of the present organism and the regular appearance of the phenomena that one usually ascribes to the drive to self-preservation.[20]

Nietzsche links the will to live with the struggle for existence, which is a Darwinian conception. The word 'struggle' does suggest a striving of the will, but Darwin stipulated that he was using the expression in a 'large and metaphorical sense'. The tendency of readers such as

Alfred Russel Wallace to take his metaphors in some literal sense, and to object to them on that basis, was a source of dispute from the start. Darwin expressed some exasperation on this point, even as he very grudgingly accepted the phrase 'survival of the fittest' as an equivalent for natural selection, less likely to provoke misinterpretation.[21]

Nietzsche acknowledges that the will to live is Schopenhauer's idea. 'It was a very happy find of Schopenhauer when he spoke of the 'will to live'; we do not want to give up this expression and hence are thankful to its inventor in the name of the German language. But that should not prevent us from seeing that the concept of a will to live has not yet acquired any rights of citizenship in science, any more than the concepts 'soul', 'God', 'life force', etc.'[22] The link with Schopenhauer is certainly there: the will to live receives a whole chapter in *The World as Will and Representation*.[23] Later, however, Nietzsche attributes the same concept to Darwin. Perhaps this is just a way of displacing a rejection of Schopenhauer by attributing his ideas to others. Just how Nietzsche came to link the 'will to live' with Darwinism is unclear. His opposition to the concept is part of his general rejection of Schopenhauer's metaphysical doctrines, but he thinks it is just as implausible if understood as a natural instinct. For, he argues, how could an individual being will to exist without existing already? Of course, this objection (which parallels the traditional Epicurean argument about death: 'Where death is, I am not, where I am, death is not') presupposes a naturalism for which there is no transcendent reality 'behind' the world of experience and from which such a will could press towards existence in space and time. If this point were conceded, the will to live might simply be interpreted as a will to *go on* living, that is a drive for self-preservation. Nietzsche does not deny that such a form of willing occurs, but he argues that it is deliberate and conscious, not an innate instinct. When we look further into motivation, what we find far more often is the will to seek pleasure and to avoid pain. Thus the fear of death, which Schopenhauer takes to be strong evidence in support of a will to live, is really only a fear of pain or else of the deprivation of pleasures.

Nietzsche rejects the will to live and to reproduce because he cannot see an immediate achievement of the goal. That is, each requires foresight of some kind which is plainly implausible in the great majority of living things. Hedonism made up for this by supplying an immediate goal which through natural selection could be linked with the (so to speak) real purpose of the behaviour. Animals eat to satisfy hunger, not to go on living, although both the drive and its reinforcement by pleasure are explained by their contribution to survival.

By the time he came to write *Thus Spoke Zarathustra*, six years later, Nietzsche's views had changed completely. He still opposed the notion of a will to live, and the same objection was put into the mouth of Zarathustra: 'For what does not exist cannot will; but what is in existence, how could that still want existence?'[24] However, the alternative now proposed was quite different from psychological hedonism. 'Only where there is life is there also will: not will to life, but – thus I teach you – will to power.'[25] This switch from a model of pleasure and pain to a new and, on the face of it, far less immediately plausible postulate is striking and puzzling. Why did Nietzsche suddenly abandon the hedonism that he had been championing vigorously throughout the previous six years?

From Hedonism to Anti-hedonism

As I remarked earlier, Nietzsche had been firmly committed to hedonism throughout his philosophical partnership with Paul Rée, even though Rée's psychology emphasised the prevalence of drives such as vanity, which drive human behaviour despite their failure to deliver happiness – hence his pessimistic conclusions. It is remarkable that the ending of their philosophical partnership was followed by an about face on Nietzsche's part. Darwin had wanted to recognize a multiplicity of natural instincts, not all associated with pleasure and pain. Of course, we can say that the satisfaction of any instinct is itself a pleasure, but that does not mean interpreting all motivation as a desire for that pleasure, taken by itself. As Darwin points out, spontaneous behaviour such as coming to the aid of someone in distress does not seem to include either immediate pleasure or pain, or any calculation of future pleasure or pain. The social instinct is one of these natural drives, found in human beings as in other species.

The philosophers of the previous century had already addressed this issue. Following Butler, Hume argues that any deliberate pursuit of pleasure presupposes an acquaintance with those pleasures that originally come out of some instinct. This applies not just to simple bodily desires such as hunger but also to passions such as vanity, vengefulness or ambition.[26] Thus, anyone who forms a deliberate plan of seeking fame must have an 'original propensity' that makes praise and admiration a source of satisfaction in their own right. Such an original passion may even be stronger than the rational pursuit of pleasure: so it is, Hume observes, that people seek vengeance even at their own cost – the same point that Rée makes in relation to vanity. What these drives are may vary from person to person: significantly, amongst them Hume mentions the desire for power, which he identifies in its more deliberate form with ambition.

After 1882 it seems that Nietzsche no longer felt obliged to up-hold simple hedonism against this belief in a multiplicity of ir-reducible drives. He now opposed hedonism by criticising the status of pleasure and pain. These were not sensations but interpretations of states of affairs.[27] One point of categorizing pleasure and pain as epiphenomena is to show that they cannot be ends of action. Nietzsche has now gone over to the other side of the argument about hedonism. Not only does he maintain that there are pleasures that consist in the satisfaction of some already existing drive. But he seems to think these are the *only* kind of pleasures, unlike (say) Hume who retains pleasures that are straightforward feelings, and which can therefore be the sole object of behaviour.

There might be several reasons for this, but I think that one was his determination to push forward with a program of removing pur-pose from a conception of the world. And that removal was closely linked with Darwinism. Nietzsche's understanding of the theory of evolution was primarily based on his familiarity with F.A. Lange's *History of Materialism*. For Lange, the importance of Darwinism has to do not with the issue of common ancestry but rather with the elimination of teleology from biological explanation. 'There can no longer be any doubt,' he wrote, 'that nature proceeds in a way that has

no similarity to human purpose; indeed, that its most essential means
is one that, measured by the standard of human understanding, can
only be compared with the blindest chance.'[28] Similarly, Nietzsche
presents himself as concerned to carry out an elimination of teleology
from psychology once and for all, and he sees the last hiding place of
that concept as pleasure and pain.

> Pleasure is only a symptom of the feeling of power attained, a consciousness of
> difference (*Differenz*) – there is no striving for pleasure: but pleasure occurs
> when what is being striven for is attained: pleasure accompanies, pleasure does
> not motivate [...][29]

Nietzsche's critique of pleasure and pain is also designed to disallow
making them a standard of value. Both pessimism (the belief that the
world contains more pain than pleasure) and optimism relied on that
standard, and were widely debated in Nietzsche's time. So conceived,
though, he thinks they make no sense. If they are by-products then
their value must be determined by the value of the real aim of the
activity.

So, why should the activity of increasing power be given a special status?

Nietzsche's Alternative Model

My hypothesis is that Nietzsche wanted to develop his own model of
natural selection. It is true that he often uses the word 'selection' to
mean some deliberate policy of breeding or training or both – hence,
the old misconceptions about his outlook – but then, so does Darwin.
The Origin of Species begins with a chapter about the human practice
of modifying animals and plants through selective breeding. As with
Darwin, the term 'selection' has two uses for Nietzsche. One is this
familiar meaning, but the other is the metaphorical counterpart that
refers to a process that is not due to a human or for that matter any
other agent. Natural selection is something that *happens*. Having said

that, we can specify what the conditions are for its occurrence. Here however there is an important issue about what is or is not required. Nietzsche believes that Darwinian selection presupposes what he calls a 'will to live'. I have not found this in Darwin and I do not believe it is necessary to his account. Nietzsche, I suspect, is displacing his rejection of Schopenhauer on to a different target.

The appeal of a reduction of all drives to some single basic drive is clearly appealing to Nietzsche. He wants to reduce all drives to the will to power.[30] This would work for inorganic nature, to which the hedonic model is hard to extrapolate, despite the efforts of some speculative thinkers to find pleasure and pain throughout nature, even in its inorganic forms. Just as the will to live and the will to reproduce inevitably imply competition, so does the will to power. Competition is the fact that has to be explained in each case.

But what is the agenda of such a theory? Presumably to *explain* some range of phenomena, such as the achievements of outstanding artists, scientists, philosophical or religious thinkers and political leaders – that is, the occurrence of exceptionality. How do we explain this? Nietzsche says there is a process of selection. Now, for selection to occur, there must be a process of competition. This is how Darwinian selection occurs. First of all there is a competition for individual survival. Second there is competition for sexual selection – the great development of the earlier model in *The Descent of Man*. Hence, Nietzsche must postulate a competition for exceptionality. It is not enough however just to observe that a struggle exists. Darwin starts by citing the testimony of naturalists on the struggle for existence, but immediately goes further by providing an explanation, which indicates that this must necessarily occur. His argument is drawn from Malthus's theory of population: the rate of increase of population will always be greater than any increase in the means of subsistence, 'Hence, as more individuals are produced than an possibly survive, there must in every case be a struggle for existence, either one individual with another of the same species, or with the individuals of distinct species, or with the physical conditions of life.'[31]

What does Nietzsche have to say about this? He has no such argument for his own hypothesis of a universal struggle for power, although from time to time he tries to support it by giving examples drawn from diverse phenomena ranging from biology to cosmology, somewhat in the manner of Herbert Spencer's supposed 'law of development.' A stepping-stone towards his theory is a critique of Spencer's work by a German writer, W.H. Rolph.[32] Rolph's model replaces the will to live (which he explicitly attributes to Darwin) with a will to nourishment. 'While for the Darwinists there is no struggle for existence wherever the existence of a creature is not threatened, for me the struggle is an omnipresent one. It is primarily a struggle for life, a struggle for the increase of life, not a struggle for existence.' Rolph argues that a will to live assumes a scarcity of resources, and so explains competition only in rare circumstances, whereas his postulate of an insatiable drive for consumption implies as much and even more competition in a situation of abundance. Hence, he concludes, the process that produces evolutionary change will proceed more rapidly in an abundant environment, since the organism will gain far more nourishment than it needs simply to maintain its own existence.

Nietzsche's idea of the will to power comes very close to this drive to expand, to take in and absorb whatever is outside, up to the limit of the organism's ability to control, at which point the elementary form of reproduction occurs. In this broadened sense, his hypothesis is that a struggle for power is found everywhere. In the resulting selection in animals and human beings, qualities of strength, boldness, aggressiveness, inventiveness are rewarded. These qualities do not necessarily increase the individual's chance of a long life or of leaving numerous descendants, nor do they contribute to the community in any direct way, although Nietzsche has previously argued for an indirect benefit to society from supposedly anti social qualities. But even if the apathetic 'last men' of *Thus Spoke Zarathustra* are both long lived and prolific, the fact remains that they have been *rejected* by this natural selection.

From a Darwinian standpoint, the weaknesses in Nietzsche's argument are evident. He overlooks the ability of the Darwinian concept of fitness to allow for different strategies, both active and passive, aggressive and defensive, in the struggle for existence. The qualities that Nietzsche identifies with the will to power can, in fact, be explained as outcomes of natural selection operating on individuals. While they are not selected for exceptionality in that context, the actual outcome of adaptation often includes features that go beyond their original function.

One final problem with the will to power is the *ad hominem* objection that it is liable to the criticisms that Nietzsche levels against its rivals. Is the feeling of increasing or decreasing power just another epiphenomenon? The same objections that he raises against hedonism seem to apply here. Further, if Nietzsche finally accepts Hume's argument that most versions of selfishness presuppose a number of given 'original passions' out of which more deliberate 'secondary motives' arise, the reduction of these to a single drive seems a quite arbitrary move, if anything showing Nietzsche's continuing preoccupation with Schopenhauer's metaphysics of the will.

Conclusion

What I have argued is that Nietzsche's conception of the will to power is part of his attempt to construct a version of natural selection which is parallel to the Darwinian model, or to what he takes that to be, and in which what is selected is individual exceptionality. The qualities that constitute 'fitness' in that sense are quite different from those occurring in Darwinian selection, especially when groups are emphasized. As we have seen, however, this alternative model faces four major objections:

1. Nietzsche's theory does not have the kind of *explanatory* power that Darwin's can claim.
2. It rests on an assumption that natural selection requires a driving force, even though no such premise figures in Darwin's argument.
3. The struggle for power is not shown to be something that occurs of necessity, unless one simply assumes the postulated will to power.
4. The doctrine of a will to power is open to the same objections that Nietzsche brought against his previous position, hedonism.

But Nietzsche's real reason for proposing this alternative is not theoretical. It has far more to do with his determination to replace the 'perspective of extreme altruism'[33] with one in which what is traditionally condemned as selfishness is held up as higher in 'order of rank' than the values of traditional morality. The new model of natural selection thus turns out to be, in the end, not so much a genuine theory as a rationalisation for Nietzsche's transvaluation of moral values.

References:
For a general bibliography of Nietzsche's works in German and English see end of volume.

Notes

1   *Ecce Homo*, Why I Write Such Good Books, 1.
2   See e.g. Jean Gayon, 'Nietzsche and Darwin', in Jane Maienschein and Michael Ruse (eds), *Biology and the Foundation of Ethics*, Cambridge: Cambridge University Press, 1999, p. 154–97; and Gregory Moore, *Nietzsche, Biology and Metaphor*, Cambridge: Cambridge University Press, 2002.
3   Robert Trivers, 'The Evolution of Reciprocal Altruism,' *The Quarterly Review of Biology* 46 (1971), p. 35.
4   Joseph Butler, *Fifteen Sermons Preached at the Rolls Chapel, & A Dissertation Upon the Nature of Virtue*, London: G. Bell and Sons, 1949, p. 24.
5   Schopenhauer does hint at an explanation: whereas the compassionate person *'makes less of a distinction than do the rest between himself and others'*, the malicious person makes *more* of this distinction than most. *On the Basis of Morality*, trans. E.F.J. Payne, Indianapolis: Hackett, 1996, p. 204. But it is hard to see how this moral solipsism, so to speak, points beyond callousness to positive malice.
6   Lucretius, *De rerum natura*, trans. W.H.D. Rouse, rev. M.F. Smith, Loeb Classical Library, Cambridge, Mass.: Harvard University Press, 1975, Book IV, lines 1–4.
7   St Thomas Aquinas, *Summa Theologiae*, IIIa, Supplement to the Third Part, Questions 94 & 97.
8   For a more complex analysis see John Portmann, *When Bad Things Happen to Other People*, New York: Routledge, 2000.

9 We need to distinguish, though. W.H. Bates's theory of biological 'mimicry', known to Nietzsche from the second edition of F.A. Lange's *History of Materialism*, has endured, whereas the evolutionary ideas of Wilhelm Roux or G.H. Schneider are historical curiosities.

10 See especially "On Truth and Lies in a Non-Moral Sense". *Kritische Studienausgabe: Werke* (hereafter: KSA), vol. 1, 881.

11 *Twilight of the Idols*, Skirmishes of an Untimely Man, 36.

12 *The Works of Charles Darwin*, ed. Paul H. Barrett and R.B. Freeman, London: William Pickering, 1986–9, vol. 21, p. 137.

13 *The Works of Charles Darwin*, vol. 15, p. 161–9.

14 See Gary Malinas and John Bigelow, "Simpson's Paradox", *Stanford Encyclopedia of Philosophy*, http://plato.stanford.edu/entries/paradox-simpson/

15 Cf. *Twilight of the Idols*, Skirmishes of an Untimely Man, 14.

16 Nietzsche wrote to Franz Overbeck: 'Each of these 3 articles discusses a single *primum mobile*; missing is a fourth, fifth and even the most essential one ('the herd instinct') – that must be left aside for the time being as too comprehensive.' Letter of 4 January 1888, *Kritische Studienausgabe: Briefe*, 8, 224.

17 *The Gay Science*, 4.

18 *On the Genealogy of Morals* I, Note.

19 *On the Genealogy of Morals* II, 12.

20 KSA 8, 23[9], 405–6.

21 See *The Works of Charles Darwin*, vol. 15 & 47.

22 KSA 8, 23[12], 406.

23 Schopenhauer, *The World as Will and Representation*, trans. E.F.J. Payne, New York: Peter Smith, 1969, vol. 2, p. 349–60.

24 *Thus Spoke Zarathustra*, On Self-Overcoming.

25 Cf. KSA 10, 5[1], 187.

26 Hume, *Enquiries Concerning the Human Understanding and Concerning the Principles of Morals*, ed. L.A. Selby-Bigge, 2nd edn. Oxford: Clarendon Press, 1902, p. 301.

27 A somewhat similar analysis of pain is found in D.M. Armstrong's *Bodily Sensations*, London: Routledge and Kegan Paul, 1962, p. 106–10.

28 Friedrich Albert Lange, *Geschichte des Materialismus und Kritik seiner Bedeutung in der Gegenwart*, Iserlohn: Verlag von J. Baedecker, 1866, p. 402–3. Despite this strong pronouncement, Lange wanted to preserve a purely heuristic notion of teleology in the necessary correspondence of form to the understanding. Ibid., p. 405.

29 KSA 13, 14[121], 300. Cf. ibid., 14 [80], 260; 14[101], 278; and 14 [174], 360.

30 KSA 11, 40[61], 661.

31 *The Works of Charles Darwin*, vol. 15 & 47.

32 W.H. Rolph, *Biologische Probleme, zugleich als Versuch einer rationellen Ethik*, Leipzig: Wilhelm Engelmann, 1882.

33 KSA 12, 10[57], 489.

HENRY STATEN

Toward a Will to Power Sociology

A good deal of Nietzsche scholarship interprets will to power in a way that parallels the base/superstructure model in Marx's theory of society, and gives rise to the same kind of conundrum. According to Marx, economics is the base, the ultimately determinative causal instance, and politics, law, what we think of as ' thought' in general, are superstructural effects of this base. In Nietzsche interpretation, it is 'drives' that are treated as the base, the final causal instance, and all of conscious thought (not only ideology) is relegated to the superstructure. The conundrum in both cases is: exactly how is the relation between base and superstructure to be conceived? Is the superstructure the mere effect or, as the Marxists say, 'reflection' of the dynamics of the base, or does it enjoy what is today called 'semi-autonomy'? On the 'semi-autonomy' interpretation, the level of ideology develops formal laws specific to the superstructural level that can exercise a substantial influence on subsequent ideological developments and even, as Engels already acknowledged, on the base itself. But then, how is such semi-autonomy to be reconciled with the underlying causality?

The clearest statement of ' reflection theory' in Nietzsche studies has been articulated by Brian Leiter, who argues that for Nietzsche thoughts issue in actions only by transmitting the underlying causality of the 'fixed' or 'immutable' set of traits, comprising the physiology and drives of the person in question [p. 91], which Leiter calls the 'type-facts' constituting the type of person one is.[1] On this view, 'Nietzsche would have us dispense with the idea of the will as causal altogether' [p. 93]. Since thoughts possess no causal force arising specifically at the level of thought, they affect neither what we do nor, a fortieri, the base itself. Consciousness is merely a passive observer of conflicts that are worked out entirely at the level of the drives, where, of course, the strongest one always wins [p. 100].

In this essay, by contrast, I will outline an account of the drives/ thoughts relation that could, at least by way of initial orientation, be called a 'semi-autonomy' account. This account stresses the socio- logical aspect of the formation of conscious thought as what the socio- logical theorist Anthony Giddens, in an analysis strongly influenced by Wittgenstein, calls 'practical consciousness.'[2] Because thought is internally structured by social forms, it has a system dynamics that is not the mere reflection of the dynamics of the drive system, and that has an important role to play in the determination of action. In no way does my argument attempt to resuscitate the transcendent 'I' that Nietzsche rejects as self-caused, nor to defend some notion of freedom against the deterministic and fatalistic trends in Nietzsche's thought that Leiter emphasizes. On my account, the system of consciousness is one set of naturalistic force-phenomena among others, with no onto- logical privilege; but it constitutes a distinctive level of causality, a specific locus at which new types of phenomena, not directly de- rivable from underlying phenomena, emerge, not as something ideal that escapes determinism but as the dialectical result of the additional layer of 'natural' determination exercised by cultural forms.

The view I am going to argue is intended as a correction not of Leiter's account but of the Nietzschean arguments that he interprets. But my intervention is itself based on Nietzsche's text – other parts of Nietzsche's text than those on which Leiter focuses, in which the theory of drives is developed sociologically and thus in ways more adequate to the problem of how one becomes what one is than the fatalism identified by Leiter. This fatalism is rooted in a 19th century biologism that will not bear scrutiny today, and, more important, this biologism implies a teleologism that compromises Nietzsche's philo- sophical radicalism in a fundamental way.

Biological Destiny?

Leiter addresses the relation between drives and social forms in a very limited way, in relation to the influence of healthy or decadent cultural values. He attempts to answer the question: If the values we encounter in our process of socialization cannot alter the physiological type-facts with which we come equipped, what difference can Nietzsche's teaching make, and for that matter, what influence can be exercised by the decadent cultural values Nietzsche opposes?[3] Leiter acknowledges a certain 'feedback' onto the development of the individual by moral values, such that, for example, a person who is potentially of the 'higher type' might turn out decadent as a consequence of the influence of ascetic morality. But, he argues, such outside influences can only have an effect on the individual in virtue of the pre-given psycho-physiological facts that constitute that individual; what one becomes is a function of 'how [one] already is' [pp. 98 & 156; cf. Richardson p. 216]. Only in virtue of her 'essential psycho-physical constitution' [Leiter p. 95] is the individual rendered susceptible to the influence of specific moral values; thus when someone comes to believe in decadent morality, this simply means that this person was already characterized by certain 'decadent type-facts,' and all the outside influence does is to activate these facts [pp. 157–8]. The individual's 'essential constitution' is not a single unitary essence but a warring community of drives; external factors can influence how the individual turns out because they will reinforce one set of drives in their struggle against another set. And yet this doesn't alter the essence that determines the individual's fate; the constitution nevertheless remains the *very same* 'essential' constitution.

This account forecloses the possibility that social forms could make a fundamental contribution to the individual's makeup. But Leiter can only insulate the level of the 'type facts' from social construction, while yet admitting cultural influence, by leaving unspecified exactly how the *essential nature* of a constitution is determined. If what is immutable is not the overall development of the individual (since the same individual can turn out healthy or decadent), the immutable must be either a) the individual elements that make up the individual's constitution (the 'type-facts') or b) a holistic principle encompassing the totality of type-facts. Leiter's phrase 'essential constitution' points toward b) as the locus of the individual person's fatality; but by definition an unalterable principle governing the whole could not be affected by external influences that could yield opposite outcomes. Leiter gets around this difficulty by attributing the variability of the outcome of individual development to the variability of the *relations among* the constituent type-facts. Overall health or decadence are possible outcomes because the type-facts are not homogeneous in type; some are healthy and some decadent. The external influences then affect the balance of power among the contending drives that are determined by these underlying 'facts.'

But this doesn't work either. If the overall balance of power is contingent on external influences, what is 'essential' cannot be the overall 'constitution' of the type facts, but only the nature of the constituent 'facts' themselves. Only the basic constituent units out of whose struggle the principle of the whole emerges, and not the principle of the whole, would be essentially impermeable to alteration. But then, if the constituent units really are unalterable in their essence, the outcome should be unalterable too; the relative strength and weakness of the entire ensemble of constituents would be fixed, and the constitution of the whole would be the result of a struggle the outcome of which was pre-determined. This would yield the desired 'essential constitution' of the whole, but only by closing off the posited openness to cultural feedback (and rendering senseless Nietzsche's project of revaluation of values). If decadent values have the power to make the *weaker* ensemble of units stronger than the intrinsically *stronger* ensemble, it makes no sense to say that these units have an unalterable essence; and if they really are unalterable, then no such influence is possible.

Nietzsche attempts to posit something like an 'essential constitution' of the whole while yet attempting to base this notion in the dynamics of struggle among a multiplicity of parts, creating contradictions that neither he nor Leiter overcome. The poststructuralist interpretation of Nietzsche took his deconstruction of the unity of the organism into a multiplicity of conflicting forces to be a definitive step beyond teleology; but if the conflicting forces are defined in Leiter's fashion as unchangeable natures tending inexorably toward the fulfillment of their essence, they are themselves guided by their own individual, quarrelsome telei. These little telei become a means of securing the dominance of teleology over the reign of contingency (to be sure, teleology of a radical new kind, much more to the taste of modernity, but still teleology), *and above all, of securing the impermeability of essential natures from the influence of the social outside.*

The teleological nature of Nietzsche's fatalism, implied but not explicated as such by Leiter, is not only acknowledged but embraced by John Richardson in his book *Nietzsche's System*, perhaps the most impressive attempt ever made to grasp Nietzsche's thought as a coherent system.[4] '[...] Nietzsche, despite his repeated attacks on (what he calls) 'teleology,'' Richardson writes, 'really has such a theory himself: the beings or units in his world are [...] end directed, and to understand them properly is to grasp how they're directed or aimed' [p. 21]. He identifies the 'unit' of will to power as the *drive* or *will* and uses the terms more or less interchangeably. Richardson's account serves as a mediation between Leiter's and my own, because he plays down the physiological nature of drives, stressing instead the profound formative influence on them of historically evolved social practices (on which more below), yet delimits a subset of drives that correspond to Leiter's fatal physiological type-facts. This subset is that of the 'most primitive wills,' which exhibit an apparently pre-cultural 'intentionality' [p. 188] of the most essential sort, a preconscious aim-directedness toward health. The primitive 'knowing' [p. 207] that is built into the most primordial unconscious drives is the most important kind of purposiveness; it is an immanent, unconscious 'reason' or 'power of discernment,' that makes the drives 'trustworthy judges' of sickness and health [p. 206]. As in Leiter's account, cultural influence can enhance the pre-cultural aim-directedness of 'the most primitive wills' only to the degree that it shares their intrinsic nature: 'these drives themselves take valuing viewpoints on the world; the 'sight' involved in their preconscious caring can be improved by stimulating and exercising that caring in a special way' [ibid.].

Presumably, then, one would, on Richardson's account as well, be fated by the physiologically given drives to either health or decadence. But Richardson realizes that the social outside reaches very deeply into the constitution of the individual, far beyond the influence of the 'moral values' that Leiter discusses. The drives themselves are for the most part not a 'common human endowment' but customs and practices into which humans are trained by their cultures [p. 48]; these practices are syntheses of more primordial wills, and once culturally established, they take on 'a life of their own' and take power over the persons who perform them [pp. 49–50]. Individual being is thus, on Richardson's account, not entirely settled by pre-existing essence; it must be brought forth by the individual's active resistance to the subject-constituting power of existing social practices. Only 'by developing idiosyncratic variations on the common practices, by weaving the latter into new syntheses, *and especially by shifting that overall practice itself through such* efforts' can I create 'a self that *is* as a will to power, in its own right [...]'[p. 161; italics added].

However, beyond appealing to the notion of ontological individuality, Richardson does not identify the precise source of such originative power. As outside the patterns of social practice, it presumably has something to do with the knowledge possessed by the 'most primitive wills'; but if that is the case, a number of crucial questions arise.

What do Drives Know?

The questions I want to explore require that we now take a closer look at the concept of drive. A good place to begin is with Richardson's notion that a drive is a 'pattern of activity' that is, as he says, 'telically' oriented toward 'its own network of ends' [p. 21].

A drive thus, according to this definition, unconsciously *knows what it aims at* and *how to get there*; the 'intentionality' of wills 'includes both a view of the goal and a view of surroundings and circumstances in and through which that goal is being pursued' [p. 188].[5] The knowledge of how to attain the end is not, in a biological drive, representational (Richardson uses the notion of 'viewing' the goal metaphorically); this knowledge is given in the structure of what ethologists call the 'behavioural program' of the organism. Thus the notion of the 'network of ends' is folded back into the 'pattern of activity' itself; an organism's instinctual pattern of activity is structured by evolution to attain certain ends, without the organism's needing to think about what it's doing. This biological definition makes good sense as well when applied to the patterns of social practice; the teleology of socially constructed drives is a derivative of the aim-directedness of the practices that impress upon the drives their pattern of activity.

But how are we to understand the *superior* will that is able to revise a social practice but is defined precisely by its *not* corresponding (in some obscure but essential way) to the typed pattern of the practice? How can it 'know' either the end at which it aims or, more important (since the aim might just be 'to shift the practice'), the path to this end? In the absence of an account of how the ends are woven into the pattern of activity, the bare 'aim' at *shifting the practice* could be nothing more than, for example, the ambition of a callow youth who dreams of being a great poet but doesn't have a clue as to how to write a sonnet.

The superior will is supposed to be based in healthy biological drives, but the only kind of 'knowledge' the biological drives have, beyond their behavioural programs, concerns 'health' [p. 206]; and *health* is not the aim of any specific biological drive and has no specific pattern of activity appropriate to it. In Richardson as in a great deal of Nietzsche commentary, health is made to do a lot of work without being given much specification. Even if health is a kind of overall tropism conditioning the individual drives – even the 'synthetic,' culturally constructed drives – only the individual drives themselves can propose the *objects* in regard to which this tropism can then operate and the *means* by which to seek or turn away from it. This knowledge belongs to the structure of the individual drive in biology and to the socially prescribed pattern of activity in the case of social practices. So how do we leap the gap between biology and culture, such that something biological is going to account for the *specific form* of a cultural production of a radically original kind?

Richardson's discussion of 'shifting the practice' itself says nothing about primordial drive knowledge; it is only his overall account that implies its relevance here. This discussion suggests, rather, that practices are shifted by the superior *power* of the one who thereby individuates her self. This self '*is* as a will to power' [p. 161]; and the discussion of individuation here articulates smoothly with the remarks on pages 212–13 about wills that command and wills that obey. We could theorize, then, that all the actual knowledge of how-to is still derived, in the superior will, from cultural patterns of practice, but that a superior quantum of force exerted by the original individual throws the practice off its customary tracks and into a new pattern. This strikes me as a promising track; here would be the required nexus between biology and culture, with no illegitimate ascription of cultural know-how to biological drive. Superior, physiologically based strength needs the social pattern, but, given the pattern, it can bring forth new forms by pouring more energy into the practice than ordinary wills can muster. Richardson, however, does not address such a possibility; he completely ignores the notion, much stressed by Nietzsche (notably in *GS* 360), that will to power is primarily the release of a 'quantum of energy' that must express itself in action; on Richardson's account, will to power is nothing but the universal tendency inhabiting all specific drives to raise their end directed activity to a 'new and higher level of effort' [p. 26], and at the limit to become something higher, more 'spiritual' [pp. 188–9]; and the notion of *strength* is assimilated very closely to that of *health* ('[...] freedom is strength or health of will.' [p. 213]).

Further, nothing on my suggested revision of Richardson's hypothesis would justify his claim that the newness, the non-belonging to the typed pattern, of the new, revised form of the practice, is the *correlate of the being of the individual qua individual* and not of some creative potential *in the practice itself*. In Aristotelian terms, the application of a superior quantity of force would be only the 'efficient cause' of the emergence of the new form and thus strictly *accidental* to its production;[6] the ontologically 'prior' cause, the *formal* cause, would be the formative power of the cultural practice itself. The notion of the 'formal cause' fell into disrepute because of its extension outside the field of human productive practice, *techne*, into the realm of physics; but it remains valid in the field of techne in which it originated.[7] In the absence of Aristotle's distinctions, or their updated analogs, Richardson's account – which is faithful to a fundamental tendency in Nietzsche – sounds uncomfortably like a biologistic recasting of the personalistic Romantic theory of creation that mystically endowed the genius creator with precisely the requisite *form-originating* power, 'hidden somewhere in the depths of the soul,' that would make the artwork a pure manifestation of something intimately proper to the essentially *culture-transcending* creative individual.

Once we recognize the practice or art itself (techne) as formal cause, by contrast, the individuated I looks less like the transcendent source of cultural innovation than its *product*. Richardson's account actually comes close to being already reversible in this sense. 'By developing idiosyncratic variations [...] I create a self' already says that it is the process of cultural production that produces the self. But by positing some quality or power of the extra cultural drives as the ontological origin of the cultural product, or rather of that about it which is really new, and therefore *valuable*, Richardson is able to suggest that the resultant individuated I is itself also *extra-cultural*, despite the necessary mediation of the act of cultural production. The kernel of ontological individuality in the most primitive drives is elaborated and amplified in the process of cultural production, and ends up as a fully individuated self, with the ontological core transmitted intact (though presumably 'unfolded'? – as a *dynamis* that attains its *energeia*? – or else?) from a *pre-cultural* to a *post-cultural* state; and the cultural product of this *extra-cultural* core acquires from its *extra-cultural* origin a special kind of *cultural* value, that of changing the form of existing practice. Apparently this is supposed to be the expression of the generalized desire for the ' higher' that will to power brings to the movement of the drives. But how do we get from the *desire for the higher* to the *cultural attainment* of the higher?

Richardson's account is vulnerable not only to the objections of incoherence that I have been raising but also to the charge that it traduces the naturalism to which he and Nietzsche adhere. As Richardson recognizes, the sociological level of explanation is part of a full naturalistic account; yet he tries to make good Nietzsche's attempt to use biology as a pretext for the introduction of a form-creating power that would govern a pattern of cultural activity from an *extra-cultural* site.[8]

Macht and Social Form

The knowledge of a cultural goal, and of the pattern of activity by which the cultural goal is to be achieved, must be culturally inscribed. No doubt there is a biological substratum to such inscription, and I am convinced by contemporary work in physiology and genetics that this substratum can involve quite rich content. But this substratum, though essential, cannot be the *formal cause* of cultural form; one cannot, for example, no matter how well one is genetically endowed, innovate on the form of the sonnet yet live in an illiterate culture, or in a literate culture in which sonnets do not exist. The appropriate cultural forms and patterns of activity supervene on those of the *pre-cultural* drives, creating new, higher-order, 'synthetic' drives oriented toward the goals these forms define and equipped with the 'knowledge' of how to pursue them – a knowledge the primary locus of which, however, remains the social matrix and not individual physiology.

For a Nietzschean social theory, the crucial point is that the primitive drives that are pressed into the service of the synthetic drive constituted by the practice are *empowered* to attain its goal by being inscribed with its pattern of activity. The *Drang*, thrust or impelling force, of the drive might have as much physiological energy as possible and yet it will lack all actual *Macht*, power that can attain its goal, if it is not equipped with the culturally prescribed pattern of activity that encodes knowledge of the pathway to the goal. This means that we must make very strongly a distinction that is implicit everywhere in Nietzsche but that he tends to elide, between the *strength of the drive*, its physiologically endowed impelling force or quantum of energy, and the *Macht* at which the drive aims. Nietzsche attempted to ground the notion of drive as *self-impelled* force in an ontological theory of force as pure explosive expansiveness, and was committed to the idea of a pure force that could produce form out of itself, by something having to do with the nature of force *qua* unformed quantum of energy.[9] But this model severs pure elementary force so thoroughly from the notion of a goal that it becomes, if we take the model seriously, impossible to see how it could indeed be *power* toward which it tends, much less toward which it would be 'telically' oriented (perhaps for this reason Richardson in his otherwise impressively comprehensive account completely ignores the 'quantum of energy' model). Power is the *effectuality* of force, and the modern or modernist obsession with innovation should not obscure the fact, well known to modernist artists, and frequently stressed by them – as against the romanticism popular with second rate artists and non-artists – that the power of a drive to effect revisions in cultural practices is entirely dependent on the complete 'in-corporation' of the practice pattern or practice form to which the drive becomes yoked. [10]

The true repository of *Macht*, power as effectual force, is not the physiological substratum of the drive but the practice form that structures this substratum with the appropriate pattern of activity. The form of practice that gives form to the activity of the drive is thus also the form of the drive's effectual force, its *Macht*. The forms of social practice thus contain the concrete *dynamis* or *potentia* that is actualized in the case of any specific practice by a human agent in order to attain the goal of the practice. In Aristotelian terms, drive energy can at best contain the 'remote potentiality' of a human agent's effectual practice, and this remote potentiality must undergo alteration by the social forms of practice that shape it into a 'proximate potentiality' capable of actualization in specific actions.[11] They could thus illuminatingly be called *force forms*.

The general theory of will to power, as various commentators have noted, was based on phenomena that Nietzsche observed in human culture; the sociological re-transcription of this theory that I am proposing returns the theory to its original conceptual basis, but with a more fully elaborated analysis of this basis. Nietzsche tried to naturalize his theory by following the model of physics all the way down to the concept of homogeneous elemental force; its sociological re-transcription by contrast begins from the concept of the *competent agent* as a concrete social phenomenon. If it is not to relapse into pure metaphysics or a form of speculative biology, human will to power must fundamentally mean this: the desire for the power to do what human beings *can do* in one's culture of reference, and supremely to do what the most able of all can do, or even to surpass these, yet while taking them as one's models. On this conception, agency is not a metaphysical puzzle but a given of human natural history. We derive our concept of agency (=power) from seeing people do things and from doing things ourselves; no one doubts that such doing occurs. But then the doubt creeps in as to whether it's *really me* that is doing this or whether I might not be the mere instrument of some other cause, and the notions of free will and metaphysical agency are introduced to stave off this doubt. Subsequently, when metaphysical agency becomes unbelievable, it seems that in its absence it must indeed not be me that is the agent of my doings, but, say, social forces or unconscious drives. But this all-or-nothing picture (either I or something else is the *real cause* of this doing) is a pure derivative of the intervening metaphysical episode. If we drop the demand that an agent be an absolute metaphysical origin, there is no problem in recognizing more modest forms of agency that are what ordinary usage calls agency (the term 'agency' is already a term of art; ordinary usage just says '*She* did it'); and these more modest forms of agency leave room for the operation on the agent and the agent's doing of prior and perhaps greater causes, yet without compromising our non-metaphysical sense that *this person here* (humanly considered) is a great pianist or an accomplished writer and that this performance or this work is – given the necessary context of physical, biological, and social causation/constitution – *their* doing.

So, then: we begin this re-transcription from the fact that an ordinary member of a human culture possesses the competencies that make her a cultural agent, someone capable of doing the things that competent adults in that culture are supposed to be able to do in order to satisfy obligations, take care of themselves, gain the respect of others – and also, in the rare case, to achieve some cultural goal superlatively well, on the level of a Shakespeare or Bach.[12] These competencies range from the ability to do a specific kind of work to the ability to carry on a conversation or tie shoelaces. It is only within the context of this rich soup of competencies that something like moral choice can be understood, concretely, in terms of will to power. Nietzsche runs too quickly over this social mediation; on one side he posits the metaphysical theory of free will as something that happens in the thin air of thought, and on the other side the hydraulics of drive. Moral choice is certainly not what Nietzsche denies it is, but neither is it the simple triumph of the 'strongest' physiological drive; it is the resolution, governed by the overall nisus toward the optimal feeling of will to power that Nietzsche best describes in an often quoted passage from *GM* III, 7,[13] of an extensive complex of drive forces that have been woven into drive syntheses deriving their structure and their effectuality from the force forms of a given culture.

I have posited as the basic model of the satisfactions of will to power the attainment of some practical goal by means of the appropriate techne (which, recall, does not only define the pathway to the goal but constitutes the goal as a goal); this model gives the thickest content to the notion of power by defining it in terms of actual formative impact on the world, and by providing a well articulated description of what it means for a drive to be structured by a pattern of activity that is oriented toward a goal. Otherwise the notion of the power that humans aim at remains under specified, as a general tendency toward control or expansion or, as in Richardson's interpretation, toward spiritualization of the basic drives. It may seem that the techne model in fact *over* specifies the nature of power in a way that cannot be generalized; but, as I will explain below, once this model is in place, the power that is sought in other, less 'technical' cases – notably in cases of moral choice – can be understood, in part as depending on, and interwoven with, techne competency, and in part as having *their own 'technical' structure*, in the sense that they involve the same kind of habituation to culturally constituted patterns of activity.[14] The agent's physiological substratum provides genetic programs of various sorts, some of them probably quite rich – perhaps 'modules' that constrain the possibilities of human behavior in very specific ways – but which nevertheless remain only the materials that must be elaborated and synthesized under the influence of the force forms into which human beings are trained in their respective cultures. And once the agent has fully incorporated a practice, become skilled in it, the *potentia* of the practice becomes the agent's 'own' *potentia*, yet not in the metaphysical sense of 'ownness' that Richardson attempts to secure for the agent's metaphysical kernel of individuation. For the power potentiality of the human agent here, *insofar as this potentiality is that of a formal cause* – which is to say, the cause of a new form with cultural value – is strictly that of the incorporated techne.

Yet there remains a great deal that is entirely individual about the process of actualization by which a human being becomes the agent: the physiological quantum of energy that a given individual brings to the table, as well as all the particularities of that individual's socio-historical location, which determine that no two individuals will appropriate a given cultural practice in precisely the same way. It is always a particular subject who carries out the behavioural program provided by a techne, and in so doing makes its potential actual; and this is enough for our ordinary attributions of *active agency* to persons. It is also enough to explain the ability of rare individuals to 'shift the practice' and leave their stamp on it for future practitioners.[15]

Once we understand agency not as metaphysical origination but as actualization of the *Macht* that lies potential in a techne there is no reason to deny, as Leiter does, that the conscious self can take an 'active part' in the process of 'self-mastery' [p. 100]. For self-mastery is only a misleading name for the process by which a self that has been equipped with the right, culturally constructed drive syntheses, with their encoded knowledge of the pathways to their respective networks of ends – and crowning them all the self-concept of the self-mastered man, along the axis of ethics the supreme social force form, and one to which no one is more committed than Nietzsche himself – is able to follow the pathways that, as it knows from experience, lead to the actualization of that *potentia* that, also from experience, it can judge to be the optimal *potentia* of which it is capable in a given situation. Understood naturalistically in this way, the conscious self is one level at which the drives are synthesized into their effectual cultural patterns of activity, a derivative or representative of the physiological drives that is more mobile and thus more quickly educable than they are, and which can therefore be educated to subserve the optimization potentials that are contained in a specific set of social forms. Conscious thought that is equipped with the appropriate training and experience can range quickly over the possible alternatives of action and their possible outcomes, and be drawn, as mere thought, toward the representation of an optimal outcome that is not present enough to the unconscious drives to be able to attract them but which thought, equipped with cultural techniques of drive discipline, is able to 'amplify' by calling up from memory the non present consequences of possible courses of action, and by so doing increase the attractive force of the option that thought has already recognized as promising the superior yield of effectuality.

Picture these Consequences

In the final section of this essay I will fill in the details of the account sketched in the preceding paragraph, but first I must reply to a possible objection: that in the preceding paragraphs I have advanced a version of the theory of action that was decisively skewered in *Daybreak* 129, the 'picture of the consequences' account. Let us take a close look at this poorly reasoned passage of Nietzsche's, often quoted but strikingly little criticized. Rather than refuting the techne account, the gaps in its argument show exactly how the idea of techne can be inserted into Nietzsche's drive theory.[16]

Nietzsche's remark begins by describing the conventional notion of motivation that he means to attack, the notion that when we deliberate over an action we present to ourselves in 'reflective consciousness' a 'picture of the consequences' of that action, and that this picture then determines the *motive* of the action.

As against this conception, Nietzsche argues that 'often enough' the true determining motive of the action is not included in the conscious 'picture,' and he gives a list of motives that remain unconsidered and unknown:

What here comes into play is the way we habitually expend our energy; or some slight instigation from a person we fear or honour or love; or our indolence, which prefers to do what lies closest at hand; or an excitation of our imagination brought about at the decisive moment by some immediate, very trivial

event; [...] caprice and waywardness come into play; some emotion happens
quite by chance to leap forth [...]. *Probably* a struggle takes place between these
as well, a battling to and fro, a rising and falling of the scales – and this would
be the actual 'conflict of motives' – something quite invisible to us of which we
would be quite unconscious. [D 129]

The notion put forth here of the unconscious struggle of motives
is obviously a precursor of the later, fully fledged drive theory that
was based on will to power. But in fact the theory of will to power is
poorly adumbrated here, for two reasons.

First, most of the possible triumphant motives Nietzsche names
are implausible candidates for 'drives.' Nietzsche of course does not
call them drives here; but Nietzsche commentary commonly treats
them so; see, for example, Leiter [p. 103]. Indolence is the opposite of
anything the theory of will to power could deem a drive; and chance
imaginations, caprice, and momentary emotion are too unstable and
momentary to qualify. Second, the idea that such motives as these,
whether 'drives' or not, could be the true determinants of moral choice
evokes as the agent an adolescent or a ninny (perhaps the protagonist
of Eichendorff's *Aus dem Leben eines Taugenichts*) rather than a
competent adult making a serious decision; so it's hard to take this as
a generalizable model of motivation. Among the proposed unconscious motives there is only one that is stable, significant, and dynamic enough to be called a drive: 'instigation from a person whom
we fear or honour or love.' Here Nietzsche at least gestures in the
direction of a real moral psychology of unconscious drives; and of
course in his work as a whole he develops such a psychology. But the
notion that the conscious 'picture of the consequences' plays an
important role in practical judgment is not so easily disposed of as
Daybreak 129 suggests.

Nietzsche is here presumably working toward the following
doctrine: 'you think you act because of your conscious, rational pro-
jection of consequences, but in truth you act because of the way that
an overall will to power emerges out of the contending drives out of
which you are constituted.' But the windblown arbitrariness of the
struggle of motives described in *D* 129 leaves it a complete mystery
how anything like a *will to power* could emerge out of it. To deal with

this problem Nietzsche in his later work tried to work out a 'systems' account of the struggle of drives, influenced by the physiologist Wilhelm Roux, according to which a person's interacting drives evolve a holistic principle of health that serves as a guardrail keeping will to power on track. But this brings us back to the problem I discussed earlier in this essay, of how the principle of physiological health is going to govern the level of human action if action is, as I have been arguing, internally structured by social force forms. It's fine to evoke 'health' as a magical formula by means of which the struggle of drives is stipulated to result in optimal cultural activity, but this notion will not yield a rigorous account of the micro dynamics by which drives are culturally 'synthesized' or of the structure of the practical judgments based on these syntheses. In the absence of such an account, the notion of the resolution of drive forces too easily arcs back into the Romantic conception of an organic 'ruling idea' that like an invisible hand guides the destiny of the higher man, as it did in Nietzsche's own thought [EH, clever, 9].

The shape of the overall drive synthesis is that of a *person* (not a mere human organism), and therefore its will to power must be understood primarily at the level of the forms of culture and society. And these forms inevitably involve the intervention of consciousness, the fact against which Nietzsche protested. But the role of consciousness in this process is much more textured and layered than Nietzsche's railing against 'reflective consciousness' will allow. On the techne account, consciousness is primarily something that opportunistically piggybacks on the practical knowledge that is historically sedimented in social practice, and only incidentally something 'psychological', belonging to the here-and-now of an individual's lucid mental presence. Nietzsche's notion that the most important knowledge is contained not in reflection but in the 'judgments of the muscles' [WP 314] is today hard to sustain on a purely biological basis, but it is plainly true of muscles that have incorporated the know-how of any given techne. Our preeminent model of muscle knowledge must be not the animal instinctively seeking optimal activity but, say, the concert pianist who has fully incorporated her techne and is at the peak of her powers.

No one could be more aware of the model of artistic power as a flow of non-reflective, 'instinctual' power than Nietzsche; and in the most important passage in which he condemns consciousness he comes very near the insight that artistic power actualizes the *potentia* of social force forms. When a group develops the art of communication to a very high degree, Nietzsche writes in *Gay Science* 354, it becomes 'a capacity that has gradually been accumulated and now waits for an heir who might squander it' – heirs who are called 'artists', but also 'orators, preachers, writers,' and who 'always come at the end of a long chain.' But Nietzsche has his eye on a different point, as is indicated by the metaphor of an 'heir' who 'squanders' his cultural heritage. As he makes clear earlier in this remark, consciousness is 'really only a net of communication between human beings' and therefore identical with herd being; the resources of communication, signs in general (including preeminently language but also 'a mien, a pressure, a gesture') that a culture accumulates are therefore the very element of herd being. The *reality* of individual action is therefore inaccessible to consciousness because, as 'incomparably personal, unique, and utterly individual', it is absolutely alien to herd being (the point that Richardson stresses). Presumably, then, the artist-heir creates not by actualizing but by *suborning* the social force forms, beginning with those of language, to the expression of his own 'utterly individual' being, and doing so in a way that destroys ('squanders') the resources it uses. Nietzsche thus always, and despite strong indications to the contrary, remains at bottom a Romantic in his view of the nature of artistic creation. *Either* conscious, and therefore of the herd; *or* individual, and therefore unconscious. This is the duality that keeps Nietzsche's thought from broaching the notion of practical consciousness.

If we now reconsider *Daybreak* 129 from the techne standpoint, it becomes apparent that one of the 'motives' listed there is incomparable to any of the others, and leads us into just the revision of Nietzsche's account that is required to articulate it with the theory of techne. 'The way we habitually expend our energy' is not one factor among others in a battle of drives; it is the general form of both drive and techne. Techne, when incorporated in a human body as a set of typed pathways in the nerves and muscles and neurons, is nothing other than a habitual manner in which the body has learned to expend energy, one which encodes the how-to of an action pattern charged with effectuality that a given culture has evolved, hence an especially effectual mode of expenditure, one conducive to optimal activity; and the 'behavioural program' of a biological drive even more clearly counts as a habitual mode of expenditure of energy.

The one solid candidate for a drive that *D* 129 mentions – 'instigation from someone we fear or honour or love' – can be analyzed along the same lines, taking fear, honour, or love as habitual modes of energetic expenditure. A drive to 'honour' someone in particular is clearly a cultural synthesis, based in physiology like all drives but dependent on the social forms that make it possible; and there is plenty of evidence that love is in large part socially constructed as well. Fear seems like the most primordial of the three, yet an established relation of fear toward another human being such as Nietzsche evokes is something that requires an elaborate cultural stage setting (for example in the relation to one's intellectual master or military superior). The 'instigation' then would derive its possibility – both its structure and its energy – from the pathways of habitual energetic expenditure that mark out the relation as one of fear or honour or love, and these pathways in individual physiology would be deeply marked by the social forms that define the identities of the persons involved, the nature of their relation, and even the character of the affective flow that traverses the relation.

Such patterns are not as such forms of techne; they are not structured as modes of how-to oriented toward a goal. For that reason they would be subordinate in importance in the analysis of action to the habit patterns derived from techne. This and other sorts of non techne patterns of expenditure might in some individual's drive synthesis be yoked to the project of power; but in order to analyze such a yoking we would need to keep clear the normative priority of the techne structure.

Thus the notion of habitual modes of energetic expenditure makes it possible to link techne with other kinds of energetic flow, integrating the theory of techne into the terms of will-to-power economics (the 'quantum of energy' aspect).

Now let us return to the key notion at issue in *Daybreak* 129, the conscious anticipation of the probable result of action ('picture of the consequences'). Since techne is the form of effectual human action, we can realistically picture as successful the consequence only of an act the pathways toward which already belong to our neuromuscular competence because we have incorporated the appropriate social force form. As I have noted, there are other forms of habitual expenditure of energy, but only those that embody or are adaptations of techne or techne like action patterns can reliably be projected as pathways toward power.[17] Habitual expenditure is oriented toward habitual consequence of the expenditure, and the more skilled I am in a techne the more habitually and justly – habitually *because* justly – I will picture as successful the probable consequence of my act. In fact, if I'm truly skilled, like the pianist mentioned above, I can dispense altogether with the picturing and do the thing with unreflective confidence, just the sort of thing Nietzsche loves. But *this* sort of 'unconscious' activity is the product of socially accumulated resources rather than an argument against them. The distinction between conscious and unconscious knowledge thus cannot be made on the basis of that between the herd and the individual. And there is no boundary of essence between conscious and unconscious implementation of social force forms. The effectuality of *unreflective* skilled activity is constituted by social forms that embody a long antecedent historical development by which the pathways to such goals have been worked out, and effectual *conscious* thought, thought that can form a purpose and carry out a series of actions designed to fulfill it is derived from the same source.[18] Thought might thus be said to have a certain causal power, one that is *delegated* to it, not from any force or energy emanating from within, whether of a *geistlich* or a physiological nature, but from the social force forms.

Thought conceived as a Drive

Techne is, so to speak, prosthetic instinct, and becomes 'instinctual' and 'unconscious' to the degree that it is successfully *in-corporated*. And the case is no different for the philosopher than it is for the crafts-man or artist; what we call 'reflection' even of a philosophical type – *especially* of a philosophical type – is constituted as a historically evolved techne, a specific art of arrangement of words. As anyone who spends his life writing knows, to the degree that one is 'in com-mand' of one's writing, so that one does not struggle but the sentences and paragraphs flow into their proper form, one after another, the activity becomes a sort of reverie that one only recognizes as such when the flow grinds to a halt and one is rudely awakened. At that point once again 'reflection' sets in, as one goes back and tests critic-ally what one has done; and yet this reflection too is a form of techne, and thus mainly 'unconscious.' Consciousness in the strictest sense, as the self-aware wakefulness of the self, only glimmers in the interstices of effectual practice, when the self-impelling energy of practice flags.

We are thus led to the apparent paradox that what we call *con-sciousness* is mostly *unconscious*. But 'consciousness' is not a *sub-stance*, much less a *homogeneous* substance, and above all it is (to the degree that we can speak of an 'it') something much rarer than Nietzsche implies in *GS* 354. There is a wide variety of mental activities that participate to a greater or lesser degree in some aspect of what we call consciousness; *knowledge*, however, belongs not to consciousness as such (which must be essentially empty) but rather to the 'unconscious' of the cunningly structured activity patterns (whether instinctual or socially inscribed) within which consciousness plays such a role as it has. Despite the fact that there is no autonomous self, (conscious) thoughts do play an active role in the system of causality by which actions are generated, and, to the degree that this causal role of thoughts (as opposed to the causal power of the 'I') is what we mean by 'will', it can be said that will plays a certain active role in action.

Nietzsche himself, in the famous dictum of *BGE* 17 that 'a thought comes when *it* wishes', implies that a thought is, like all other drive phenomena, an energetic quantum seeking discharge, a self-originating spontaneity; and since thought is on this account essentially alien to the I, we could conclude that it is intrinsically 'unconscious'.[19] According to this line of thought, then, the energetic flow of quanta called 'conscious thought' (or more strictly, the varieties of psychic function that can, in a specific context, be differentially characterized as conscious) would be just one more drive synthesis or family of drive syntheses, and would participate in the causal relation to action of the drive system in general; conscious thought would be, like unconscious, instinctual thought, 'pure effecting, pure willing' [GS 354].

BGE 17 in fact throws the doctrine of *GS* 354 into a cocked hat. The usual way of reconciling the two is by assimilating what *BGE* 17 says to the orthodox idea that thoughts are caused by underlying drives; but this reading is forced in the extreme. How can the notion that 'a thought comes when *it* wishes' mean: comes when a causality of a different and underlying type causes it to emerge? Moreover, in the continuation of the remark, Nietzsche says that even this form of statement is misleading; to say that 'it' wishes is already to posit an agent of the deed. Thus this remark is linked to the famous doer/deed analysis of the *Genealogy*, where Nietzsche links it closely to the cause/effect split; it is therefore implausible to suggest that he rejects 'it wishes' because he thinks thought is really the *effect* of an underlying cause. The more natural reading of *BGE* 17 is that it manifests his persistent effort to get beyond the notion of cause and effect to a conception of the pure spontaneity of every moment of universal becoming. That this conception contradicts the 'physiological drives cause thoughts' model is in my view all to the good, given the limitations of that model that I have been pointing out.

However, despite its attractions as metaphysics, and its aptness to describe a certain undeniable fact of experience (the fact that we cannot anticipate a thought in order to choose it – cannot think it *before* thinking it, so that it takes us as it were by surprise), the notion of pure spontaneity will not take us far into the naturalistic understanding of thought. For even if I can't pre-think a thought before thinking it, there is nevertheless an *order* of thought that implies something other than a pure spontaneity. In Wittgenstein's phrase, 'the place is prepared' for the thought before the thought comes; neither I nor anyone else knows what the thought will be before it appears, but we can reliably predict, given a specific discursive context, what kind of thought it will be, and we will be able, *if the thought is an effectual one*, retrospectively to perceive very strong links to the preceding chain of discourse out of which it emerged. Only a random thought, one that 'came out of nowhere,' and therefore would not express will to power – or much of anything, for that matter – would not be strongly determined by the structuring generative force of a socially well established linguistic techne.

But let's stay with *BGE* 17, because the doctrine of spontaneity is essential to the suture between will to power and techne. Commenting on the wedge Nietzsche drives between the I and its thoughts, Leiter says the I is merely a passive observer. Even mere observation could be construed as noetic activity, but to neutralize this possibility Leiter calls the observing I an 'epiphenomenon' of drive dynamics. We might accordingly picture the wakeful I as a sort of light that thought throws off at its surface, the fitful coruscation of an essentially unconscious flow.

This I, however, according to the doctrine of Zarathustra, *is not the 'self'* which is identical with the body and its drives. The I that Nietzsche declares null and void is thus what me might call a 'thin' I – an *extremely* thin one in *BGE* 17. It's one thing for Nietzsche to identify the conscious I with the flow of conscious thought while depreciating the significance of conscious thought, and quite another to sever the I *even from conscious thought*. Once this has been done, there is no reason to depreciate thought, which can now be reintegrated into nature.

The overall strategy that determines both moves is to show that consciousness is not 'master in its own house.' What Nietzsche is feeling his way towards is a new, richer, thicker conception of the self. This self would not be divided like the Platonic horse and rider but would be, let's say, *all horse*, yet a horse who possesses the rider's knowledge. This analogy will not bear much weight, but the ways in which it threatens to break down are as instructive as those in which it

works. For what does a horse need with a rider's knowledge, if it can't
share a rider's purposes? The senselessness of the suggestion that the
horse could incorporate the rider's knowledge is precisely that of
Nietzsche's attempt to make the reality of human action something
entirely non social and individual, belonging to the darkness of the
individual body.[20]

Once the I has been evicted even from the flow of articulated
thought and declared wholly ineffectual, the entire realm of human
experience is free of the baneful spell of 'reflective consciousness'
and the Christian/idealist philosophy of *Geist* that sponsored it.[21] Body
and mind can now be considered on what Deleuze calls 'the plane of
immanence' of mere nature, but with no need for the adventitious
distinctions between consciousness and unconsciousness, drive and
culture, group and individual, that lead Nietzsche's thinking back into
Romantic and vitalistic mystifications. The self can now be identified
with the spontaneous flow of self-originating thought; it comes into
being at the point of that emergence, *is* that emergence (not its epiphenomenal effect). But it is not isolated thought entities that emerge;
the spontaneity of the thought flow must be conceived not as the
absence of all before and after but simply as the absence of any
transcendent, *geistlich* master of the flow. 'A thought comes when *it*
wants' must be revised into 'the flow of thought is self-moved, it is,
like the physiological drives, spontaneous flow of will to power; and
this immanent flow has structure, the structure of the habitual modes
of energetic expenditure of various types.'

Now I can fill in the details of the new 'picture of the consequences' model that I adumbrated earlier. The dynamics of the model
are now entirely immanent to the drive system, which has now been
expanded to include the flow of 'conscious' thought as merely another
level of structured energetic flow, with its structure now understood as
derived not only from physiology but from social forms as well. And
the energy that drives thought and the conscious will is not that of
transcendent spirit but that of will to power. But the energy of will to
power, contrary to what Nietzsche's quantum theory would have it be,
cannot be an absolute, non relational quantity; will to power always
exists in a determinate environment of expression, in relation to which
it is able to will optimal activity in accord with the specific pattern

that constitutes that activity as such. The notion of complete 'discharge' or 'release' of energetic quantum only makes sense in a human context as actualization of the energetic potential constituted by the relation between *bio-energy* and the social force forms that constitute the possibility of optimal forms of human activity.

As I have already suggested, when (what Nietzsche calls) reflective consciousness is at work, this work need not involve the wakeful self-awareness of the I since it is primarily a product of the techne of reflection to which thought has been trained, and may be applied quite without the wakeful 'presence' of the thinker.[22]

Yet there is another, more flexible and mobile role 'thought' plays, when it is not bound to any specific techne but moves from one to another and plays in the spaces between them. This is a special kind of 'improvisation,' different from the kinds specific to particular arts, but it can exist only if the specific technai exist, and is patched together out of the skills constituted by their prior incorporation. Varying Aristotle's notion that the soul is the form of forms, we could say that thought in this sense is the techne of technai, the most cunning and adaptable of pathway finders, which seeks the optimal pathways through the panoply of technai that structure the drive system of any given subject. As it ranges over the possibilities made available by its techne motivated powers, thought gravitates toward those that promise the optimal release of energy; and when it finds the optimum, the 'choice' follows as an energetic consequence. Consciousness is thus a sort of go-between or Pandarus of energy. As Pandarus perceives the potential energies that are embodied in Troilus and Crisseida, and places himself between them to serve as catalyst of their interaction, thought serves as a kind of conduit between force flows that would otherwise not communicate.[23] And when it finds this point, when the energetic system of the individual is situated at this locus, then it 'discharges' its energy in an effectual manner that yields the pathos of power. What makes all this possible, of course, is that the goal is posited for thought, and that it has been culturally provisioned with the cunning of means by social force forms. And, as in the case of the specific technai, thought as general improvisation involves wakeful self-presence, thought as a conscious lighting-up, only in special moments when it does not more or less effortlessly slide into the most attractive energetic locus.

Thus consciousness comes into play primarily in hard cases, in which there is no obvious optimal pathway, so that I feel that I must exert myself, must willfully rouse a quantum of energy, like putting my thumb on one side of the scale to make it fall. These are the cases that suggest the pure willed activity of an agent; but they submit to the same analysis as the normal cases. Consider: I'm trying to get myself to do my workout (this means: I notice that it's four o'clock, and this sets in motion the habitual chain of thought). I really don't feel like it; but I know I will be better off if I do; and I've learned from past experience that if I can only get over the threshold of the initial movement toward doing it, the rest will follow more or less automatically; this is the technique on the basis of which I will be able to carry through my willing. It's the mental picture of all that effort and sweat that is deterring me; but I know an energy saving trick: I can stop thinking about that, and concentrate only on getting up off this couch. That is, I know (consciously or not) that my current state is non optimal, and I am drawn to the alternate picture of optimal activity and its results; this picture arouses the drive energy in me to put strategies into effect that will bring about the alternative. I therefore withdraw my attention from the non optimal that is sapping my energy because it is too much for me and focus on a much smaller, more manageable task that attracts me because I recognize it as the first step on the path toward increased power. The first step is to switch off the TV. Now, with the TV off, my energy already begins to shift. I can get up and move toward the bedroom and start putting on my workout clothes. Now my habits take over, and the workout ensues with no further struggle of 'will.'

That is what agency looks like when it is properly analyzed in terms of will to power. It remains true, as Nietzsche says, that the fundamental dynamic is that of one drive overcoming another; my drive to health overcame my addiction to political talk shows. Even if we say that not consciousness but the drive made my finger push the off button, it remains that, in order to be strong enough to move my finger – in the face of the countervailing intertia – the drive had to be placed in an energetically advantageous position, had to have its energy 'leveraged,' by the economic calculation that was carried out by (more or less conscious) thought; and that this thought is itself a drive, drawn like any other drive by the pull of the optimum, where 'optimum' is finally defined in relation not to the specific goal of a specific practice but to the *self* that my overall drive complex has cathected as the organizing principle constituting the fullest possibility of actualization of the will to power of that entire complex.

We might still be inclined to attribute to 'will' a tiny, subtle, very strategic power all of its own that exerts a very tiny influence calculated to snowball into action by showing blind drive the direction in which it is strong enough to flow. Here in this minute action of psychological interiority it seems we could still find ineliminable the moment of pure spontaneity of will. But this is an illusion created by isolating the single moment of button pushing from the before and after that constitute its possibility. My will doesn't have any intrinsic interest in me working out; it's a function of the discipline of my drive system in relation to a specific system of goals. Will is just another drive formation, a specific drive synthesis, one with a special function but a function that is formed and an energy that follows the same pathways of drive energy, and is incited by the same drive activation system of goals, as the other drives.

At this point my discussion might be evoking the eerie sensation of mere zombie being that the denial of 'free will' seems to stimulate in some people. From the Nietzschean standpoint, however, the unmotivated wisping about of some essence of spirit-being is a very pale image of freedom compared to *optimal activity* – the fullest exercise of power, experienced as complete absence of constraint and as complete (or the maximum feasible) release of one's energetic quantum. I have argued that this definition of agency is itself a little pale when conceived in terms of purely physiological drives; thought, conceived primarily as 'practical consciousness', sometimes conscious but mostly not, plays a role that is certainly not 'active' in the sense of *geistlich* activity, but is just as certainly not that of a mere 'passive observer'. This dichotomy, like that of consciousness/unconsciousness, belongs to the metaphysics Nietzsche was trying to leave behind; the sociological theory of will to power introduces a new conception of the structure and effectuality of thought that is indifferent to these dichotomies. Drives do not *cause* thoughts; more elementary drives are part of the synthesis of which culturally formed drives, including the thought drive, are made. The autonomy of consciousness is overthrown in a new way, open to the determinations of culture and culture history as well as to those of biology and evolutionary history, yet which unlike structuralist theory understands action in terms of the will to power.

The I is a sequence of power events that occur as self-moved coalescences of constellations of force that are social and symbolic as well as physiological. Each of these events constitutes a 'relative center of individuation,' connected by what the *Genealogy of Morals* calls the 'memory of the will' (which may be conscious or unconscious, or any mixture of the two) with the sequence of such events that together constitutes the history of a person's actions and thus her effectual personhood. The conscious I that is experienced as agent is the locus of actualization of a particular flow of power events that is organized as a *person* or *self* by the constitutive forms of a given culture. Without this center of the action individuation the drives would not come together in the effectually organized form that they do.

The opening to the social makes possible a productive new avenue of engagement between the theory of will to power and ethical theory. Because the force form of selfhood is the supreme organizing principle by which historical societies hierarchically integrate the incorporation by individual subjects of the technai of the culture, and thus constitute truly optimal modes of activity for their members, the account I have given readily articulates with 'virtue ethics' of the steadfastly naturalistic type developed in her recent book *Ethical Formation* by Sabina Lovibond, who places at the center of her argument Nietzsche's notion of the 'memory of the will'.[24]

In fact, it was the original theorist of virtue ethics, Plato or Platonic Socrates who first defined virtue as power and as actualization of power [Republic 352e–353e], and the way to virtue as a form of techne. One who 'knows', in the sense of having incorporated the techne of virtue at the level of full mastery, cannot, in Socrates' view, do other than that which his knowledge reveals to him as the good.[25]

In this essay I have done little more than transcribe this theory into the register of will to power.

References:
For a general bibliography of Nietzsche's work in German and English see end of volume.

Notes

1   '[...] the 'will' so conceived is nothing but the effect of type-facts about the person [...] the type-facts [...] explain both consciousness *and* a person's action.' Brian Leiter, *Nietzsche on Morality*, London: Routledge, 2002, p. 92.

2   Giddens clear, brief description of the notion of practical consciousness may be found in an essay, 'Action, Subjectivity, and the Constitution of Meaning,' in *Aims of Representation: Subject/Text/History*, Stanford University Press, 1987. A full account of his theory of society may be found in *The Constitution of Society*, Cambridge: Polity Press, 1984.

3   The type-facts are 'psycho-physical,' but the only 'psychological' facts involved are 'facts about the person's unconscious drives or affects' [p. 91], which are a direct derivative of physiology.

4   John Richardson, *Nietzsche's System*, New York: Oxford University Press, 1996.

5   Richardson's book, *Nietzsche's New Darwinism*, which makes an essential advance on the clarification of the concept of drive, appeared when this essay was well underway and could not be taken into account here. But I cautiously assert that the fundamental points I am making here are not invalidated by Richardson's new work.

6   I think Jonathan Lear is right that the post-Humian sense of 'efficient cause' on which I draw here is actually not Aristotle's. See Jonathan Lear, *Aristotle: the Desire to Understand*, New York: Cambridge University Press, 1988, pp. 30–3. But this is the sense in which the term is commonly understood today.

7   In fact, formal cause has been enjoying a widespread resurgence in recent decades in every field touched by 'complex systems theory.' See, among the multitude of works that could be cited, Alicia Juarrero, *Dynamics in Action*, Cambridge, Mass.: MIT Press, 1999; and Robert E. Ulanowicz, *Ecology, the Ascendant Perspective*, New York: Columbia University Press, 1997.

8   A great merit of Richardson's discussion is that it brings starkly to light the stakes of Nietzsche's teleologism: the preservation of an impermeable, onto-

logical boundary of identity around the will of the superior individual. The reason we need ontological individuation of selfhood on this account is that it makes practice shifting possible, and practice shifting is necessary if healthy will to power is to manifest itself. Merely cultural individuation is no individuation at all; it is merely repetition of the type and participation in common being. The definition of cultural practice as mere repetition means that by definition the new must have an extra cultural origin. But on a truly naturalistic account, any cultural form and its attendant cultural value must be explained in a way that does not beg the question regarding its true cause. If we grant that before the creation of the work, the I is intra cultural, it might be possible to make a case that somehow the process of creation would then lift the self out of cultural being, in the sense that the self of the great creator might attain a degree of individuation denied to others. But the 'self' created would not be identical with the physio-psychological individual but only with a 'formal' self that is the correlate of the power of the techne involved. As Aristotle says, 'The cause of the statue is not Polyclitus but the sculptor.'

9   I discuss this question at length in 'Will to Power: A Socio-Historical Critique,' in *The Blackwell Companion to Nietzsche*, ed. Keith Ansell-Pearson, 2006.

10   The most famous and influential statement of this principle was made by T.S. Eliot in his essay 'Tradition and the Individual Talent.'

11   Aristotle, *De Anima* 417a21–b2. Explicators also call the two grades of potentiality 'first' and 'second' or 'first-level' and 'second-level' potentiality. See, e.g., T.H. Irvin, *Aristotles's First Principles*, Oxford, Clarendon Press, 1988, pp. 230–3; Lear, pp. 103–5.

12   The example of Bach is, incidentally, a good one to pose against that of Beethoven. Nietzsche's imagination, and that of much Nietzsche scholarship, is limited by the Romantic image of artistic greatness that Beethoven epitomizes. Bach by contrast is much easier to see as attaining his greatness by actualizing the *potentia* of the force forms of the art in which he was trained (which, on the present account, must also be what Beethoven did, however much his achievement might be mystified by Romantic mythology).

13   'every animal [...] instinctively strives for an optimum of favorable conditions under which it can expend all its strength and achieve its maximal feeling of power; every animal abhors, just as instinctively [...] every kind of intrusion or hindrance that obstructs or could obstruct this path to the optimum (I am *not* speaking of its path to happiness, but its path to power, to action, to the most powerful activity, and in most cases actually to its own unhappiness).'

14   For example: I must decide whether to leave town to give a prestigious lecture or stay home and help my wife with our newborn. Neither of these alternatives can be properly understood except in terms of the cultural structures that constitute them as realities, and the history of my involvement with these structures, such that I have tremendous libidinal investments in both, and also a highly articulated sense of the pattern of activity that each involves and of my

own competence in regard to it, as well as tropisms of my will to power determined by the successes and failures that have resulted from my previous involvements with these culturally-set patterns of activity. Presiding over the entire ensemble of these tropisms, there is, in the person who has achieved some measure of competence as a person, the form of selfhood. This form both constitutes my will to power as such, as the will to power of this person that I am, and, when I posit it to myself as a mental representation, serves as an 'attractor' of my energetic quantum. To be 'master of myself' means to have the habit of subordinating drives that do not conduce to the optimal actualization of my selfhood to those that do. My optimal self-conception does not include abandoning my wife and child under these circumstances for a bauble of academic recognition; so my choice is inevitable. But this depends on my *knowing*, firmly and steadily (though not necessarily in 'reflective consciousness,' as I will explain below), where my greatest degree of actualization lies. If I were unsure, then so would be my choice.

15   Even epochal shifts in the nature of a symbolic practice can be analyzed in terms of the system dynamics of the practice itself. The practice James Joyce inherited, for example, was already, before he came to it, a heterogeneous multiplicity of forms, genres, and styles, and this heterogeneity, far from constituting a fixed type pattern that can only be shifted from outside, as Richardson suggests, can be described by adapting the very terms that Nietzsche used to describe physiology, as a struggling multiplicity of formed forces or force forms out of which new forms can emerge because no simple line of causal determination can govern the dynamics of the system.

16   Of course Nietzsche had not yet struck on the theory of will to power when he wrote *Daybreak*, a fact too little taken into consideration by Nietzsche commentary that often cites it as though the drive theory it develops were thoroughly homogeneous with the later theory.

17   It is important not to fall for misleading forms of description of the action in question. Huck Finn is obviously not skilled in 'helping runaway slaves,' yet he chooses to help Jim and actually does help him. This is possible because he does possess the characteristic 'picaresque' skills that are easily adapted to such a project. The notion of picaresque skills evokes a dimension of the present analysis that I do not have the space to develop here: that of a range from the most 'crystallized' level of techne to the most 'fluid' level, at which individuals cobble together nonce forms of practice that at first sight have little discernible relation to the socio-historical accumulation of know-how that I have been describing. But a little reflection serves to undo this impression, as does a reading of the history of the original *picaro*, Lazarillo de Tormes – the history, precisely, of how he slowly *learned his craft* from a series of teachers. On the relation between the crystallized and fluid levels of social practice, see V. I. Volosinov, *Marxism and the Philosophy of Language*, trans. Ladeslav Matejka and I.R.Titunik, Cambridge, Mass., Harvard University Press, 1986 [1973].

18   I use the term 'pathway' as shorthand. It should not be taken to imply that
      social practices have the simplicity of a physical pathway, or lead to a fixed,
      self-identical actualization. Nevertheless, regardless of the complexity and vari-
      ability of even the simplest social practice, it remains the case that all of its
      complexity is governed by the notion of *correctness*, a notion of which the
      community of those who carry on the practice are the judges (and this claim
      again must not be taken simplistically, as implying that agreement is always
      possible). The 'pathway' defined by a practice is the ideal thread around which
      all competent judgments of correctness are entwined (judgments which, in the
      case of practices aimed at dealing with the physical world, above all those dir-
      ectly related to survival, are themselves normed by the nature of that world – a
      correctly made hunting arrow, made to be actually used for hunting, must in
      fact fly true).

19   Leiter takes Nietzsche's denial that the I causes thoughts to be a denial that
      thoughts cause actions; but this ignores the cleavage between *thoughts* and the *I*
      that Nietzsche explicitly makes here. Leiter claims that Nietzsche is attacking
      the '(autonomous) causal power of our conscious mental life', a power that he
      identifies with that of the I. But if thoughts are spontaneous phenomena, not
      willed by an ego but arising out of a coalescence of forces, the denial of the
      causal power of the I does not translate into a denial of the causal power of
      thought. Leiter then suggests that if I don't cause my thoughts, they must be
      caused by underlying drives; but if thoughts are self-caused they cannot be
      caused by drives. Nietzsche's subsequent reflections in *BGE* 17 link his line of
      thought here to the famous doer/deed analysis of the *Genealogy*. The least
      forced reading of *BGE* 17 leaves us with the idea that thoughts are a spon-
      taneous occurrence analogous to lightning – hence a part of the 'plane of
      immanence' of pure phenomenal becoming.

20   Nietzsche's notion of infinite individuality by the way doesn't even make
      biological sense, since biological drives are a property of the species and only
      derivatively of the individual. The same logic that makes him reject social
      being in *GS* 354 should make him reject physiological instinct.

21   There still, however, remains a residual question, of great philosophical interest,
      as to how such a peculiar, utterly non functional phenomenon as this reflective I
      is to be conceived, and how it could ever have gotten into the world to play its
      ghostly non-role. Hans Jonas argued that the notion of a purely epiphenomenal
      I that is all effect and causes none itself would be an exception to the universal
      rules of naturalistic explanation and therefore 'an assertion of the occult.' 'It is
      meant to denote an effect which unlike all other effects in nature, does not
      consume the energy of a cause; it is not a transformation and continuation of
      such energy, and therefore, again unlike all other effects, it cannot become a
      cause itself. It is powerless in the absolute sense, a dead end alley off the high-
      way of causality, past which the traffic of cause and effect rolls as if it were not
      there at all. Even to call to mind an 'iridescence' on the material substratum

would be too much, since in exchange for the appearance of an iridescence in the physical sense some quantity present in the preceding physical transaction will have disappeared, and again another will replace it on its disappearing in turn (and these successive replacements will be found to be quantitatively equivalent), whereas no equivalent is deemed missing from the material account with the appearance of the epiphenomenon.' Hans Jonas, *The Phenomenon of Life: Toward a Philosophical Biology*, Chicago: University of Chicago Press, 1966, p. 128.

22   I am, in other words, extending a welcome to that quality of *wissenschaftliche* practice that Husserl decried in *The Crisis of European Sciences and Transcendental Phenomenology*. I should say, however, that I think the problem with which Husserl was concerned, of spiritual and intellectual 'inauthenticity' in the actualization of existing techniques, remains real, though it is beyond the scope of the present discussion.

23   Consciousness has the same tropism as the other drives; it is drawn by the pull of optimal activity; but the optima to which it is drawn, when it is engaged in practical deliberation, are those of other drives. Practical consciousness attains its own optimality in doing this; but there's also the optimum of 'pure thought' described by Aristotle, which is the practice of the optimal activity constituted by the techne (or more accurately, technai) of philosophy.

24   Sabina Lovibond, *Ethical Formation*, Cambridge, Mass.: Harvard University Press, 2002.

25   See W.K.C. Guthrie, *Socrates*, Cambridge: Cambridge University Press, 1971, pp. 136–7.

HERMAN SIEMENS

The first Transvaluation of all Values: Nietzsche's *Agon* with Socrates in *The Birth of Tragedy*

Any attempt to examine Nietzsche's relation to Ethics must at one point or other confront the concept of transvaluation or *Umwertung*. Without question, it is a key category in Nietzsche's philosophy of values, and if we take our cue from his late works, is used by him as a general description of his philosophical life-project. How are we to understand transvaluation, not just as a philosophical project, but also *in concreto* as a specific kind of philosophical practice? What kind of discourse on values does it name, and what kinds of pressure does it operate under? This essay is an attempt to shed some light on these questions.

Nietzsche's project of critical transvaluation is dedicated to a contestation of values. Against the prevailing values of European (Christian-Platonic) culture, whether metaphysical, moral or religious, Nietzsche attempts, time and again, to raise life as the highest value. This I take to be the basic and recurrent task of *overcoming*: to overcome metaphysical, moral and religious values *in the name of life*, its affirmation and elevation or 'greatness'.

This task originates in a critical diagnosis of the present, which in turn raises a number of problems for it. If the later Nietzsche is right that Western values originate in a 'decadent' form of life, a sick and impoverished will, then there is more than just values at stake in the question of overcoming. Overcoming must not only raise new values geared towards life affirmation; it requires a new *form* of evaluating, a new process of idealisation. Nietzsche's strategy of overcoming must somehow address, not just Western values, but their origin in the body, the affects, a dissolute will. The problem is: how can this be done through discourse, an ideal medium if ever there was one? Even if we grant that Nietzsche's discourse *can* somehow address the body, then *how* exactly is it to engage the condition of decadence? If, as Nietzsche claims, it is not possible to 'screw back humankind towards an *earlier* measure of virtue' [TI, Expeditions, 43], to reverse decadence, then how is his writing to serve the elevation or enhancement of life? What exactly would it mean to 'overcome' decadence?

On closer analysis, decadence raises a further problem. This centres on the question of closure. If Nietzsche is right that Western values originate in a life form that is turned against life: the attempted closure of theoretical discourse[1] against time and the senses *in the name of eternal truth* (as in metaphysics); and the concurrent war of annihilation against the instincts, *in the name of virtue* (as in the moral demands of religion and metaphysics); if, in short, these values originate in a willing that is turned against the will, then they cannot be effectively challenged through a purely theoretical discourse that neglects the body and closes itself off against the will. Such a discourse, even if it pitted life, its affirmation and elevation, against Western values, would fall prey to a performative contradiction: in its performance – as a discourse of values – it would undermine its discursive intention.

How, at the level of discourse, is Nietzsche to deal with this problematic of values and take the side of life? A strictly conceptual discourse of values will just replicate what Nietzsche is contesting – the illusory closure against time and the life of the body, the theoretical and moral denial of the will on the part of the Christian-Platonic will. To lay claim on an eternal future by proclaiming a redeeming set of beliefs or evaluations clearly will not do the job of inaugurating a 'counter-movement' to modern nihilism [WP, Preface, 4].

What Nietzsche needs is to confound the Socratic will to closure endemic to discourse, to open up his discourse towards life *without* undoing its discursive force. He needs to *supplement* his discursive challenge with a *performative* challenge that enacts the concept of life raised and pitted against Western values. Nietzsche's response is, I believe, best understood if we recur to his account of ancient Greek culture, and in particular its signature institution of the contest or *agon* as described in *Homer's Contest*.[2] At its most ambitious, my claim is that Nietzsche's philosophical practice of transvaluation is modeled on the Greek *agon*. In the *agon* Nietzsche finds a principle for organizing his critical discourse on values, one that is responsible for his peculiar, adversarial style of critique and for several puzzling, yet recurrent features of his textual confrontations that tend to get ignored or written off as inessential. More importantly: what Nietzsche finds in the *agon* is a way to address the problem of life affirmation and discursive closure. Understood as a law of production governing Nietzsche's critical discourse on values, the *agon* both regulates Nietzsche's discourse and *supplements* it, as a performative enactment of the highest form of life and life affirmation. In short, Nietzsche's text *is* itself *agonal* culture, as the affirmative interpretation of life thematised throughout his work as the highest form of life: (the rebirth of) tragic culture.

It is important to clarify at this point what I am *not* claiming. The claim is not that Nietzsche single-handedly revives ancient Greek culture, nor that he is able to transcend the modern condition, to embody *agonal* drives and express them in his text. Such clumsy readings of Nietzsche's *agons* are undone by the feint of writing, the emphatically fictive style of his *agonal* confrontations. I do maintain, on the other hand, that the dynamic form peculiar to the Greek *agon* operates as a principle that organizes and regulates his critical confrontations. We can thus speak of an *agonal* law of production governing Nietzsche's text, as long as production is not separated from interpretation, so that Nietzsche's textual antagonists and his readers are implicated together within its jurisdiction. As such a productive hermeneutic principle, the *agon* is a good model for trying to think the discursive and performative aspects of his challenges to prevailing values *together*. If we restrict ourselves to a discursive analysis, we often get stuck in dualisms such as life/truth, becoming/being, health/sickness, active/reactive etc. Clearly, this is unsatisfying in the light of Nietzsche's own critique of metaphysics as the 'belief in the oppositions (*Gegensätze*) of values' [BGE 2]. But it also seems inadequate to the task of posing a radical challenge and alternative to the metaphysical and moral values under attack; it seems as if Nietzsche remains tied to what he is criticising. Finally, a purely discursive analysis is unsatisfying, because it fails to confront what Blondel has called the 'enigma' of Nietzsche's text.[3] This means to confront them in a way that connects the thematic dimension, amenable to discursive synthesis and analysis, and the performative dimension, those elements which resist discursive synthesis: the narratives, mythologies, breaks, polemics, music, the surface play and comedy of Nietzsche's texts, commonly relegated to the extra-philosophical domains of rhetoric, style, art or literary history. Until we find a way to link the discursive themes with this 'rest', we have failed to address their unique status in the history of European philosophy and culture. Only if we consider Nietzsche's discursive critique *together with* the performative dimension of his writing – the attempt to *enact, through agonal confrontation*, the concept of life pitted against metaphysics and morality – can we make a decisive break from these dualisms, and reach a fuller, more adequate understanding of his challenge.

Finally, the *agon* is a good model for considering the cultural, collective presuppositions and implications of Nietzsche's critique of values. Nietzsche reacts to the status quo with the demand that things be changed or transformed. Only, this demand is *not* addressed to individuals as the movers and agents of this change; it is pitched, rather, at a transindividual level of *mores*: customs, social practices and collective belief structures that govern individual values and action. Culture in this broad sense is the framework of analysis for Nietzsche's critique of values, and the site for the new values he deploys, not just in the early work, but throughout.[4] Although his work is characterized by a personal, individual pathos and an increasing preoccupation with the individual, its constitution and disintegration, its pathology and potential, this does not exclude a transindividual, cultural dimension from his thought. This unfolds more at a performative than a thematic level: in his *agonal* confrontations, and the we's and you's that occupy the pages of his texts.

In what follows these claims will be instantiated and filled out through an interpretation of Nietzsche's first published *agon*: his critical confrontation with Socrates in *The Birth of Tragedy* [BT]. In *Twilight of the Idols*, Nietzsche refers to this text as his 'first transvaluation of all values' [TI, Ancients, 5]. He goes on in *Ecce Homo* to describe his project of transvaluation as 'my formula for an act of supreme self-examination on the part of humanity became flesh and genius in me' [EH, destiny, 1]. While a good deal has been written about Nietzsche's relation to Socrates,[5] not enough attention has been given to the complexity, precision and penetration of Nietzsche's engagement with Socrates in *BT* as an articulation of his 'first transvaluation of all values'.

Overcoming Socrates: *Birth of Tragedy* as Nietzsche's first Transvaluation

At stake in *BT*, as always in transvaluative texts, is the question of overcoming: what would be the overcoming of Socrates and Socratism, conceived broadly as theoretical discourse and culture? This question breaks down into two. On the negative or critical side: what is required to pose a radical challenge to theoretical discourse and culture? What kind of confrontation is *open* to us? And on the positive side: what would a counter-position look like, a standpoint beyond theory, a culture beyond Socratism?

For preliminary orientation on the questions, I shall draw on Nietzsche's famous claim, in the 1886 *Attempt at a Self-Criticism*, that he dared '*to see Wissenschaft through the optic of the artist, but art through that of life*' [BT, Attempt, 2].[6] The basic terms of Nietzsche's transvaluative contest with Socrates and Socratism are, then, theoretical discourse (*Wissenschaft*), art and life. The precise relation between them is, however, unclear, and we need to look more closely at the two 'optics' named in Nietzsche's formula.

The contours of Nietzsche's 'optic in life' are, without doubt, shaped by Schopenhauer, not Socrates, and the more intimate contest with his thought. As *philosopher of life*, Nietzsche's tasks are defined against Schopenhauer in two ways. Schopenhauer's fundamental questions are a questioning of life: what is existence (*Dasein*) worth? Why live (*Wozu leben*) [cf. GS 357]? These questions represent a *theoretical* (*metaphysical and moral*) interrogation of life, its value and meaning. They are informed by the assumption that the negativity of life – the preponderance of pain, suffering, violence – constitute an argument *against* life: they ought not to be (*sollten nicht sein*). Whence the practical negation of life: the claim that the world ought not to be.[7] Nietzsche attempts to invert and transvaluate this procedure. His gesture is to put himself on the side of life and existence in order to evaluate both life and theory; that is, to substitute the theoretical evaluation of life for a perspective whose standard of evaluation is determined by life, in order to evaluate the value of theoretical discourse (*Wissenschaft*, as embracing scientific, metaphysical and moral interpretations of life), as well as the value of life. In the context of *BT*, this takes the form of a critical interrogation of Socratism from a perspective in life, on one side, and a positive evaluation or 'justification' of life from a perspective in life on the other. Against the central charge that Socrates initiated a fateful strategy of theoretical denial or closure against life, Nietzsche claims to *open theory up to life*, to *bring discourse back to life* by making his text be the *saying and yes-saying* of life. But what does it mean to take 'the side of life' against theory? What kind of discourse is it that promotes a standard of evaluation determined by life against the claims of theory? How is it to be constructed and organized? Or to sharpen the problem with a little Nietzschean suspicion: what is to say that, under the guise of an anti-theoretical standpoint in life, he does not actually offer just another theoretical discourse, another metaphysics that again denies the life it claims to embrace?

This is, of course, the charge that Nietzsche will level against his earlier notion of 'metaphysical consolation' in the *Attempt at a Self-Criticism*.[8] But is he right? If, as I maintain, *BT* avoids the trap of replicating what it is contesting, then one thing is clear: it cannot do so *as a theoretical discourse*, a conceptual discourse of metaphysics or science; a purely theoretical discourse is inadequate to the task of saying and affirming life against the claims of theory. This is *not* to deny that Nietzsche engages in discourse: he clearly does conceptualize life as the highest value and deploys it against Socratic discourse. On pain of self destruction, however, Nietzsche's discourse needs to be transgressed and *supplemented* by a *performative* challenge that *enacts* the concept of life raised against the claims of theory. Here, the 'optic of the artist' enters into his transvaluative contest.

Nietzsche's two-fold optic in the *Attempt* suggests an opposition between theory on one side, and life and art on the other: against the claims of theoretical discourse, Nietzsche's text opposes art as the saying of life. This certainly conforms to a dominant reading of Nietzsche as a romantic advocate of art as the *Other* of reason. On this view, the 'artist's optic' names an impulse to abandon theory on the wings of art, a totalisation of the aesthetic as the way to a total, unreflective submersion in life. In another well known line from the *Attempt*, Nietzsche expresses the regret that in practice he betrayed this impulse: 'it should have *sung*, this 'new soul' – not spoken! What a shame that I did not dare to say what I had to say then as a poet' [BT, Attempt, 3]. But is he right to regret that he spoke instead of singing? Perhaps not, for art can only exacerbate the problem of discourse. Against theoretical discourse, as we saw, Nietzsche faces the problem of making his text be the saying and yes-saying of life without getting trapped in the very discourse it would supplant. Art or song may well offer an alternative to metaphysical or scientific discourse: but does it offer any more than a mute limit on the perimeter of discursive thought? To displace theory with art would certainly rob him of the means to make any truth claims; for art is, in the Platonic terms that still dominate our thinking, no more than an illusion.

Nietzsche is, it seems, faced with two equally unattractive options. If, in opposing theory with life and art, he remains trapped in a metaphysical discourse of life, then the radicality of his challenge is undermined. If, on the other hand, he seeks to avoid this trap through an artistic challenge to theory, then he banishes himself to the realm of illusion, robbing himself of the means to pose a powerful challenge. The value of Nietzsche's 'first transvaluation' hinges on whether he can avoid the horns of this dilemma. The key to Nietzsche's contest with Socrates, I shall argue, lies less in a flight from theory to art, than in a holding together of disparate powers, the kind of synthesis without reconciliation often ascribed by Nietzsche to the dionysian artist or the tragic philosopher.[9] *BT*, I shall argue, combines theoretical discourse and art in a way that avoids the pitfalls of either on its own. Ultimately, it occupies an undecidable, ambivalent space between theory/discourse and art. This 'duplicitous' position names a different kind of romanticism in Nietzsche, who sees art, not as a substitute for theory, but as its necessary *supplement* and *correlative*, the medium in which to overcome or make good the failure of theory to meet *its own demands*.

The claim I will advance is, then, that Nietzsche's two-fold 'optic' assigns a two-fold role to art: i) art *enacts* the concept of life raised against Socratism, through a *performative* challenge that *supplements* his discursive confrontation with theory from a perspective life; and ii) art makes good the failure of Socratism to meet its own demands, as its necessary *supplement* and *correlative* through which alone the claims of theory can be realized.

Art never serves simply to replace theory; as its *supplement* and *correlative* it bears both an external challenge to theory from a perspective in life, and an internal challenge from a perspective in theory. These functions come together in what I will call 'the art of listening'. As I will try to show, this posture or practice can be ascribed to Nietzsche's authorship of *BT*. But it is also thematized in the text itself at the end of chapter 14 under the sign of the 'music-practising Socrates'. Here Nietzsche engages in a narrative contest with Plato's *Phaedo* from which he draws his figure. Unravelling this contest will yield a preliminary formulation of the relation between art, theory and life in Nietzschean transvaluation, as an *inversion* of Platonic determinations. The first step is, then, a brief examination of the *Phaedo*.

Plato's Socrates: Art, Philosophy and the Practice of Dying in the *Phaedo*

At issue in the *Phaedo*, as always for Plato, is the question of the best human life. As in the *Republic*, he will advocate philosophy as the life devoted to wisdom, eschewing, as far as possible, the claims of the body and the passions. One passion in particular is central to the dialogue: our fear of death. In the figure of Socrates, Plato presents philosophical activity as 'charming away the fear of death'.[10] With his usual cheerfulness, Socrates devotes his full attention to the arguments, after which he drinks the cup of poison, meeting his death with perfect composure. He thereby demonstrates the philosophical detachment of the intellect from the body for which he argues as the best life.

Yet, in the opening exchanges this is far from clear. Socrates appears to hesitate, hanging a question mark over his life long dedication to philosophy; what is more, the threat comes from poetry, condemned in the *Republic* for nourishing the passions [Rep. 606]. The occasion is some poetry which, for the first time in his life, he writes while awaiting execution. When questioned, Socrates explains:

> I did it in the attempt to discover the meaning of certain dreams, and to clear my conscience, in case this was the art which I had been told to practice. It is like this, you see. In the course of my life I have often had the same dream, appearing in different forms at different times, but always saying the same thing, 'Socrates, practice and cultivate the arts [*mousiken poiei kai ergazou*].' In the past I used to think that it was impelling and exhorting me to do what I was actually doing; I mean that the dream, like a spectator encouraging a runner in a race, was urging me on to do what I was doing already, that is, practicing the arts, because philosophy is the greatest of the arts, and I was practicing it. But ever since trial [...] I have felt that perhaps it might be this popular form of art that the dream intended me to practice, in which case I ought to practice it and not disobey. I thought it would be safer not to take my departure before I had cleared my conscience by writing poetry and so obeying the dream. I began with some verses in honour whose festival it was. When I had finished the hymn, I reflected that a poet, if he is to be worthy of the name, ought to work on imaginative themes, not descriptive ones, and I was not good at inventing stories. So I availed myself of Aesop's fables which where ready to hand and familiar to me, and I versified the first of them that suggested themselves to me.' [Ph. 60e–61b]

How is Socrates' music to be taken? Is there a question concerning the philosophical life, a genuine hesitation provoked by – his fear of death? Answering these questions requires an understanding of the relation of philosophy to art developed across the dialogue.

The main body of the text is concerned with proofs of the immortality of the soul. These are crucial to Socrates' chief purpose: to advocate the philosophical pursuit of wisdom through a progressive detachment of the soul from the body. Certain knowledge, he argues, comes only when the realm of invisible, constant entities is apprehended through intellectual activity, untainted by sensory receptivity or other distractions of the body [Ph. 65a–c; 66b]. In our lives, we should therefore cultivate a distance from our bodies, closing ourselves off in pure intellectual activity against the body and the other receptive areas of personality (emotions, desires) and directing our attention towards the soul instead [Ph. 64d–e]. But it is death alone that promises the fulfillment of wisdom: by releasing the soul from the 'shackles of the body', death gives it passage to a place which is 'like itself, invisible, divine, immortal and wise' [Ph. 66e] – provided, of course, it *is* immortal. The life of philosophy is only viable if it can be proved that personal identity is contained in an immortal, intellectual soul, which unites with the forms after death. In this sense, Socrates claims that 'those who really apply themselves in the right way to philosophy are directly and of their own accord preparing themselves for dying and death.' [Ph. 64a]. Hence Nietzsche's equation of the theoretical with '*the dying Socrates*', as the new 'ideal of noble Greek youth' – including Plato [BT 13, KSA 1, p. 91]; for he is the 'first who could not only live, guided by the instinct of science, but also – and this is far more – die that way'. As 'the human being whom knowledge and reasons have liberated from the fear of death' he becomes the 'emblem' of science [BT 15, KSA 1, p. 99].

Yet the 'practice of dying' is more than a theoretical ethos. The language of redemption, from 'contamination', the 'prison' of the body, from 'uncertainty and folly, from fears and uncontrolled desires, and all other human evils' [Ph. 81], betrays a deeper religious interest, a hatred of embodied existence animating the theoretical life. Philosophical wisdom is 'a sort of purification' akin to religious initiation.[11] Accordingly, Socrates demands the ritual sacrifice to Asclepius for convalescence from the protracted illness of his life, for his 'return to 'virtue', to 'health', to happiness' through death: 'living – that means to be a long time ill: I owe a cock to Asclepius the healer.'[TI, Socrates, 1].

This is how Nietzsche spins out Socrates' last words in *TI*. But he does so in a way that is true to the pessimistic, religious animus of the *Phaedo*. And it is in the same spirit that Plato's Socrates writes his hymn to Apollo, or at least interprets it, after the event. With clear reference to his own music, he reinterprets the swan's lament as a celebration:

> I believe that the swans, belonging as they do to Apollo, have prophetic powers and sing because they know the good things that await them in the unseen world, and that they are happier on that day than they have ever been before. Now I consider that I am in the same service as the swans, and dedicated to the same god, and that I am no worse endowed with prophetic powers by my master than they are, and no more disconsolate at leaving this life. [Ph. 85b]

Socrates' artistic swan song is thus subsumed under philosophy as preparation for death. It joins the philosophical initiation in death, as its joyful celebration.

There is nothing, therefore, in Socrates words to suggest that through his music he laments or falters in the ascetic life he advocates, and he goes with serene confidence to his death. But what about his disciples – and us? Can philosophy cast a spell over the child in us and charm away his fear of death [Ph. 77f]? There is a marked contrast between Socrates' composed self-sufficiency and the dependence of his devastated disciples: 'But Socrates', said Simmias, 'where shall we find a magician who understands these spells now that you – are leaving us?' [Ph. 77f]. In the repeatability of Socrates' performance lies the real test for the life of philosophy; and in this space, art re-enters Plato's conception of the best human life in the form of myth-ology.

After advising his disciples to seek out the magician by their 'own united efforts' [Ph. 77f], Socrates offers another proof of the soul's immortality, and then another. With trepidation, Cebes and Simmias then raise objections to Socrates' arguments and after these are countered, both declare themselves satisfied with the truth of his arguments. 'All the same,' Simmias continues in true Socratic style, 'the subject is so vast, and I have such a poor opinion of our weak human nature, that I can't help feeling misgivings.' [Ph. 107f]. 'Quite right' Socrates replies and, after telling them to re-examine the as-sumptions, he launches into a lengthy and detailed mythology recount-ing the transcendent rewards awaiting the souls of those who philosophize, and the punishments awaiting those souls which neglect

philosophy for bodily pleasures and adornments. Upon concluding,
Socrates remarks:

> Of course, no reasonable man ought to insist that the facts are exactly as I have
> described them. But that either this or something very like it is a true account of
> our souls and their future habitations – *since we have clear evidence that our*
> *souls are immortal* – this I think is a reasonable contention and a belief worth
> risking, for the risk is a noble one. *We should use such accounts to inspire ours-*
> *elves with confidence*, and that is why I have drawn out my tale so long. [Ph.
> 107d; emphasis added]

Once again, it is clear that Socrates' poetry in no way threatens or
challenges the claims of his philosophical activity; it serves, rather, to
support the philosophical evidence for the immortality of the soul. In
this subordinate role, art has a positive meaning for the man of reason:
by prefiguring truths to which reason alone can lay absolute and
exclusive claim, it guides his soul towards theoretical enquiry. Art,
Plato suggests, is a useful ancilla to the best human life, the life of
philosophy. Or is he suggesting a little more – that art can also do
something philosophy cannot? Socrates himself performs the ideal of
courage described in the *Republic*: altogether self-sufficient in his
pure contemplative activity, he is in need of no-one and nothing from
without to complete the value, happiness and goodness of his life.[12]
Having overcome the fear of death, art is for him not only ancillary; it
is superfluous. Not so for his disciples, as he clearly appreciates. For
them, one, two or more philosophical proofs of the immortality of the
soul are *insufficient* to overcome the fear of death, and mythology
must be adduced to 'inspire [...] confidence' in the philosophical life.
What is more, there seem to be good *philosophical* reasons for their
misgivings: practically quoting from Socrates' defence, Simmias invokes the worthlessness of human wisdom, the knowledge of ignorance which Socrates claims to practise, in order to point out the
inconclusiveness, the limits of philosophical enquiry.[13] Who is to say
that, on the day after Socrates' death, someone will not come up with
a devastating proof of the soul's mortality? In the gap dividing Socrates from the rest of us, Plato deploys mythology as a *necessary sup-*
plement to reason in the philosophical life. At the very least, art leaves

a dent – a lingering doubt – in the ideal of self-containment, the pure intellectual activity promoted by Socrates in Plato's middle dialogues.

Nietzsche's Socrates: the Practice of Music in *The Birth of Tragedy*

It is evidently to Socrates' myth at the end of the *Phaedo* that Nietzsche refers when invoking 'the dying Socrates', as

> the emblem that above the entrance gate of science, reminds all of its mission – namely, to make existence appear comprehensible and thus justified, and if reasons do not suffice, *myth* must also at the end serve – myth which I just designated as the necessary consequence, indeed as the purpose, of science. [BT 15, KSA 1, p. 99]

This passage resonates with Plato's view of myth as a *necessary supplement* to the *insufficiency* of theory, casting doubt on its capacity to inspire confidence. For a precise grasp of Nietzsche's view of myth as the 'necessary consequence' of theory, we need to examine *his* version of Socrates' death in *BT* 14.

Nietzsche begins with a seemingly accurate report of Socrates' explanation of his poetry in the *Phaedo*: how a recurrent dream urging him to practice music provoked, for the first time, a hesitation concerning his contempt for art and his life long conviction that philosophy is the highest art of the muses. Only Socrates' sense of 'duty' or 'conscience' [Ph. 60e, cited above] regarding the dream becomes in Nietzsche 'the feeling of a gap, a void, a half-reproach' [BT 14, KSA 1, p. 96]; then the dream itself becomes a 'dream apparition' (*Traumerscheinung*) and, likened to Socrates' renowned 'daemonic warning voice', is cast as a daemonic voice of conscience throwing his philosophical practice and identity into question. Socrates is made to see that

> like a barbarian king he did not understand [*nicht verstehen*] a noble divine image and was in danger of sinning against a deity – through his lack of

understanding [lit. understanding- nothing: *Nichtsverstehen*] [BT 14, KSA 1, p. 96].

In this mythological scenario of hubris, Socrates' philosophical vocation of not-knowing or understanding nothing (*Nichtsverstehen*) is portrayed as a sin. The account concludes with Nietzsche's interpolation of Socrates' thoughts:

> These words of the Socratic dream apparition are the only sign of a misgiving concerning the limits of logical nature: perhaps – so he must have asked himself – what is incomprehensible to me [*mir Nichtverständliche*] is not as such without comprehension [*Unverständige*] after all? Perhaps there is a realm of wisdom from which the logician is banned? Perhaps art is even a necessary correlative and supplement to theory [*ein nothwendiges Correlativum und Supplement der Wissenschaft*]?' [loc. cit.]

There is no question here of art confirming Socrates' philosophical practice. Predicated on a unique, daemonic hesitation concerning the limits of his 'logical nature' and understanding, it signifies a dramatic switch of practice, a reversal or peripeteia. In *BT* the switch from dialectical to musical practice takes on a meaning radically at odds with the *Phaedo*. In the first instance, Socrates' hesitation signifies an intervention in philosophical practice. As a response to the daemon of music, Socrates' music marks a unique transformation of his *hearing*: for the first time, he allows a 'gap', a 'void' to disrupt his life long dialectical practice, a moment of receptivity to override his intellectual activity. And in listening beyond the capsule of his intellect, he hears the 'limits of logic', the limitations of pure intellectual activity, suspending his conviction that philosophy is the highest art of the muses: he learns for the first time the *art of listening*.[14]

In putting the limitations of Socrates' theoretical practice to his own ears, Nietzsche is subjecting him to doubts like those surrounding Plato's treatment of myth at the end of the *Phaedo*. But Plato's doubts about the form and feasibility of the Socratic life are radicalized by Nietzsche: in Socrates' ears the very *meaning* of the philosophical life are put into question. Socrates' musical practice becomes the moment when the true significance of his philosophical practice recoils upon him and he discovers his real philosophical identity – as the music practising Socrates.[15] By radicalising Plato's mythological hesitation and writing it into Socrates' speech, Nietzsche twists the relation between art and theory/philosophy in the *Phaedo*. Art is transformed from a useful ancilla of the philosophical life into a threat that challenges its form and value as the best life, confounding Socrates' philosophical identity. The music practising Socrates, far from celebrating the practice of dying, is turned against his philosophical counterpart, confronting him with new questions concerning the limits and meaning of his enterprise. In short, *BT* revises the *Phaedo*, casting Nietzsche into confrontation with theoretical Socratism.

The precise contours of Nietzsche's confrontation can be determined with reference to the words he puts into Socrates' mouth:

> Is art perhaps 'a necessary correlative'[BT 14, KSA 1, p. 96], that is, the 'necessary consequence' [BT 15, KSA 1, p. 99] or *conclusion* of philosophical practice?

Here, Socrates' words elevate art from the handmaiden [ancilla] of philosophy into its true goal or ultimate meaning: philosophical practice, conversely, is humbled from the telos of art into its handmaiden, a preparation for artistic practice. As Socrates' philosophical life recoils upon him in its true significance, it appears as something that points beyond itself, guiding his soul towards art. What, then, becomes of the telos of philosophical practice: wisdom-in-death?

> Is art perhaps 'a necessary [...] supplement' [BT 14, KSA 1, p. 96] to the philosophical life?

Philosophy is *grounded*, not in the lack of wisdom-in-death, but *in the lack of art*, in a 'neediness of art' [*Kunstbedürftigkeit*: BT 15, KSA 1, p. 102]. Art forms the conclusion of Socrates' life as the fulfillment of his desire for wisdom, the hidden telos of his lack of wisdom finally exposed through the 'feeling of a gap' by the daemon of music – a voice of remembrance. Thus wisdom-in-death is displaced by wisdom-in-art, or the art of listening, as the end of philosophical desire.

For Plato, the love of wisdom or *philosophia*, as a form of eros, desires what it lacks; arising out of lack, its satisfaction spells the end of desire. In line with this negative concept of desire, the art of listening inscribed in Nietzsche's text terminates philosophical desire in satisfying it. As Diotima points out, 'None of the gods philosophize, nor do they desire to become wise – they are; nor if anybody else is wise does he philosophize' [Symposium 204a]. But does it spell the end of *all* desire – of desiring life – in death, like Socratic wisdom? Or does Nietzsche's Socrates, through the art of listening, come to hear a new, positive sense of desire in *excess*, rather than lack?[16] The recurrent conjugation of 'excess' with the task of 'aesthetic justification' throughout *BT* indicates clearly what figures as the object of desire in the text: *art-as-life*, or *life-as-art* drowns the siren voice of death as the new 'inspiring genius', the 'muse' or daemon of philosophical thought. Like Plato's mythological supplement, it comes to 'inspire [...] confidence' in the philosophical life, even in its final moments. Only, for Nietzsche's Socrates, it celebrates an initiation (*Einweihung*) in life, not death.

We are now in a position to settle the precise terms of Nietzsche's first transvaluation. The contest of narratives enacts a confrontation between two positions:

For Plato [Plato's Socrates]: *art [as ancilla] serves philosophy [theory] as a preparation for wisdom-in-death.*

For Nietzsche [Nietzsche's Socrates]: *philosophy or theory [as ancilla] serves art-as-life or life-as-art.*

Thus, philosophy or theory prepares *not* for death, but for a new kind of life: *the art of listening*. In these terms, *BT* performs a *redetermination* of the relation between art and theory (philosophy) in Platonic/Socratic thought. It challenges the subordination of art to theoretical truth as the highest value, and its subordination to theoretical practice as the best human life. But is this just an *inversion* of Platonic-Socratism? Plato's Socrates grounds art in the lack of theory: as the ancilla of theory, an indeterminate yearning, a preparation, a prefigurement of theoretical insight, art derives its meaning and value from theoretical contemplation as its end and true purpose. Does

Nietzsche merely invert the terms of this definition, maintaining the theoretical logic of opposition and subordination controlling them? Does *BT* offer no more than a mere theoretical opposition to theory, an inversion of Platonic/Socratic values?

The Problem of Inversion and Nietzsche's Duplicitous Optic in Art

The question of mere inversion returns us to the opening problem of discourse. In this section, I will try to sketch a response to inversion in connection with the duplicitous optic of art claimed by Nietzsche in the *Attempt*. For clearly, it is the artistry of Nietzsche's contest with the *Phaedo*, its form *as narrative*, if anything, that takes it beyond mere inversion. And yet, as argued earlier, a purely artistic challenge does not resolves the problem of discourse. The first step, then, will be to argue that, at one level, Nietzsche's narrative 'encodes' an internal, epistemic critique of Socrates' epistemic practice. I will then argue that Nietzsche's narrative is organized by an *artistic cultural practice*, the *agon*, which enacts the concept of life-as-excess limned by the musical Socrates in *BT* 14. In this way I hope to give flesh to the initial thesis that Nietzsche adopts a duplicitous optic in art as a *supplement* to theory, bearing both an external challenge from a perspective in life, and an internal, theoretical challenge. Guiding both readings is the question of Nietzsche's standpoint as narrator, and in specific: as narrator of the 'necessary' switch from Socratic theory to art. In what sense *must* theoretical practice turn into art, as its 'necessary' conclusion and supplement?

The epistemic reading

The co-ordinates for my first reading are: a) the discussion of the
Socratic daemon and the monstrous deformation of Socrates' instincts
in *BT* 13 [KSA 1, p. 90]; and b) the discussion of his daemonic hesitation in *BT* 14 [KSA 1, p. 96]. In the latter passage, as we saw, the
target of divine repulsion is Socrates' hubristic '*Nichtsverstehen*'.
More than just a 'lack of understanding', this term refers to the active,
critical programme of 'knowing-nothing' through which Socrates
sought to establish the limits of human understanding:

> The sharpest words for that new and unprecedented glorification of knowing
> [*Wissen*] and [conscious] insight were spoken by Socrates when he found him-
> self to be the only one who would admit to himself that *he knew nothing* [*nichts
> zu wissen*]. [BT 13, KSA 1, p. 89]

These lines, from *BT* 13, already indicate that something is amiss.
Concealed in Socrates' critical programme is a critical deficit, an unquestioned positive belief or 'instinctive wisdom' ascribed by Nietzsche to his 'abnormal' 'logical nature': while 'excessively developed', it is also a 'monstrous defect' [BT 13, KSA 1, p. 90]. The
key to this paradox lies in Socrates' 'daemon': in their 'unbridled
flooding' his critical instincts were turned on the claims of others; yet,
as Nietzsche emphasizes, his 'logical drives were completely incapable of turning against themselves' [BT 13, KSA 1, pp. 90f.].

Turning, with this remark in mind, to Socrates' death bed, we
find him attending to 'something similar to the daemonic warning
voice' [BT 14, KSA 1, p. 96]. Yet the difference is critical; for the
daemon of music *does* enable the 'logical drives' to turn against
themselves, provoking Socrates' hesitation. For the first time he has
'misgivings about the limits of the logical nature'. For once, his logical nature throws itself in question: 'perhaps there is a realm of wisdom
from which the logician is banished?' [loc. cit.].

Taken together, these passages indicate that Nietzsche's story of
daemons and instincts intends or encodes an *epistemic* critique of
Socratic practice from an *internal* Socratic standpoint: Socrates' dialectic fails to realize his own promise of critique, his own demand to

limit knowledge. While critical of others' claims, it is incapable of being self-critical, until disrupted by an other practice, the art of listening. It is, then, by realizing the promise of critique that Socrates' music forms the 'necessary' conclusion and supplement of his theoretical practice. The root necessity is a '*Sollen*', an intellectual imperative: if the demand to limit knowledge is to be met in full, then active critique *must (soll)* turn into the art of listening. In order to clarify the latter as the key to self-critique, it helps to draw on the unpublished text, *Sokrates und die Tragödie* [1870], where Nietzsche specifies Socrates' epistemic failure as follows:

> Never did a doubt occur to him concerning the correctness of the entire form of questioning [*Fragestellung*]. 'Wisdom consists in knowing [*Wissen*]', and 'one knows nothing as long as one cannot express it and convince others of it.' [KSA 1, p. 541].

By taking issue with Socrates' form of questioning, Nietzsche is contesting the entire ontology implied by the question: What is...? For, as Deleuze points out, 'the opposition of essence and appearance, of being and becoming, depends primarily on a mode of questioning, a form of question.'[17] And with this ontology goes the standard of knowledge deployed by dialectical critique: whatever cannot be conceptualized articulately, 'the continuity of concrete objects taken in their becoming' [loc. cit.], is worth nothing. The claims of sensuous particularity, articulated best in narratives like Nietzsche's, are excluded from wisdom. Nietzsche's critical point in these lines is that Socrates' form of question and his standard of knowledge are both removed from critical questioning by the dialectic. Active contention of others' claims goes half way to meeting the demand to limit knowledge; in order to be met in full, it must *(soll)* recoil upon the critic's standard of critique, throwing his form of questioning into question. How, then, is the art of listening, as the moment of self-critique, supposed to supplement the dialectical contest and meet these conditions? It is, I want to suggest, as a breach of practice, a momentary stillness that exposes theoretical discourse to its other.

The *agonal* reading

The successive combination of active contention and receptive retraction is not just Socrates' signature trajectory for Nietzsche. In *Homer's Contest* [HC], a short essay or 'Preface' written shortly after *BT*, it appears in dynamic terms as the signature practice or institution of pre-Socratic culture: the *agon*. Here Nietzsche describes the *agon* as a 'play of forces' (*Wettspiel der Kräfte*): a dynamic interplay of mutual affirmation and negation, empowerment/disempowerment, among a plurality of forces or 'geniuses who rouse (or stimulate: *reizen*) one another to action, as they also hold one another within the bounds of measure' [HC, KSA 1, p. 789]. This text thematizes in a generalized form the dynamic conditions for self-critique glimpsed in *BT*. But in *BT* they already inform Nietzsche's authorship, which exceeds the internal, Socratic critique of Socratism outlined above. At a performative level, his critique of Socrates enacts an *agonal confrontation* with the dialectic. Nietzsche does not simply oppose theory or (Platonic) Socratism within theoretical discourse; he contests it from within an *artistic cultural practice*, the *agon*, which sustains, i.e. drives and organizes, his discourse. *Agonal* discourse occupies that ambivalent space between theoretical discourse and art proposed as Nietzsche's response to the problem of discourse. As an artistic practice, it plays the two-fold role for art claimed by Nietzsche in the *Attempt*: on the one hand, it enables him to raise life against theoretical discourse without falling into the trap of discursive closure – mere opposition. Nietzsche's *agon* is a *performative* challenge that *supplements* his discursive confrontation by *enacting* the concept of life-as-art raised against the claims of theory; Nietzsche's text becomes the saying and yes-saying of life, less by offering a series or system of designating signifieds, than through its movement, the very process of *signifying*, which replicates, feigns, or enacts the dynamic and mobile character of life or Becoming. On the other hand, *agonal* discourse is also Nietzsche's performative response to the problem of self-critique: the *agonal* dynamic of empowerment/disempowerment engages Nietzsche in a process of signification, but also a retraction of signifieds, a process of saying and unsaying, an unstable discourse that also undoes its own discursivity, exposing itself to the other of discourse.

In order to illustrate this thesis, I shall draw out certain aspects or moments of Nietzsche's critique of Socrates which, on a discursive reading, are incoherent, but in *agonal* terms begin to make sense. After Socrates' death scene, *BT* 15 opens by reiterating his dying question: 'whether art is not a necessary correlative and supplement to theory?' [BT 14, KSA 1, p. 96]. Only here, it is no longer a question, but a futural 'guarantee', an extravagant, mythological claim concerning Socrates' endless influence on 'all futurity' and how it 'always again necessitates the recreation of art [...] in the metaphysical and broadest sense' [BT 15, KSA 1, p. 97]. If this is not strange enough, the chapter ends by reiterating this claim, or rather reopening it as an anxious question:

> Will that 'turning' [of theory into art – HS] lead to ever new configurations of genius and indeed of the *music-practising Socrates*? Will the net of art spread over existence, whether under the name of religion or theory, be woven ever tighter and more delicately, or is it destined to tear into shreds in the restless barbaric whirl of activity that goes by the name of 'the present'. [BT 15, KSA 1, p. 102]

At issue, as these lines show, is the question of closure: the Socratic belief in the possibility of a completely closed and coherent interpretation or discourse on life is contested by a bold claim on the future that would determine or enclose it within the necessity for theory to turn into dionysian art. Why, then, retract this contention? Why should Nietzsche reopen a fate which he initially presented as sealed? Why end the chapter by calling the necessary recreation of dionysian art, announced at the start, into question? It is tempting to dismiss these contradictions as examples of an uncontrolled, '*impossible* book' [BT, Attempt 2, KSA 1, p. 13]. Alternatively, the logic of this move can be approached from two angles:

1) First, we can ask: what is required to mount an effective critique of closure? Clearly, a direct counter-claim asserting the impossibility of closure would itself presuppose closure, building defeat into the challenge. Nietzsche's opening move is to contest the claim to closure with a powerful counter-claim that would enclose the future within the necessary failure of closure, turning theory into art; a move which, however, remains trapped within the circle of opposition or

inversion. He therefore goes on to reopen his own attempt at closure, throwing his own counter-claim into question. In this light, Nietzsche's question enacts the moment of self-critique found lacking in the dialectic, whereby the demand to limit knowledge recoils upon the critic, putting his critical standard and his form of questioning into question. In the frayed or fractured form of *BT* 15, we can glimpse what Nietzsche means by the art of listening, as a breach of critical practice where critique is sharpened into self-critique and the active contention of another's claim is disrupted by a retraction of one's own counter-claim, an unsaying of what is said.

2) From a second angle, this response can be placed within a fuller, positive account of Nietzsche's critical practice, as one side of an *agonal* confrontation with the dialectic. This reading takes off from the affirmation or empowerment of Socrates into 'the one turning point and vortex of [...] world history' [BT 15, KSA 1, p. 100]. In *BT* 15, the theoretical Socrates is affirmed as the symbol and 'progenitor of the theoretical human', who deflected an 'incalculable sum of energy' from destructive, egoistic conflict towards the pursuit of truth. Yet, at the very turning point, the transition to the theoretical age, Socrates negates or disempowers himself as philosopher, turning into a musician. On the verge of being transported into immortality as 'the dying Socrates' [BT 13, KSA 1, p. 91], he senses danger; transfixed by the envious eye of a god resting upon him and bowing in a vertiginous fear of victory to the divine envy, he makes his offering of music. Socrates' undoing is, in fact, Nietzsche's own empowerment into a mythologist able to determine or enclose the future within the necessity for theory to turn into art: Nietzsche aligns himself with the music practising Socrates as a mythological figure of (Dionysian) necessity, so as to overcome the philosophical Socrates and his hold over the present. And yet, within the *agonal* play of forces, this victory must also be contained, Nietzsche too must reach a limit where his own claim to closure is undone or opened to question. Nietzsche's question at the end of *BT* 15 thus inscribes the limits of his victory over Socrates into the text.

The logic of this confrontation is *agonal* through and through: a dynamic of mutual affirmation or empowerment drives each to a limit where it negates itself and limits its victory over the other. *Agonal* critique can be summarised as an open-ended to-and-fro of two moments:

1) the active contention of the opponent's claim, in response to the demand to limit knowledge (suspicion): can we really suppose that theoretical closure is possible? As an act of contention it is also a positing (*Setzen*). Like dialectics, it posits a standard of critique; but the *agonal* critic is roused and empowered by his opponent to go further, to op-pose (*Gegen-setzen*) the opponent's claim with a counterclaim (the impossibility of closure). Insofar as this counter-claim itself presupposes closure, it is strictly speaking self-defeating. *Agonal* critique does not, however, rest here. Instead it is followed by:

2) the recoil of critique, whereby the demand for critique folds back upon the *agonal* critic and his standard of critique. A retraction to disrupt his active contention, a moment of stillness that enables him to question his form of questioning, to reopen his attempt at closure and check his limitless desire for power over the antagonist. It is this moment of limitation that offers the strongest measure of the gap dividing *agonal* from dialectical critique. For it gives to the former the openended, inconclusive repeatability of all play, in sharp contrast to the will-to-closure animating the dialectic. If, as Nietzsche claims, 'the Socratism of our times is the belief in being finished' [1[8], KSA 7], then *agonal* critique opens the horizon of the future as an invitation to contest Socratism under the sign of endless repeatability.

References:
For a general bibliography of Nietzsche's works in German and English see end of volume.

Notes

1   For the concept of theoretical disourse I take my bearings from Blondel, E.:
     Nietzsche: The Body and Culture, Sean Hand [tr.], Athlone Press, London,
     1991, pp. 23–30, who points to two aims of classical rational discourse:

univocity or 'clarity', and logical continuity. Clarity is achieved by inscribing in rational discourse a code that fixes univocal relations between its terms (signifiers) and the concepts they signify. As an attempt to master or contain within discourse the code that regulates its understanding, this procedure aims to establish thoertical discourse as a stable, self-contained, closed and coherent signifying whole that imposes a fixed meaning on reality or life.

2   *Homer's Wettkampf* [KSA 1, pp. 783–92]. The best English translation of the text is by Christa Acampora: 'Homer's Contest', in: Nietzscheana, North American Nietzsche Society, 5, 1996. Together with the notebook PII8b [= notebook 16, KSA 7], *Homer's Contest* is the most important source for Nietzsche's thought on the *agon*. As one of *Five Prefaces for Unwritten Books* given to Cosima Wagner for Christmas 1872, it was 'finished on the 29. December 1872' [KSA 1, p. 792]. But the drafts in notebook 16 show that Nietzsche was working on it in the period of summer 1871 to early 1872, i.e. during latter stages of *BT*. The folder MpXII 3 [= notebook 20, KSA 7], containing first draft, is dated summer 1872.
       In this paper the translations of Nietzsche texts are mine. Italics have been used to render Nietzsche's emphases.

3   Blondel, E.: *Nietzsche: The Body and Culture*, Introduction.

4   See note 10[28], KSA 12, p. 470: '[…] in place of 'society' the *culture-complex [Kultur–Complex]* as *my* primary interest (as a whole in relation to its parts, as it were)'.

5   To mention only a few: Dannhauser, W.: *Nietzsche's View of Socrates*, Cornell U.P., Ithaca/London, 1974; Kofmann, S.: 'Nietzsche's Socrates: 'Who' is Socrates?', in: *Graduate Faculty Philosophy Journal* 15/2, 1991, pp. 7–30; Schmidt, H-J: *Nietzsche und Sokrates – Philosophische Untersuchungen zu Nietzsches Sokratesbild*, Hain u. Meisenheim, 1969.

6   '[…] die Wissenschaft unter der Optik des Künstlers zu sehn, die Kunst aber unter der des Lebens....' [KSA 1, p. 14]

7   See especially *The World as Will and Representation*, vol. II Ch. 17: *On the Metaphysical Need of Man*, Ch. 41, 46 and 48. See also Nietzsche's critique of this line of thought in *BT, Attempt*, 5. Also note 1[161], KSA 12: '[…] Whoever feels that suffering is an argument against life counts as superficial in my books, including our pessimists […]'.

8   See *BT, Attempt*, 7. The underlying problem – first worked out against Socrates in *BT* – is that metaphysics, according to Nietzsche, denies the reality it claims to embrace ('denies' in both the epistemic sense of 'falsifies' and the ethical sense of 'negates') in the name of a fictional realm of static Being responding to our wishes. It is just such a wishful falsification that Nietzsche attacks in the notion of 'metaphysical consolation', used to articulate the affirmation of life offered by tragedy in *BT* 7.

9   The tragic philosopher 'seeks to let the total sound of the world resound within himself and to re-project it in concepts: while he is contemplative like the plas-

tic artist, compassionate like the religious, in search of purposes and causalities like the man of science, while he feels himself swelling out into the macrocosm, he all the while retains the composure to view himself coldly as the mirror of the world: that composure which the dramatic artist possesses when he transforms himself into other bodies, speaks out of them and yet knows how to project this transformation outwards in written verses.' [PTG 3 (1872), KSA 1, p. 817].

10   The *Beschwörung der Todesfurcht*, as Nietzsche translates it in his lecture on the *Phaedo* in his *Einleitung in das Studium der platonischen Dialoge* [1871–2, KGW II/4, p. 85]. Nietzsche continues: 'Death was called the real inspiring genius of philosophy or the muse of philosophy: according to Plato, philosophy is really *thanatou melete*.' See also *BT* 15, KSA 1, p. 99 and note 6[14], KSA 7. All of this refers to *Phaedo* 77e–78, where Socrates speaks of saying 'a magic spell over him' who is afraid of death, and of 'charming his fears away'.

11   'You know how the initiation practioners say, 'Many bear the emblems, but the devotees are few'? Well, in my opinion these devotees are simply those who have lived the philosophical life in the right way – a company which, all through my life, I have done my best in every way to join, leaving nothing undone which I could do to attain this end.' [Ph. 69d]. A paraphrase of this passage occurs in *Das griechische Musikdrama* [KSA 1, p. 522] but it is referred to the devotees of Dionysos in the proto-tragic cult. As we shall see, this prefigures the twist given to philosophy in *BT*: from an initiation in death, to an initiation in art.

12   See the description of courage in *Republic* Bk. III, culimiating in the claim that the good man 'is most of all men sufficient unto himself for a good life and is distinguished from other men in having least need of anybody else.' [Rep. 386e]. See also Nussbaum, M.: *The Fragility of Goodness*, CUP, Cambridge, 1986, Ch. 5 [& 7] on the ideal of self-sufficiency through pure contemplative activity in Plato's middle works.

13   As quoted above, Simmias says 'the subject is so vast, and I have such a poor opinion of our weak human nature, that I can't help feeling misgivings.'. Cf. the *Apology*, where Socrates' account of his divine, peripatetic mission, culminating in his negative claim to wisdom of ignorance [21d], is presented as a form of human wisdom: 'I have gained this reputation, gentlemen, from nothing more or less than a kind of wisdom. What kind of wisdom do I mean? Human wisdom, I suppose. It seems that I really am wise in this limited sense' [20e]. The narrative concludes with the claim that 'real wisdom is the property of God, and this oracle is his way of telling us that human wisdom has little or no value. It seems to me that he is not literally referring to Socrates, but has merely taken my name as an example, as if he would say to us, The wisest of you men is he who has realized, like Socrates, that in respect of wisdom he is really worthless'. [23b].

14   Cf. PTG 3 [cited above] on the tragic (pre-Socratic) philosopher who lets 'the total sound of the world resound within himself'. Also note 6[15], KSA 8: '*Comparison* of the older philosophy with the post-Socratic [...] it is *not* the negation of the *other* life [des *andern* Lebens], but grew out of it as a rare blossom [...]'.

15   The contention here is that, in transcribing Socrates' speech, Nietzsche *mythologises* it into a tragic drama: 'It is only when the drama is over that actions take on their true significance and agents, through what they in reality accomplished without realizing it, discover their true identity.' [Vernant, J.P.: *Myth and Tragedy in Ancient Greece*, Zone Books, New York, 1990, p. 45]. Nietzsche transforms the meaning of this episode not simply by distorting it, but by giving it the structure of tragic action, of which Vernant writes 'that it is not so much the agent who explains the action but rather the action that, revealing its true significance after the event, recoils upon the agent and discloses what he is and he has really unwittingly done' [op. cit., p. 32].

16   On the difference between Plato's negative concept of desire as lack and Nietzsche's dionysian concept of desire as excess, see Rethy, R.: 'The Tragic Affirmation of the *Birth of Tragedy*', in: Nietzsche-Studien 17, 1988, pp. 1–44, esp. pp. 26–31. A clear measure of this difference and the gap dividing Nietzsche from Plato's concept of philsophy is the supposition in *BGE* 294 'that gods also philosophize'.

17   Deleuze, G.: *Nietzsche and Philosophy*, H. Tomlinson [tr.], Athlone, London, 1983, p. 76.

CAROL DIETHE

Nietzschean Sexual Ethics

In this study, I shall first describe my understanding of Nietzsche's sexual ethics before demonstrating how Nietzschean sexual ethics, nearly always distorted, influenced the class of bourgeois intellectuals who were his initial target audience in Germany, and who carried through his code of conduct according to their own lights in the first years of the twentieth century.

Nietzsche was at pains to relieve us of the doctrine of guilt and sin inculcated by Christianity's moral teaching. He began this task with the publication of *Human, All Too Human*,[1] promptly alienating the Wagners, who were turning increasingly pious, and ended with a flourish in *The Antichrist*.[2] It is important to know what Nietzsche was objecting to. The sexual ethics in the Old Testament rested on the misogynic base that Eve had tempted Adam and brought about their fall and expulsion from Eden. This contrasted with Christ's tolerant attitude towards the fallen woman in the gospels, an attitude nullified by subsequent acolytes from St Paul to St Augustine, who reverted to the Old Testament mistrust of women but added a new stricture that men, too, should despise and quell the pleasures of the flesh. Nietzsche singled out the ascetic priest as chief culprit in poisoning our natural instincts, but he had no time either for Christ's doctrine of weakness, such as the instruction to turn the other cheek when under attack.

Clearly, Nietzsche's critique of Christian ethics embraced many other topics besides sexual ethics, but few could be more timely: Nietzsche rode the crest of the wave which saw the founding of the new science of sexology on the one hand, in the work of writers like Krafft-Ebing (whose *Psychopathia Sexualis*, 1886, concentrated on deviant sexuality), and the emergence of psychoanalysis on the other. Indeed, Freud would eventually come to share with Nietzsche a deep

mistrust of monotheistic religions, including his own Judaism,[3] because the morality in such religions is founded on guilt.[4] Ironically,
Freud's 'talking cure' often upheld the Christian-based paternalistic
ethical *status quo* in society, especially when it came to female sexuality,[5] in much the same way as Nietzsche's insistence on woman's
domestic role very much dampened his dynamite. Meanwhile,
Nietzsche's *Übermensch* has remained an unworkable hypothesis. For
how is the *Übermensch* to emerge, become flesh, as it were; and how
can he or she struggle to create a new morality? How many new
moralities can society countenance? Who is to judge what is good and
evil in society? Nietzsche does not provide answers to any of these
questions, the initial task of breaking tablets being his chief concern.

Nietzsche's starting point on sexuality is that the two sexes are
fundamentally antagonistic. Nietzsche did not deviate from this view,
derived from Arthur Schopenhauer and deeply entrenched in Wilhelminian thought and manners, even when he spewed scorn on Schopenhauer and lambasted contemporary German culture. Nietzsche
acknowledged that a truce has to be effected so that intercourse and
the resultant offspring can come about. But how? In *The Birth of
Tragedy*, where the polarities of Apollo and Dionysus are brought
together, Nietzsche disparages the way Dionysian orgiastic excess
leads to cruelty and lust.[6] However, he overlays his discussion of
Greek aesthetics with an awed stress on the Dionysian, even while
deploring it, leaving Apollo stranded in much the same way that
Milton's deliciously wicked Satan eclipses Adam and emerges as the
potent sexual force in *Paradise Lost* (1667).[7] In terms of early
Nietzsche reception (from the mid-1890s), Dionysianism, or rampant
orgiastic excess, was seized on as the main 'message' of the book and
taken, quite wrongly, to indicate Nietzsche's approval of libertarian
sexuality.

A decade after publication of *BT*, Nietzsche trained the spotlight
on his own society in the *Gay Science,* frowning to see the hypo-
critical upbringing of the well-bred young woman which kept her
ignorant of the facts of life and left her unprepared for marriage.[8] He
felt this was bound to wreck her self-esteem and spoil her relationship
to her children. His comments on women in *GS* veer from the sympathetic to the downright rude, but his conviction that the sexes are

different, and that women love in a different way from men, emerges very strongly. Nietzsche vacillates between a biological critique whereby women are declared incorrigibly 'giving' in their love,[9] much to their detriment, and a social critique which argues that women are badly served by the dictates of decorum within a paternalistic society. Only one fact is non-negotiable: Nietzsche propounds a direct discussion of the passions as the healthy way forward, since verbal prudery has the effect of suppressing passion.[10]

Nietzsche's belief that the body should be released from the snares set up by religiously dictated mores was similar to that of the visionary poet William Blake of a century earlier. Blake challenged the Ancient of Days:

> Why art thou silent & invisible
> Father of jealousy.[11]

But Blake was serenely happy with the Christ of the New Testament, albeit seen through the visionary prism of Emanuel Swedenborg,[12] while Nietzsche blamed the 'warm-hearted' cult of Jesus for taming men's passions. The most zealous Christian ('the warmest heart') will call loudest for his own destruction.[13] Blake thought both sexes had the right to sexual satisfaction in equal proportion,[14] and those who cheated others out of it, particularly priests with false ethics,[15] were a pestilential plague. Nietzsche held these views too, although it was more controversial for him to do so in the late nineteenth century than in the less prudish eighteenth century. However, Blake never muddied the waters by insisting on the connection between female sexual desire and the drive for motherhood, as Nietzsche would do with increasing stridency. The result was that Nietzsche was forced to divide women into wives and whores, remarking that the respectable wife and mother would scarcely have time for sexual pursuits, even though a hetaerist lifestyle might well suit her.[16] Blake conceded that the inevitable transition from sexual innocence, *Songs of Innocence*, 1789, to experience, *Songs of Experience*, 1794, involved a certain amount of corruption, but this did not denote a shift in his ethics. Freedom to enjoy the god-given body remained his base line.

Ostensibly, Nietzsche was even-handed on the question of the human right to sexual bliss, certainly in his earlier work, where he tended to blame sexual problems on men, or at least, patriarchal society, rather than women, but this position would be reversed later. In reality, his stance on female sexuality was more akin to that of Freud than Blake, positing a masochistic strand in female sexuality – in that woman fundamentally wants to give herself to man – long before Freud made female masochism a plank of his theory.[17] The corollary, for Nietzsche, is that man simply wants to 'have' a woman sexually, but 'wanting to have always ends once one has *had*.'[18] Hence there is always a sexual struggle between the sexes because the target of desire is different for man and woman. Up to 1882, Nietzsche refrains from saying whether this confusion as to the desired end of coitus is either good or bad, it is just the way things are between man and woman, in his view. As we shall see, his position changed after his encounter with Lou Salomé, so that by the time he wrote *Ecce Homo*, he states the case much more harshly: 'Love – in its methods, war; at its heart, deadly hatred of the sexes.'[19] We are at liberty to disagree. In *The Will to Power*, Nietzsche is even more stridently pro-scriptive:

> N.B. A woman wants to be a mother; and if she does not want this, even though she can, she almost belongs in prison, so great is her innermost degeneration as a general rule.[20]

In telling women what they want, physically, Nietzsche has actually turned into the ascetic priest he so reviled. He is far less explicit with his suggestions for male enjoyment of their sexual desire, partly because men could enjoy the sex act without the constant risk of pregnancy, and partly because his attention was fixed on man's metaphysical progeny. If Nietzsche had really intended to include women in his plans for the *Übermensch*, as many feminists of his day believed he had, there would have been no need for him to stress woman's breeding role at the physical level. One seeks in vain for Nietzschean examples where the metaphor of pregnancy could be applied to the creativity of a female genius, since he was constantly at pains to point out his mistrust of the intellectual woman.

Rather than enter the postmodern debate on 'woman as truth', as I have done elsewhere,[21] I would like to point readers in the direction of Johann Jakob Bachofen's *Das Mutterrecht* (*Mother Right*) that appeared in 1861, eight years before Nietzsche came to Basle, where he was subsequently a frequent visitor at the Bachofens' home. It was Bachofen's thesis that there had been three seismic shifts in the social relations of the sexes: the promiscuous telluric stage of pre-history, the era of matriarchal Demeter worship and moon cults, and finally the patriarchal, sun worshipping stage of Greek society. Our current civilisation is a refined version of the third stage, and is, Bachofen infers (for all his apparent enthusiasm for detecting the origins of matriarchy), the right and proper system:

> If the principle of maternity is common to all spheres of telluric creation, the human being, man, can quit that connection through the superior weight he gives to fertilising potency, and become conscious of his higher calling. Intellectual existence is superior to the physical, and a connection with the lower circles of creation is now limited to the latter. Maternity belongs to the physical side of humanity; only for its sake does it maintain a relationship with other beings; the paternal-intellectual principle is unique to itself.[22]

The above goes a long way towards explaining Nietzsche's apparently biased sexual politics: women's physique hampers their intellect.

I would now like to examine typical *fin de siècle* reactions to Nietzschean sexual ethics in the following fields: the arts, philosophy, eugenics and feminism. The arts in Germany at this point were heavily influenced by every aspect of Nietzsche's thought, not just that of sexuality. Put briefly, the Nietzscheans fell into two camps: the Dionysians tended to be mystics who drew inspiration from *BT,* while the Zarathustrans hailed the *Übermensch* of *Thus Spoke Zarathustra*[23] as their model. I propose to take just one example of what Dionysian sexual ethics meant in German cultural life at this time. The *Kosmiker* ('Cosmics') had formed a group in Munich in 1897 which included Ludwig Klages, Karl Wolfskehl, Rudolf Pannwitz, Alfred Schuler, who later became implicated with the National Socialists, and Franziska zu Reventlow, a free living aristocrat who had been disowned by her family because of what they saw as her sexual extravagance.[24] Most of the *Kosmiker* were writers, and all venerated the poet Stefan George, though he held himself aloof from their worst antics (which had all the hallmarks of Dionysian orgiastic frenzy, or so they liked to believe). The group had a quirkily occult cosmological theory that need not detain us here,[25] beyond a mention of their notion of *Blutleuchte* or 'flash of blood', denoting some great and rare personage in German cultural life; so rare that there are only one or two per century. The *Kosmiker* classed the haunted Ludwig II of Bavaria as such a one in the nineteenth century; and Nietzsche as another.

Alfred Schuler and Ludwig Klages were rabidly anti-Semitic,[26] and this brought about the group's final dissolution when Schuler threatened to kill Wolfskehl, who was a Jew. Just as importantly, Klages was unable to master his resentment when he discovered that he had to share Reventlow with Wolfskehl. Lest this should appear irrelevant gossip, we should note that the *Kosmiker* had a theory of hetaerist sexual practices and advocated sex on demand within the group. Sexual jealousy was outlawed and guilt was supposedly eradicated. Moreover, this eccentric group believed that the new sexual ethic they had agreed upon was thoroughly Nietzschean. They also borrowed heavily from Bachofen's description of the matriarchal social structure of antiquity. Indeed, Bachofen influenced a number of would-be visionaries, including the young artist and dramatist Oskar Kokoschka. Kokoschka's concept of the threatening, sexually potent 'moon lady' (as distinct from the 'earth mother',[27] subsequently developed as the archetype of the *anima* by the convinced Nietzschean Carl Gustav Jung[28]) derives straight from Bachofen,[29] as does the *Kosmiker's* belief that in the most ancient stage of Greek culture, life was lived in swamps and a hetaerist sexual culture consisted of random copulation. The *Kosmiker* tried to formulate a sexual ethic in which free love was seen as good and normal, but eventually they had to bow to the realities of human mating, with all its complications and disappointments, and the group dispersed.

In their clumsy way, the *Kosmiker* had tried to put free love into practice, and one thing they seem to have avoided is the strong misogyny that permeated all the arts at the turn of the century, portraying the sexually attractive woman as a dangerous *femme fatale,* and for which Nietzsche was *nolens volens* partly responsible. In literature, one thinks of August Strindberg; in painting, Ernst Ludwig Kirchner;

and in philosophy, the hapless Otto Weininger, who tried and failed to inhabit a Kantian realm of ideas, viewing life itself as a dualistic struggle between the divine (*das All*) and chaos (*das Nichts*). A Jew by birth, Weininger converted to Protestantism on the day he passed his doctorate (July 2nd, 1902). From then on, he portrayed Jesus as the best of men,[30] berating the God slayer and Jesus basher Nietzsche in *Über die letzten Dinge* (*On Last Things*), completed in August 1903, two months before Weininger shot himself. By contrast, Wagner is praised for his subtle sexual politics in *Parsifal* (feminists beware!).[31]

Weininger makes a distinction between eroticism, a dangerous game in which man can be in thrall to woman, and sexuality, the nuts and bolts of coupling. In his main work *Geschlecht und Charakter* (*Sex and Character*, 1903), Weininger reduces sexuality to a mathematical formula; for example, a very masculine woman (W) (3/4) could mate with a very effeminate man (M) (1/4). Typecasting the entire female sex as either mothers or prostitutes, he declares prostitutes to be lascivious by nature and unfit for motherhood.[32] But even mothers (– all body and no brain –) are unfit for motherhood. He cautions men not to let their wives bring up their children because they are not capable of rational thought. Lacking a soul, they cannot even appreciate men properly.[33] Perhaps directly echoing Nietzsche's joke that a woman's problems are solved by making her pregnant,[34] Weininger declares in *Über die letzten Dinge* that women only have an 'inner life' for nine months at the most.[35] He seems to share with Nietzsche a view that the quest for maternity makes woman a predator on man, but whereas Nietzsche held motherhood to be ethically good as well as biologically necessary, it alarms and disgusts Weininger. He cautions that it is possible for a man to fecundate a woman 'not just through coitus but also by a single glance',[36] or even by his voice, a belief not inconsistent with Bachofen's views on male *Potenz*, discussed above, which Weininger cites with approval in a long footnote.[37]

Up to this point, a Wilhelminian sexual ethic divorced from religion has been shown to be a rarity; even the paganism of the *Kosmiker* bore the hallmark of a pseudo-religious cult. Things would change as the tenets of the newly founded eugenics movement became widespread. Eugenics rested, not on religion, but on the concept of improvement through breeding. The German eugenics movement was pioneered by Alfred Ploetz to promote 'the well born' by scientific selection. Ploetz merged socialist and Darwinist thought in his monograph on racial hygiene, *Die Tüchtigkeit unserer Rasse und der Schutz der Schwachen. Ein Versuch über Rassenhygiene und ihr Verhältnis zu den humanen Idealen, besonders zum Sozialismus (The Industriousness of our Race and the Protection of the Weak: An Essay on Racial Hygiene and its Relationship to Humane Ideals)*, which appeared in 1895. The title of the monograph gives a clear enough indication of the intended direction of the new movement, though the racist undercurrent was no doubt harder to detect in 1895, when the term *Rasse* had some positive connotations, as in 'pedigree'. Fired up by the discovery of the fundamentals of genetics, the eugenicists at first focused on social reform and hereditary improvement, but their efforts to found a new sexual ethic soon became more sinister when directed towards population control.[38]

Ploetz prefaced his monograph with an aphorism from Nietzsche, although the latter, languishing at that time in Naumburg in the care of his mother and sister, had written nothing but insults regarding both socialism and Darwinism. Thus, the bow to Nietzsche was as misleading as it was unwarranted, but many of Nietzsche's fans in the late 1890s were prepared to embrace the new science of eugenics, believing that, with his aspiration for a new man with the birth of the *Übermensch,* Nietzsche would have supported the movement had he remained sane. I do not think Nietzsche's vision of the *Übermensch* gave the eugenicists any grounds to believe that he would have upheld their views, still less their methods. The *Übermensch* heralded human intellectual and moral self-improvement, not a better-bred race of *Germans.*

Furthermore, unlike leading eugenicists such as Magnus Hirschfeld, who persisted in viewing male homosexuals as deviants for whom a cure might be found, Nietzsche did not view male homosexuality as a social misfortune *per se.* That role was reserved for female homosexuality, which, according to Nietzsche, had latterly become dangerously rampant within the campaign for female emancipation. For Nietzsche, all feminists were lesbians and therefore physical freaks, 'the ill-born'.[39] They contaminated his vision of the new breed of *Übermensch.* Nietzsche thus stands accused of unethical treatment of women in his sexual ethics. That said, Nietzsche could also make homophobic remarks at the level of innuendo, as in *On the Genealogy of Morality*,[40] where his scurrilous attack is aimed specifically at Eugen Dühring, a man whose thought he thoroughly disliked. Effeminacy is the worst insult he can dredge up within the context of dismissing 'modern' German culture.

This discussion has so far mainly centred on the early male reception of Nietzschean sexual ethics; I would now like to examine how voluble female Nietzscheans reacted by examining the sexual theories of Helene Stöcker and Lou Salomé. Here again, the examples I choose merely scratch the surface of the subject.[41]

Helene Stöcker's connection with the eugenics movement was of benign intent in so far as she did not wish to police anyone's sexuality, but merely to improve social conditions, especially for unmarried women. Even this was enough to make her the scourge of the bourgeois feminist movement (moderate in name only, since it was actually virulently conservative). As early as 1897, Stöcker had stresssed that in eroticism, it is not the way things are but the way things are valued that is important.[42] So convinced was Stöcker of the value of Nietzschean precepts that she even argued that an individual woman can adopt the Zarathustrian '*er will*'[43] to '*ich will*'[44] (as did Ellen Key, see endnote 80). At all events, no woman of intellect should deny herself the advantage gained from reading Nietzsche's work.[45] Like many radicals in the women's movement at the time, Stöcker chose to ignore Nietzsche's patent misogyny because she approved of his overall strategy. In 1905, Stöcker took over the running of the *Bund für Mutterschutz* (League for the Protection of Mothers), founded the previous year by Ruth Bré, who had thought up an unpleasant programme of social engineering which Stöcker promptly overturned with a new sexual ethic, *die neue Ethik,* that would grant all women the right to sexual enjoyment, even single women and prostitutes. Paying homage to Nietzsche in her manifesto to re-launch the movement on her own lines, drawn up in 1905,[46] Stöcker stressed that female sexuality should now be re-valued, by which she meant that it should be rid of its negative connotations. She pointed out that female sexuality had habitually been poisoned by the view of the libidinous woman as a witch or a whore.[47]

Stöcker's insistence that the unmarried mother should not be a
pariah in society, but should receive extra help, which it would be the
task of the *Bund für Mutterschutz* to provide, left her with few friends
within the mainstream of the feminist movement, now growing ever
more conventional after a decade of radicalism from 1898–1908. In
fact, the leadership of the *Bund deutscher Frauenvereine* (League of
German Women's Associations) bitterly hated Stöcker, although she
had plenty of support among the intelligentsia.[48] In particular, Helene
Lange, a leading light in the *BDF*, carried out a sustained vendetta
against the notion of a *neue Ethik*. Lange blamed Stöcker's monism
for the latter's irresponsible belief that sexuality was an individual
concern, with little to do with social mores, declaring that the result
was bound to be *Gedankenanarchie* [intellectual anarchy][49] and a descent into the glorious sounding (but unkindly meant) '*hurra-Erotik*'.[50]
Lange argued that the new morality was nothing short of an attack on
the institution of marriage.[51] It offered the respectable middle class
woman nothing, for if circumstances were propitious for a sexual relationship, they were also propitious for marriage – a patently specious
remark that ignores extra-marital affairs.[52]

To be fair, Lange made her derogatory comment in an article
written originally in 1908, two years before it became common knowledge that Stöcker was involved in a love affair with Dr Bruno
Springer, one of her chief supporters in the *Bund für Mutterschutz* –
and a married man.[53] The relationship scandalised the more straight-
laced of Stöcker's feminist colleagues, notably Adele Schreiber, who
brought it to light, and the scandal contributed to the collapse of trust
in the *Bund für Mutterschutz*. When the written word failed to utterly
crush the *Bund für Mutterschutz*, Lange initiated a cluster of lawsuits
against it, seven in all in 1910. The result was a scandalous public row
that did none of the combatants any service. Stöcker responded to her
critics with remarkable moderation,[54] but was left to discover that
former friends, such as Elisabeth Förster-Nietzsche, wanted nothing
more to do with her.[55] However, she kept on good terms with Lou
Salomé and followed the latter's principle of '*sich ausleben*', discussed below, in her own life.

With the outbreak of the Great War, Stöcker turned her attention
to the pacifist movement and drew up a sexual ethic for German

women who might fall in love with enemy soldiers. She openly disagreed with the view that such love affairs would be tantamount to treason,[56] citing a number of immoderate statements made by both men and women to engender hatred of the enemy. True to her conviction that Nietzsche's life affirmation was the starting point for all ethics, Stöcker cited Nietzsche as an example of a patriotic soldier who had every right to criticise his fatherland:

> We must not forget that the same Nietzsche who, alongside Bernhardi, and who, when a Professor in Switzerland in 1870/71, sacrificed his health trying to serve the Fatherland as a volunteer, is nowadays paraded as the intellectual instigator of the war, especially abroad, – this same Nietzsche was at the same time the *strongest campaigner* against the overweening *un-German* mood that manifested itself in the intoxication of victory after the 1870/71 conquest.[57]

By a strange sequence of events, this discussion of Nietzschean sexual ethics has brought Nietzsche, often seen, wrongly, as a warmonger, into the pacifist debate. Nietzsche's letters to Carl von Gersdorff, for example, tell of his horror at the suffering caused by war,[58] and remind us that Nietzsche had a vulnerable and compassionate side, however much he might wish to harden himself.

We may perhaps allow ourselves to assume that Nietzsche and Salomé discussed sexual ethics during the time they spent together at Tautenburg in 1882. At all events, their views on woman's domestic and maternal destiny are almost identical, and were, incidentally, acceptable to the main body of German feminists. The divergence came with Nietzsche's claim that all women had the right to sexual bliss, echoed by Salomé but not by her fellow 'moderate' feminists, who held the prevailing view that the respectable woman had little libidinous desire, and who tended to equate prostitution with female lust, in line with medical opinion at the time.[59] Even the Abolitionist programme in Germany (initiated by Josephine Butler's noble minded campaign to abolish legalised prostitution) was essentially repressive, arguing that respectable men should be as chaste as their wives.[60] Since we cannot doubt that many of these same respectable women nevertheless enjoyed sexual activity, we must presume that a number of them acted against their own self-interest by sublimating their desires, or at least pretending to, in obedience to the belief that the overt enjoyment of sexuality was the realm of the prostitute.

Such deception played no part in the sexual ethics of Lou Salomé. For her, to be a woman represented the pinnacle of earthly bliss, and was not to be compromised. According to Salomé, the prime function of the erotic is to lead us to ourselves. So far, so Nietzschean, but Salomé's thought verged away from that of Nietzsche when she argued that for love to be truly consummated, the intellect must be satisfied as well as the body.[61] Salomé's arguments on female eroticism are found in three essays, *Der Mensch als Weib* (The Human Being as Woman, 1899), *Gedanken über das Liebesproblem* (Thoughts on the Problem of Love, 1900), and *Die Erotik* (Eroticism, 1910). Woman's physiology, bestowed by nature, has made woman maternal without her actually having to give birth,[62] a notion that was perhaps a convenient conceit in the mind of the childless Salomé.[63] It is fair to add that in spite of an unconsummated marriage, she had a number of affairs in accordance with her philosophy of '*sich ausleben*' (which included free love under the umbrella of full self-expression), ensuring thereby a lifetime's devotion to her husband built on a firmer foundation than sexual attraction.[64]

There can be few sexual ethics in which goodness lies in the mere fact of existence, but this is what Salomé proposes: 'Woman just goes on living out the sexual in the structure of her whole being.'[65] For Salomé, no woman in her natural state of grace could fail to submit to her womanly calling; hence she *must* resist the temptations of education and a career. Since Salomé went on to make a career out of telling women about her own sexual code, which she developed and refined under the tutelage of Freud, she drew down upon herself the despair of radicals in the German feminist movement like Hedwig Dohm, who accused her of manifest bad faith.[66] However, this did not trouble her by one hair's breadth. She lived out her life as a free spirit with breathtaking aplomb.

Salomé exulted in her free lifestyle while retaining a profoundly conservative stance on contemporary sexual politics which, in common with mainstream male and female opinion at the time, discussed above, saw woman as less intellectual than man. Salomé argued that woman was part of a universal psychic experience of sex: a paradox that, according to Salomé, resulted in woman's natural tendency to sublimate her sexuality.[67] In the essay *Die Erotik*, Salomé's preference for mystical statements sometimes endangers her point, which is to assert that a woman's experience of eroticism puts her in touch with the pulse of the universe;[68] she urges women to live in tune with the 'rhythms of universal life' (*Rhythmen des All-Lebens*).[69] She comes close to suggesting that this is almost an experience of divinity, a view Nietzsche would most certainly not have shared, notwithstanding Salomé's controversial attempt to argue, in *Friedrich Nietzsche in seinen Werken* (*Friedrich Nietzsche in his Works*, 1894), that Nietzsche retained a sort of 'religious aesthetics' in his works, where ethics and aesthetics became merged.[70] Salomé's stress on the devastation caused to Nietzsche through his early loss of faith was nothing if not controversial: not surprisingly, Nietzsche's friends Erwin Rohde and Franz Overbeck resented this analysis of their friend's philosophy,[71] especially as Nietzsche could no longer defend himself.

Salomé's exultant *jouissance* ranks woman's experience of sexuality above that of man, and might explain why some of Nietzsche's comments seem to make the same value judgement, albeit in a tone of ill-disguised resentment. In *Friedrich Nietzsche in seinen Werken*, Salomé argues (as Weininger had done when he cited 'lack of religion' as the reason for Nietzsche's *Untergang*),[72] that it was Nietzsche's self-hatred rather than a truly original iconoclasm that fuelled his attack on Christian morality. Her thesis is that Nietzsche's loss of faith informed the whole of his thought;[73] his agonizing quest for a God-substitute inevitably resulted in his self-deification: 'The yearning for God, transformed by torture into a drive to create God, expressed itself by necessity in self-deification'.[74] Salome's attempt to rationalize Nietzsche's *oeuvre* as an expression of repressed and unresolved *religious* conflict is neither completely fair to Nietzsche nor to Salomé, since she wrote of repression in sexual terms only when she turned to psychoanalysis.[75] That said, in this early work on Nietzsche, Salomé anticipates Freud's revelations on the Oedipal conflict when she stresses the adverse effects on Nietzsche of his father's early death.

As we saw at the outset, Nietzsche's sexual ethics grew increasingly strident in tone, arguably because he never recovered from the loss of Lou Salomé, the love of his life. As Sarah Kofman has pointed out with regard to the severity of some of Nietzsche's maxims on women: 'are they not symptomatic of a deep love for women, all of whom abandoned him?[76]

I would argue that Nietzsche, somewhat ruefully, concurred with Salomé that woman's biology best fitted her to luxuriate in life itself, although he could not resist the temptation to claim credit for men in the field of intellectual procreation, describing contemplative natures in the *GS* as 'die männlichen Mütter' (male mothers).[77] Salomé also reinforced the similarity of creative genius to procreation,[78] but we must not forget that she also condemned female writers and all career women as a disgrace to their sex. Thus, in effect, she uses the pregnancy metaphor for creative men only, just as Nietzsche did. Men have their brains and women have their bodies; but Salomé sees this as an enormous plus, putting woman in touch with the ecstasy of the universe.

Much of Salomé's mysticism sounds like a pseudo-scientific interpretation of Bachofen's tale of a pre-history dominated by female divinities and matriarchal cults. Once again, Bachofen forges a missing link with the sexual ethics of late Wilheminian culture via his premise that when women ran society in prehistoric times, their sexuality, if non-thinking, was gloriously unpoliced. Something was lost when civilisation became male dominated, with a new iconography typified by the preference for the right hand over the left, the sun over the moon, and the mind over the body. Bachofen tacitly infers that the gain in sexual ethics does not quite outweigh the loss of freedom. Thus, we can better understand why Nietzsche gives with one hand and takes away with the other when he supports the principle of maternity by granting women full rights to the enjoyment of copulation, yet denigrates the female intellect à la Bachofen. To that extent, Salomé understood the nub of Nietzsche's sexual code and elaborated upon it in her own unique fashion.

As we have seen, sexual ethics in Wilhelminan Germany were generally seen as either black or white, signifying rigid moral standards in marriage or loose behaviour outside it. It was a stark choice.[79] In the art world, loose behaviour won, however un-Nietzschean it really was. Orgiastic Dionysian excesses, as exemplified by the

Kosmiker, were as ill-conceived as the notion of Zarathustra as a priapic Tarzan. Some women intellectuals like the socialist Lily Braun embraced Nietzschean sexuality in the belief that it constituted free love. More conservative thinkers such as Ellen Key,[80] and indeed, Lou Salomé, noted Nietzsche's kind words on motherhood with approval, as did the majority in the women's movement, even if they disagreed with his other comments on women. This simply serves to show that the feminists pursued their own factional agendas, with Salomé's insistence that she was opposed to feminism as a case in point; for what does her sexual ethic do for a woman chained to domestic drudgery and childbearing, and forced into work?

Clearly, then as now, the term 'feminist' was provocative and divisive. Bourgeois feminists of the 'moderate' mainstream such as Helene Lange frowned on Nietzsche's insistence on individualism, preferring to highlight the domestic virtues of woman's nature or *Persönlichkeit*. In 1931, Lange's successor as leader of the feminist movement at that time, Gertrud Bäumer, blamed the chaos of moral standards in Germany squarely on individualism; for her, women's lack of self-discipline caused moral chaos in the state.[81] We now know that the chaos in German society at that time had plenty of much deeper ideological causes than a faulty (or otherwise) sexual ethic.[82] In the main, though, German middle class married women accepted their domestic status in the Third Reich and many relished the prominence of their role as mothers within the state, vigorously promoted by Hitler himself.[83]

There is no space here to discuss middle class women's false consciousness under National Socialism, beyond noting the staggering complacency with which Aryan women tolerated anti-Semitism in German society prior to Hitler's rise to power, a topic that has been discussed by Claudia Koonz.[84] What is depressing is that Nietzsche's work exerted considerable influence on the emergence of this ideology of motherhood. Of course, society needs mothers, but this does not mean that motherhood needs an ideology, still less one that is inherently nationalistic. Whether deliberately or not, Nietzsche seemed to voice views on female sexuality identical to those held by the conservative majority of men (and women) in the Germany of his day, the same generation that would gradually adopt a jingoistic nationalism.

Nietzsche's misogynic comments in *Beyond Good and Evil* cannot be laughed off as pure irony.[85] Nietzsche's long-lived sister typified the complacency of this generation: the mere fact that this strong woman (to put it mildly), childless, like the woman she hated most, Lou Salomé, could obsequiously agree with Nietzsche's anti-feminism, is enough to make us pause.[86] By this yardstick, Nietzschean sexual ethics were doomed to fail, if only because nobody understood them. We cannot duck the issue that Nietzsche led an attack on women's emancipation that was sure to go wrong, and that this was bound to vie with the liberating potential of his sexual ethics. Feminists and sexologists alike struggled with these contradictions until the Great War burst into their lives, finishing off all traces of the *fin de siècle* headiness and libertinism that derived directly, if mistakenly, from Nietzschean sexual ethics.

References:
For a general bibliography of Nietzsche's works in German and English see end of volume.

Notes

N.B. All translations from German in this text are my own; I have used the de Gruyter edition of Nietzsche's work, *Kritische Studienausgabe,*de Gruyter, 1967-.

1   *Menschliches, Allzumenschliches , Human, All Too Human* [I &II, 1878–9; III, 1880].

2   *Der Antichrist, The Antichrist* [1895].

3   Jacob Golomb has recently touched on this topic in *Nietzsche and Zion*, Ithaca, New York, Cornell University Press, 2004, especially pp. 189–214 *(Hillel Zeitlin: From Nietzschean Übermensch to Jewish Almighty God)*. For Renate Müller-Buck, Nietzsche wanted the death of God to mark the end of the whole of Western morality, while Freud just wanted it to mark a new beginning for the individual. See 'Psychologie' in *Nietzsche-Handbuch*, ed. Henning Ottmann, Stuttgart and Weimar, Metzler, 2000, pp. 509–14, p. 512.

4   Freud battled with these ideas in *Der Mann Moses und die monotheistische Religion: Drei Abhandlungen* (1938) (Moses the Man and Monotheistic Reli-

gion: Three Essays), where he tried to establish the provenance of Moses' religion to explain the shift from the Egyptian worship of many gods to the Judaic worship of the one true God.

5 For example, Freud and his collaborators counselled blue stockings that their desire for education was merely penis envy. See Sigmund Freud, *Die Weiblichkeit* (Femininity), in Studienausgabe, eds. A. Mitscherlich and others, Frankfurt am Main, Fischer, 1982, 10 vols, I, pp. 544–65, pp. 564f.

6 *Die Geburt der Tragödie, The Birth of Tragedy* [*BT*]: sections I and II, KSA 1, pp. 25f and pp. 30–3.

7 Now is the moment to express my view – not provable – that both Nietzsche and Milton were prudes in sexual matters, though unlike Milton, Nietzsche did not marry and appears to have had little actual experience of sex, if any at all. Philosophers are not expected to slavishly live out their philosophy in their lives, but in Nietzsche's case, his insistence on inserting his own opinions, jokes and prejudices into his writing makes it harder to divorce his life from his thought.

8 *Die fröhliche Wissenschaft, The Gay Science* [*GS*], II, 71, *Von der weiblichen Keuschheit* (On Feminine Modesty), KSA 3, p. 429.

9 *GS* V, 363, *Wie jedes Geschlecht über die Liebe sein Vorurtheil hat* (How Each Sex has its Prejudice on Love), KSA 3, pp. 610–13.

10 *GS* II, 47: *Von der Unterdrückung der Leidenschaften* (On the Supppression of the Passions), KSA 3, pp. 412f.

11 William Blake, 'To Nobodaddy', in *The Oxford Anthology of English Literature: Romantic Poetry and Prose*, eds. Harold Bloom and Lionel Trilling, Oxford and New York, Oxford University Press, 1980, p. 60. Blake detested the pseudo-rationalism and prohibitions of Urizen ('your reason') as much as the resentment of Nobodaddy ('nobody's daddy').

12 See Harvey F. Bellin and Darrell Ruhl, eds, Blake and Swedenborg: *Opposition is True Friendship*, New York, Swedenborg Foundation, 1985.

13 *HH* I, V, 235, *Anzeichen höherer Kultur* (Tokens of Higher and Lower Culture), KSA 2, p. 197: *Nun will das warme, mitfühlende Herz gerade die Beseitigung jenes gewaltsamen und wilden Charakters, und das wärmste Herz, das man sich denken kann, würde eben darnach am leidenschaftlichsten verlangen [...] das wärmste Herz will also Beseitigung seines Fundamentes, Vernichtung seiner selbst, das heisst doch: es will etwas Unlogisches, es ist nicht intelligent.* [Now the warm, sympathetic heart wants to eliminate that powerful and wild characteristic, and the warmest heart that one can imagine would be the most passionate in demanding this [...] so the warmest heart wants the elimination of its base, the destruction of itself: it wants something illogical, it is not intelligent.]

14 Blake, in 'Bloom and Trilling', p. 60:
What is it men in women do require?
The lineaments of Gratified Desire.

What is it women do in men require?
The lineaments of Gratified Desire.

15   Blake, 'The Garden of Love':
     And Priests in black gowns, were walking their rounds,
     And binding with briars, my joys and desires.
     In *Songs of Innocence and Experience*, Oxford, Oxford University Press, 1972
     [1789 and 1794], 'The Garden of Love', p. 43.

16   See *HH* I, VII, 424, *Aus der Zukunft der Heirat* (From the Future of Marriage),
     KSA 2, pp. 278f.

17   Freud, *Die Weiblichkeit*, p. 547: *Der Masochismus ist also, wie man sagt, echt
     weiblich.* (Masochism is, then, as they say, genuinely female).

18   *GS* V, 363, *Wie jedes Geschlecht über die Liebe sein Vorurtheil hat* (How each
     sex has its Prejudice about Love), KSA 3, p. 612.

19   *Ecce Homo, Warum ich so gute Bücher schreibe*, 5 (Why I Write Such Good
     Books), KSA 6, p. 306: *Liebe – in ihren Mitteln der Krieg, in ihrem Grunde der
     Todhass der Geschlechter.*

20   Nietzsche, *Nachgelassene Fragmente* (Posthumous Fragments) 1884–5, KSA
     11, p. 472 [*N.B. Ein Weib will Mutter sein; und wenn sie das nicht will, ob sie
     es schon sein könnte, so gehört sie beinahe in's Zuchthaus, so groß ist dann ge-
     wöhnlich ihre innewendige Entartung*]. *Der Wille zur Macht, The Will to Power*
     was first published under the supervision of Elisabeth Förster-Nietzsche as vol.
     XV of the *Grossoktavausgabe*. The material is now available in KSA 11 and
     12.

21   Carol Diethe, 'Nietzsche Emasculated: Postmodern Readings', in *Ecce Opus –
     Nietzsche Revisions in the Twentieth Century*, eds. Rüdiger Görner and Duncan
     Large, Vandenhoeck and Ruprecht, 2003, pp. 51–63, passim.

22   Johann Jacob Bachofen, *Das Mutterrecht*, Stuttgart, Krais and Hoffmann, 1861,
     p. XXVII (Introduction).

23   *Also sprach Zarathustra, Thus Spoke Zarathustra*, [Z], 1883–5.

24   'Franziska zu Reventlow' in Diethe, *Towards Emancipation: German Women
     Writers of the Nineteenth Century*, New York and Oxford, Berghahn, 1998, pp.
     190–7, p. 192.

25   See R.J. Roteuscher, *Die Wiederkunft des Dionysos: Der naturmystische Ir-
     rationalismus in Deutschland*, Bern, A. Francke, 1947, pp. 223ff.

26   Steven Aschheim, *The Nietzsche Legacy in Germany 1890–1990*, Berkeley, Los
     Angeles and Oxford, University of California Press, 1992, pp. 79ff.

27   On matriarchy in Bachofen, see Uwe Wesel, *Der Mythos vom Matriarchat*,
     Frankfurt, Suhrkamp, 1980.

28   See Paul Bishop, *The Dionysian Self: C. G. Jung's Reception of Friedrich
     Nietzsche*, Berlin and New York, de Gruyter, 1995, p. 205, on the anima as 'the
     archetype of life'. According to Bishop, 'Jung developed the idea that the way
     out of the modern psychological impasse is *via* the archetypes, and in particular,
     that of the Anima', p. 200.

29   J.J. Bachofen, *Das Mutterrecht*, p. VIII. On the 'Moon Lady', see: Carol Diethe, *Some Aspects of Distorted Sexuality in German Expressionist Drama*, New York, Lang 1988, pp. 129–46.

30   Otto Weininger, *Letzte Aphorismen* (Last Aphorisms), in *Über die Letzten Dinge* (On Final Things), Vienna and Leipzig, Braumüller, 1912 (1993), p. 177.

31   Kundry refuses to be 'saved' by Parsifal, since she will not or cannot be 'chaste'; hence, there is no place for her in God's kingdom and she must die. Weininger, 'Zum Parsifal' (On Parsifal), in *Über die Letzten Dinge*, p. 89.

32   Otto Weininger, *Geschlecht und Charakter* (Sex and Character), Vienna, Braumüller, 1926 (1903), p. 298.

33   *Geschlecht und Charakter*, p. 270.

34   *Z I, Von alten und jungen Weiblein* (Of Old and Young Women), KSA 4, p. 84: *Alles am Weibe ist ein Räthsel, und alles am Weibe hat Eine Lösung: sie heisst Schwangerschaft* [Everything about woman is a riddle and everything about woman has one solution: it's called pregnancy]. We are justified in assuming that Nietzsche agrees with this remark (strategically placed in Zarathustra's mouth) because he returns to the subject in *Ecce Homo, Warum ich so gute Bücher schreibe*, 5, *Die Schlechtweggekommenen* (The Ill-Born): *Hat man meine Antwort auf die Frage gehört, wie man ein Weib kuriert – erlöst? Man macht ihm ein Kind* [Have you heard my answer to the question how one cures a woman – 'saves' her? You make her pregnant].

35   Weininger, 'Über Henrik Ibsen und seine Dichtung "Peer Gynt"' (On Henrik Ibsen and his Play 'Peer Gynt'), in *Über die Letzten Dinge*, p. 27, n 2.

36   *Geschlecht und Charakter*, p. 276.

37   *Über Henrik Ibsen und seine Dichtung 'Peer Gynt'*, p. 47, footnote.

38   As Paul Weindling has pointed out in *Health, Race and German Politics Between National Unification and Nazism* (1989), pp. 377f, 'the German eugenics movement was fundamentally two-edged: on the one hand the intentions of many eugenicists were genuinely reformist. They wished to relieve the burden of moral guilt and social pressures on groups such as homosexuals. The choice of a scientific strategy had points of weakness, since once racial categories permeated science, then science could change from a means of emancipation to a justification for persecution'.

39   *EH, Warum ich so gute Bücher schreibe*, 5: *Die Schlechtweggekommenen* (The Ill-Born), KSA 6, p. 306.

40   *Zur Genealogie der Moral* On the Genealogy of Morality III, 26; KSA 5, p. 406: *[...] ich wüsste Nichts, was so sehr ekel machte, als solch ein 'objektiver' Lehnstuhl, solch ein duftender Genüssling, vor der Historie, halb Pfaff, halb Satyr, Parfum Renan, der schon mit dem hohen Falsett seines Beifalls verräth, was ihm abgeht, wo es ihm abgeht, wo in diesem Falle die Parze ihre grausame Schere ach! allzu chirugisch gehandhabt hat!* [I know of nothing as nauseating as this type of 'objective' armchair scholar and perfumed sensualist towards history, half-priest, half-satyr, Renan-scented, who reveals, by the mere falsetto

of his approval, all that he lacks, where he lacks it, where the fates in his case have been, alas! rather too surgical with their cruel scissors!]. The section ends with a crude reference to masturbation: [...] *hier thut Eins nur Noth, eben die Hand, eine unbefangene, sehr unbefangene Hand* [...] [one thing only is needful, a hand, an uninhibited, very uninhibited hand], p. 408.

41   As Brigitte Helm has recently pointed out: 'The Course of History did not allow feminist discourse to resolve its ambivalence toward Nietzsche.' See 'Combating Misogyny? Responses to Nietzsche by Turn-of-the Century German Feminists', *Journal of Nietzsche Studies*, 27, Spring 2004, pp. 64–84, p. 65.

42   Helene Stöcker, 'Unsere Umwertung der Werte' (1897) (Our Revaluation of Values), reprinted in *Die Liebe und die Frauen*, Frankfurt, Sauerländer, 1905, pp. 6–18, p. 7.

43   Z I; KSA 4, p. 85.

44   Helene Stöcker, 'Nietzsches Frauenfeindschaft' (Nietzsche's Misogyny) (1901) in *Die Liebe und die Frauen*, (Love and Women) pp. 65–74, p. 72.

45   *Nietzsches Frauenfeindschaft*, p. 73.

46   Helene Stöcker, *Bund für Mutterschutz* (League For the Protection of Mothers), relaunch manifesto, Berlin, Pan, 1905, p. 20.

47   *Bund für Mutterschutz*, p. 5.

48   The list includes Iwan Bloch, Max Marcuse, Alfred Ploetz, Bruno Wille, Ricarda Huch, Isolde Kurz, Gabriele Reuter, Ellen Key, Lily Braun, Hedwig Dohm. Adele Schreiber and Marie Stritt.

49   Helene Lange, 'Feministische Gedankenanarchie' (Feminist Intellectual Anarchy) in *Kampfzeiten: Aufsätze und Reden aus vier Jahrzehnten* (The Years of Struggle: Essays and Talks from Four Decades), Berlin, Herbig, 1828, 2 vols, II, pp. 1–8, p. 3. The article was first published in *Die neue Rundschau* (The New Review), 1908, and helped to discredit the *Bund für Mutterschutz*. Nietzsche is also attacked for encouraging libertinism on page 1.

50   *Feministische Gedankenanarchie*, p. 8.

51   Helene Lange, 'Die Frauenbewegung und die moderne Ehekritik' (The Women's Movement and the Modern Critique of Marriage) in Gertrud Bäumer, ed, *Frauenbewegung und Sexualethik: Beiträge zur modernen Sexualethik* (Women's Movement and Sexual Ethics: Essays on the Modern Sexual Ethic), Heilbronn, Salzer, 1909, pp. 17–102, pp. 87f.

52   *Feministische Gedankenanarchie*, p. 4.

53   Richard J. Evans, *The Feminist Movement in Germany 1894–1933*, London and Beverly Hills, Sage, 1976, p. 137.

54   Helene Stöcker, *Zehn Jahre Mutterschutz* (Ten Years of the Society for the Protection of Mothers), Hanover, Haag Verlag, 1915, p. 54.

55   Diethe, *Nietzsche's Sister and the Will to Power: A Biography of Elisabeth Förster-Nietzsche*, Urbana and Chicago, University of Illinois Press, 2003, pp. 122f.

56 Helene Stöcker, *Lieben oder Hassen?* (Love or Hate?) Hanover, Haag Verlag, 1915, p. 15.

57 *Lieben oder Hassen?*, p. 119: *Wir wollen nicht vergessen, daß derselbe Nietzsche, den man jetzt, besonders im Ausland, als den intellektuellen Urheber dieses Krieges neben Bernhardi nennt, und der mit Aufopferung seiner Gesundheit als schweizerischer Professor dem Vaterlande 1870/71 als freiwilliger Krankenpfleger zu dienen versucht hat, doch zugleich der stärkste Kämpfer gegen den überheblichen undeutschen Geist war, der sich nach dem Siege 1870/71 im Siegestaumel der Gründerjahre in Deutschland breit machte.*

58 Nietzsche to Carl von Gersdorff, 20.10.1870, KSB, vol. 3, pp. 147ff. Actually, Nietzsche only spent a month in active service (12 August–11 September 1870), but he found that quite bad enough.

59 H. von Schrenck-Notzing, *Die Suggestions-Therapie* (Suggestion-Therapy), Stuttgart, Ferdinand Enke, 1892, p. 32: *Die häufigste Form leichterer Formen von Nymphomanie ist die Prostitution* [The most common form of mild degrees of nymphomania is prostitution].

60 At the 1903 meeting in Berlin of the *Internationale Abolitionistische Föderation, Deutscher Zweig* (International Abolitionist Federation), (an offshoot of the *Verein Frauenwohl* or Society for Women's Welfare), Helene Stöcker argued in favour of contraception. Since the Abolitionist programme was essentially dedicated to sexual repression in the name of 'morality', this put her on a collision course with the German branch of the movement which, under the leadership of Anna Pappritz, argued that men ought to be as chaste as women, and disapproved of birth control methods.

61 See Diethe, 'Lou Andreas-Salomé and Female Sexuality' *in German Women Writers 1900–1933*, ed. Brian Keith-Smith, Lampeter, Mellen, 1993, pp. 25–40 passim.

62 By the same token, woman can retain her virginal characteristics even when sexually mature. Lou Andreas-Salomé, 'Der Mensch als Weib' (Human Being as Woman), in *Die Erotik: Vier Aufsätze* (Eroticism: Four Essays), ed. Ernst Pfeiffer, Frankfurt and Berlin, Ullstein, 1985 (1899), pp. 7–44, p. 18.

63 Salomé possibly aborted a child by her lover Zemek (Friedrich Pineles). She did not allow her husband to consummate their marriage, but had several long-standing affairs. See Angela Livingstone, *Lou Andreas-Salomé*, London, Gordon Fraser, 1897, p. 131.

64 Michaela Wiener-Bangard and Ursula Welsch, *Lou Andreas-Salomé: 'Wie ich Dich liebe, Rätselleben': Eine Biographie* (Lou Andreas-Salomé: 'How I Love You, Life of Riddles': A Biography), Leipzig, Reklam, 2002, p. 88.

65 *Der Mensch als Weib*, p. 18.

66 Hedwig Dohm, *Reaktion in der Frauenbewegung* (Reaction in the Women's Movement), *Die Zukunft* (The Future), 1899, pp. 279–91, p. 197.

67 *Der Mensch als Weib*, pp. 16f.

68   Salomé, 'Gedanken über das Liebesproblem' (Thoughts on the Problem of
      Love) (1900), in *Die Erotik: Vier Aufsätze*, pp. 45–82, p. 54.
69   Salomé, 'Die Erotik' (1910) in *Die Erotik: Vier Aufsätze*, pp. 83–146, p. 129.
70   See Diethe, 'Lou Salomé's interpretation of Nietzsche's Religiosity' in *Journal
      of Nietzsche Studies*, 19, Spring 2000, pp. 80–8, pp. 82ff.
71   Nietzsche's friends Franz Overbeck and Erwin Rohde were dismayed by
      Salomé's arrogance in setting herself up as judge over Nietzsche. See Franz
      Overbeck and Erwin Rohde, *Briefwechsel* (Correspondence), Berlin and New
      York, de Gruyter, 1990, p179 (Overbeck to Rohde, 9.3.1895), p. 182 (Rohde's
      reply, 17.3.1895).
72   Weininger, *Über Henrik Ibsen und seine Dichtung 'Peer Gynt'*, p. 32: *Gerade
      bei Nietzsche entsprang der Haß gegen sich selbst dem stärksten Willen zur
      Bejahung. In ihm konnte darum dieser Haß schöpferisch und tragisch werden
      [...] Darum ist er nie zur Religion angelangt: als er das Leben am leiden-
      schaftlichsten bejahte, da verneinte das Leben ihn – jenes Leben nämlich, das
      sich nicht belügen läßt* [Self-hatred arose precisely in Nietzsche out of the
      strongest will to affirmation. Therefore this hatred could become either creative
      or tragic in his case [...] So he never arrived at religion: when he affirmed life
      most enthusiastically, life rejected him – that very life which allows no self
      delusion].
73   Lou Andreas-Salomé, *Friedrich Nietzsche in seinen Werken* (Friedrich
      Nietzsche in His Works), Vienna, Carl Konegen, 1891, p. 38: *In der That ist
      eine echte Nietzsche-Studie in ihrer Hauptsache eine religionspsychologische
      Studie [...] Seine ganze Entwicklung ging gewissermassen davon aus, dass er
      den Glauben verlor.* [In fact, a genuine study of Nietzsche is in the main a study
      of the psychology of religion [...] The starting point for his whole development
      was to a certain extent the fact that he lost his faith].
74   *Friedrich Nietzsche in seinen Werken*, p. 40. [*Die Gottessehnsucht wird in ihrer
      Qual zu einem Drang der Gott-Schöpfung, und dieser musste sich notwendig in
      Selbstvergottung äussern*].
75   For example, see Lou Salomé: 'Psychosexualität', the fourth essay in *Die Erotik*,
      pp. 147–83.
76   Sarah Kofman, *Nietzsche et la scène philosophique* (Nietzsche and the Philoso-
      phical Scene), Paris, Inédit, 1979, p. 298: *ne sont-elles pas symptomatiques
      d'un amour profound pour les femmmes, qui l'ont toutes abandonné?*
77   *GS* II, 72: *Die Mütter* [The Mothers].
78   *Der Mensch als Weib*, p. 22. Also *Die Erotik*, pp. 104–7, section entitled 'Die
      Erotik und Kunst' ('Eroticism and Art').
79   Helene Lange, *Die Frauenbewegung und die moderne Ehekritik*, pp. 17–102,
      pp. 87f.
80   Key, in common with many German feminists of her day, decided to revise
      Nietzsche's statements on women to make them palatable: 'The finest young
      girls of today are penetrated by the Nietzschean idea, that marriage is the

combined will of two people to create a new being greater than themselves. But their joy does not consist in the fact "that the man wills"; they are themselves "will", and above all they have the right to choose the right father for their children, not only for their own sake but for the sake of the children.' Ellen Key, *The Woman Movement* (1912), published in *The Sexuality Debates*, ed. Sheila Jeffreys, London and New York, Routledge, 1987, pp. 573–601, p. 573.

81   Gertrud Bäumer, 'Das sexualethische Chaos' (The Chaos in Sexual Ethics) in *Die Frau im neuen Lebensraum* (Woman in Contemporary Life), Berlin, Herbig, 1931, pp. 87f.

82   George L. Mosse, *The Crisis of German Ideology: Intellectual Origins of the Third Reich*, London, Weidenfeld and Nicholson, 1966 – still the best overview.

83   See Michael Burleigh and Wolfgang Wippermann, *The Racial State: Germany 1933–1945*, Cambridge, Cambridge University Press, 1991, pp. 242–66, 'Women in the Third Reich'.

84   Koonz argues that Aryan women at the beginning of the Third Reich were more complacent than ill-intentioned: 'Whatever their views about men and politics, middle-class women generally believed they could establish their own harmonious "living room" (*Lebensraum*) cleansed of diversity and dissent within national life'. Claudia Koonz, 'The Competition for Women's Lebensraum', in Renate Briedenthal, Atina Grossman and Marion Kaplan, *When Biology Became Destiny: Women in Weimar and Nazi Germany*, New York, Monthly Review Press, 1984, pp. 199–236, p. 200.

85   *Jenseits von Gut and Böse*, VII, *Unsere Tugenden*, KSA 5, pp. 151–78; *Beyond Good and Evil*, VII, Our Values.

86   *Nietzsche's Sister and the Will to Power*, p. 113 (on feminism) and pp. 237–40 (on nationalism).

JAMES WILSON

Nietzsche and Equality

During my lifetime I have dedicated myself to this struggle of the African
people. I have fought against white domination, and I have fought against black
domination. I have cherished the ideal of a democratic and free society in which
all persons live together in harmony and with equal opportunities. It is an ideal
which I hope to live for and to achieve. But if needs be, it is an ideal for which I
am prepared to die. Nelson Mandela[1]

[...] what they sing – 'equal rights', 'free society', 'no more masters and no
more servants' – has no allure for us. We hold it absolutely undesirable that a
realm of justice and concord should be established on earth (because it would
certainly be the realm of the most profound levelling down to mediocrity and
chinoiserie); we are delighted by all who love, as we do, danger, war, and
adventure; who refuse to compromise, to be captured, to reconcile, to be
castrated; we consider ourselves conquerors [...] Nietzsche, *Gay Science* 377

The idea that there is something ethically corrupt or ethically cor-
rupting about Nietzsche's work is an anathema to Nietzsche scholars
today. Although there are some serious moral philosophers, such as
Philippa Foot, Jonathan Glover and Martha Nussbaum[2] who write
about Nietzsche whilst finding his position ethically deplorable, most
Nietzsche scholars tend to focus rather more heavily on his positive
aspects. This means that negative ethical assessments of Nietzsche
now tend to be relatively few and far between, and given that they
tend to be composed by people who know the texts less well than the
dedicated Nietzsche scholars, these criticisms can usually be swatted
away quite easily.[3]

So is there still anything ethically problematic about Nietzsche's
work that we must face up to and disown? The assumption in play
amongst Nietzsche scholars seems to be that there is not. I think we
can detect three broad camps:

Camp A: there is nothing revealed in a sensitive interpretation of Nietzsche's views that need count as ethically problematic.

Camp B: the ethical views of Nietzsche that are ethically problematic are of only minor concern (akin, for example to Aristotle's defence of slavery), so that the interpretation of his ethical contribution can sideline them.

Camp C: one need not take an ethical stance on the rightness or wrongness of Nietzsche's ethical views: it is enough to study them, and to find them challenging and interesting.

My interest is, if you like, in forming a Camp D: composed of anyone who thinks that, despite Nietzsche's undoubted interest and brilliance as an ethical thinker, at the deepest level we must think of him as an *opponent*. For what he is trying to achieve is to dislodge the idea of the equality of all human beings from its central place in our ethical thinking; but to allow this to happen would be a deep mistake.

There are two halves to this essay. The first half sets up the problem for the Nietzsche interpreter: the moral equality of human beings is the basic idea through which we (now) think about morality; and Nietzsche's views on the nature of human ethical life commit him to opposing the moral equality of human beings. Given that Nietzsche's views bring him into direct conflict with the most basic principle of morality that we have, it is implausible to hold to a Camp B or a Camp C interpretation. The Camp B interpretation must wildly underestimate either the centrality of the idea of the moral equality of human beings to our interpretation of morality or the extent to which Nietzsche opposes this ideal. The Camp C interpretation imports a failure of moral nerve; a failure to condemn what ought to be condemned. So we face a straight choice between Camp D and Camp A: between supporting the moral equality of human beings against Nietzsche's attack on it, or supporting Nietzsche against the moral equality of human beings. You cannot serve two masters: you must choose between Nietzsche and the idea of the moral equality of human beings.

The second half of the essay examines Nietzsche's critique of moral egalitarianism in more detail. Nietzsche's critique, I suggest, is composed of two parts: a negative and a positive. The negative part (the *slave morality thesis*) argues that (a) we should make a distinction between *moralities of affirmation* and *moralities of* denial;[4] and (b) all moralities which have the equality of human beings as their fundamental value are moralities of denial. The positive part, which, following Nietzsche, I shall call the *pathos of distance thesis* claims that human greatness requires a feeling of great height from which the great person looks down in lofty contempt on others.

I shall argue that it is false to claim that *all* moralities which have the equality of human beings as their fundamental value are moralities of denial, and that the pathos of distance thesis is either false or question begging or both. Hence there is no reason, even being as generous to Nietzsche as we can be, to think his critique should force us to give up moral egalitarianism. However, even if not *all* egalitarian moralities are moralities of denial, it is certainly true that some are, which leaves us with a very difficult question: how do we ensure that *our* belief in the moral equality of human beings forms part of a morality of affirmation rather than one of denial?

The Conflict between Nietzsche and Egalitarianism

The Ubiquity of Egalitarianism

The concept of moral equality – the idea that every human being has a right to be treated *as an equal* to all other human beings and has a corresponding duty to treat others as equals – forms the horizon within which we debate about what is morally right and what is just.[5] Debate, both within philosophy and outside, focuses on what the best *conception* of moral equality is: what does it mean to really treat one another as equals, rather than whether it is in fact a good thing for the concept of equality to play such a central role in our moral and political thinking.[6]

This has by no means always been the case; but the depth and pervasiveness of our commitment to it can be seen by the fact that when moral equality *is* challenged we find it difficult to take the challenger's argument seriously. (We simply do not take seriously any arguments that would defend slavery, or show that it is better that certain groups of people's interests (Blacks, Jews) *not* be taken into account when deciding what to do.)

One reason for this may be the ubiquity (at least within moral and political philosophy) of reflective equilibrium as a model of ethical thinking. The model of reflective equilibrium requires that we test our moral theories against our considered judgements – that is, judgements about which we are most confident that we are not judging wrongly.[7] The judgement that we ought, in some sense, to treat one another as equals, is now our most fundamental considered moral judgement. Any theory of right and wrong which is in disagreement with such a deep and fundamental part of our intuitive moral framework will tend, if we apply the standard of reflective equilibrium, to discredit itself through this very fact.

Thus, if we stick to the model of reflective equilibrium, it is rather difficult to set up a useful confrontation between Nietzsche and the views of someone who takes for granted the moral equality of human beings (someone who in Kymlicka's words stands on the 'egalitarian plateau.')[8] For his part, Nietzsche is simply not bothered with debates which seem important to anyone who believes that the concept of equality should play a central role – such as whether a utilitarian or a Rawlsian society better fulfils the promise of treating human beings as equals. Conversely, for the moral egalitarian, Nietzsche, by the very fact of not adhering to the principle of moral equality, puts himself beyond the pale.

In this essay I do not appeal to our moral intuitions or our considered moral judgements in an attempt to refute Nietzsche. Instead I look at Nietzsche's arguments against egalitarianism from a perspective that is friendly to Nietzsche's: one which allows that a scepticism about the value of our values is necessary; but which argues that *pace* Nietzsche, moral egalitarianism survives such a searching examination.

Nietzsche's Objections to Egalitarianism

Nietzsche puts forward his objections to egalitarianism most clearly in the chapter 'What is Noble' of *Beyond Good and Evil.*[9] His basic objection requires us to compare two different types of society: societies where aristocratic values predominate, and societies where non-aristocratic values predominate. A system of values is aristocratic if it maintains *orders of rank*: that is, if it maintains that there is a natural pecking order of human beings, and that those at the top of the pecking order are superior *as human beings* to those at the bottom of the pecking order. Non-aristocratic values systems are egalitarian value systems: they believe that there is no *order of rank*: all human beings are equal *as human beings.*[10]

We are so steeped in non-aristocratic values that it is easy for us to miss what Nietzsche has in mind. In Nietzsche's conception of an aristocratic society, those lower on the order of rank are not deemed important for their own sake. They are entirely expendable: creation of beings of the highest rank enjoys a lexical priority over the comfort or flourishing of those of lower rank.[11] Nietzsche's argument aims to persuade us that societies in which aristocratic value systems hold sway are necessary for the flourishing of the kind of people he is interested in (those of higher rank):

> Every elevation of the type 'man' has hitherto been the work of an aristocratic society – and so it will always be: a society which believes in a long scale of orders of rank and differences of worth between man and man and needs slavery in some sense or other. Without the *pathos of distance* such as develops from the incarnate differences of classes, from the ruling caste's constant looking out and looking down on subjects and instruments and from its equally constant exercise of obedience and command, its holding down and holding at a distance, that other, more mysterious pathos could not have developed either, that longing for an ever-increasing widening of distance within the soul itself, the formation of every higher, rarer, more remote, tenser, more comprehensive states, in short precisely the elevation of the type 'man', the continual self-overcoming of man. [BGE 257]

Conversely, societies in which egalitarian value systems predominate thwart the creation of the kind of people Nietzsche is interested in:

To refrain from mutual injury, mutual violence, mutual exploitation, to equate one's own will with that of another: this may in a certain rough sense become good manners between individuals if the conditions for it are present (namely if their strength and value standards are in fact similar and they both belong to *one* body). As soon as there is a desire to take this principle further, however, and if possible even as the *fundamental principle of society*, it at once reveals itself for what it is: as the will to the *denial* of life, as the principle of dissolution and decay. [BGE 259]

Nietzsche, then, is attempting to establish a two-way link between the prevalence of norms of moral equality and human flourishing: on the one hand, human beings can only reach their highest potential in highly stratified societies which bow before order of rank; and on the other egalitarian values have a deadening effect on life when they come to have precedence.

There is a long running dispute about what Nietzsche intends the metaphysical status of these claims to be: does he think that those he denominates as 'higher' really are better in some objective sense than those he denominates as 'lower', or does he merely think of himself as expressing his own perspective – one which others (particularly those whom he has denominated as 'lower') may disagree with if they wish? But this dispute is not to the point here. What is important for our purposes is how *we* interpret our values, not how Nietzsche thinks about his values: *we* take the belief in the moral equality of human beings to be something that *everyone* should acknowledge.[12] Nietzsche's stance is incompatible with the principle of moral equality regardless of whether we take his claims about the badness of egalitarian value systems to be put forward as objectively true, or as only perspectively so.[13]

Four Approaches to Nietzsche's Anti-egalitarianism

What attitude should we take to Nietzsche's anti-egalitarianism? I think, as I laid out earlier, we have four options. We can either (a) approve; (b) attempt to downplay the importance of it, but potentially disapprove of it; (c) not pass ethical judgement; or (d) disapprove. Any reasons to approve of Nietzsche's anti-egalitarianism would have to be parasitic on the soundness of Nietzsche's views. These we shall examine in part two. The rest of this section aims to show that positions (b) and (c) are untenable.

I shall begin with the claim that we can safely downplay the importance of Nietzsche's anti-egalitarianism. Someone who wants to hold this view might object as follows:

(1) Nietzsche is not opposed to equality per se: he is willing to admit that equality can sometimes be a useful value.[14] He is opposed to equality only when it is put forward as the fundamental value.

(2) Nietzsche is an esoteric moralist: he is not demanding (or even suggesting) that *everyone* should read his writings. He wants to be read (and to have an effect on) only by a few – the nascent higher types.[15] As for those who are not 'higher types', he is willing to allow their ideas about morality to carry on undisturbed.[16]

(3) Where Nietzsche is opposed to equality, this is not because he thinks that there is too much respect and consideration in the world, and not enough domination and humiliation; but because the prevalence of egalitarian *values* will tend to thwart the flourishing of higher men.[17]

(4) Given the central place of (a) freedom from resentment, and (b) acceptance of one's fate in Nietzsche's ethical system it seems plausible to suggest that a flourishing life of a higher type is likely to be self-contained and will not in fact lead to very much treating others as less than equal.

(1) and (2) do not succeed in lessening the impact of the disagreement with Nietzsche. This is because of the nature of the value that *we* place on equality. (1) Equality for us is the centre of morality and so if one's belief is only that equality can be valuable in *some* contexts then you are still in fundamental disagreement with the principle of moral equality; and you are still putting yourself beyond the pale. (2) The claim that the moral equality of human beings is a useful idea only for the weak, whilst the strong should adopt a different approach to thinking about values, also puts you beyond the pale: the moral equality of human beings purports to be a universal value. So neither suggestion reduces the gulf between Nietzsche and what we take to be morally decent. (3) Is based on a somewhat contentious reading of

Nietzsche. Even if we accept this reading, I don't see that it does much to reduce the conflict between Nietzsche and moral egalitarianism: even if Nietzsche objects only to the *effects* of egalitarian values on higher types and not to the effects that egalitarian values have on those who benefit from them, then his so objecting would still put him beyond the pale. (4) There are two problems with the claim that living the life of a Nietzsche 'higher type' will not conflict living the life of a moral egalitarian: one empirical, the other conceptual. First, given the way in which Nietzsche insists on the *differences* between people, it seems highly implausible to argue that every higher type is going to find his or her personal maximum in a peaceful and self-contained manner. Some people (Cesare Borgia or Napoleon, say) may just be built for dominating others rather than sublimating this drive into a shaping of the self. (And, of course it doesn't take very many tyrants to make the world a much worse place). Second, even in the limiting case where pursuit of the individual's flourishing *never* interfered with equal relations with their fellow human beings, this would still be a *contingent* fact. And from the perspective of moral egalitarianism it is wrong to hold principles which do not count others as equals even if in ordinary circumstances these principles do not lead to different actions from genuinely egalitarian principles.

So I take it that it is untenable to claim that Nietzsche is not in direct contradiction to our main moral value.

Avoiding taking a Moral Stance on Nietzsche's Work

This leaves the possibility that, despite the fact that *Nietzsche* is clearly opposed to the idea of moral equality, and the fact that *we* are firmly committed to it, we, as scholars and as Nietzsche interpreters do not need to take a moral stance on Nietzsche's views.

The first thing that we should note is how far this position is from Nietzsche's view of philosophy. For Nietzsche, real philosophy is about the creation of value systems: the philosopher proper is a commander and a law giver, who seeks to determine where mankind should be going. So if we were to approach Nietzsche's work in a way that *he* would regard as genuinely philosophical, then we would treat his work as merely a 'means, an instrument, a hammer' [BGE 211] as we reached for the future and created new values. So avoiding taking a moral stance can at best be true to the letter, but not the spirit of Nietzsche's philosophy.

Second, treating the interpretation of Nietzsche's texts as a purely scholarly endeavour without any implications for what we *ought* to think about morality diminishes both Nietzsche and ourselves. It diminishes Nietzsche, because it treats him merely as a figure in the history of ideas, rather than as someone who is making serious claims about how we should live, claims which contradict and seek to undermine what we believe in the rest of our lives, and who therefore sets us the task of determining whether what he says is *true*. It diminishes us if we are unwilling to challenge views we take to be wrong.

So much for the attempt to avoid taking a moral stance on Nietzsche's work. This leaves us with a straight fight between Camp A and Camp D: we can either approve or disapprove of Nietzsche's anti-egalitarianism. We cannot simply ignore it.

Why Nietzsche's Anti-Egalitarianism is Unconvincing

Nietzsche's views on morality, whether we interpret them in a objectivist or a subjectivist way, presuppose that it is only the flourishing of 'higher types' which matters. This of course is a claim that the egalitarian denies. But even if we grant Nietzsche's claim for the sake of argument, it does not follow that the right kind of system of values and the right kind of society to have is one which systematically disregards the claims of 'lower' types. For it might be the case that higher types require an *egalitarian* society to flourish; that it is aristocratic (inegalitarian) societies which stifle the flourishing of nascent higher types.

Nietzsche, of course denies this. There are two factors driving Nietzsche in this direction: (a) a claim about the nature of value systems that take moral equality as their fundamental value, namely that they are based on resentment (*the slave morality thesis*) and (b), the claim that human greatness requires a feeling of great height from which the great person looks down in lofty contempt on others (*the pathos of distance thesis*).

I shall argue that neither part is convincing. The slave morality thesis has the virtue of alerting the moral egalitarian to a potential problem: *if* belief in the moral equality of human beings were invariably based on resentment, then moral egalitarianism would indeed be highly suspect. But this is not the case: belief in the moral equality of human beings need not be reactive or resentful, and can be just as affirmative of human life as the master morality adhered to by those Nietzsche would describe as 'higher types'. Hence the slave morality thesis provides no reason to object to moral egalitarianism as such. As we shall see, the pathos of distance thesis depends for what plausibility it has on the slave morality thesis: without it, it can be seen to be either false or question begging, or both.

So Nietzsche's critique does nothing to force us to give up on moral egalitarianism; but nonetheless, Nietzsche's critique leaves us with a problem: how do we combine our belief in the equality of all human beings with a morality that is affirmative rather than denying?

Moralities of Affirmation and Moralities of Denial

Nietzsche's argument requires us to agree to his distinction between *master* and *slave* moralities. Master moralities are those which are formed by higher types out of an overflowing self-confidence and as a means of glorifying their own positive traits.[18] Slave moralities are those which are created by lower types in reaction to their feelings of powerlessness and their resentment at the higher types' superfluity of strength. Slave morality is always negative: it starts not with anything that it takes to be good and worthwhile, but with what is bad and to be avoided.[19] And it is a jealous and envious form of evaluation: at base, once decoded, slave morality's evaluations come to the following: 'We weak people are just weak; it is good to do nothing *for which we are not strong enough.*' [GM I.13]

I shall use the phrases 'moralities of affirmation' and 'moralities of denial' in preference to 'master moralities' and 'slave moralities'. The terms 'master' and 'slave' moralities run together claims about the type of person who creates a value, with the psychological effect of holding a value and thus imply that the psychological effects of holding a value are determined by the power position of those who hold it. But this begs the question against the position I shall be arguing for, namely that the value of the equality of human beings is both a value for everyone, and (in some cases at least) has the psychological profile that Nietzsche associates with a master morality. Hence I shall split the slave morality thesis into two claims: (1) there is an important distinction to be drawn between *moralities of affirmation* and *moralities of denial.* Moralities of affirmation make the life of the person living them more worthwhile to that person: in a morality of affirmation, the performance of actions that are mandated by the morality increase the joy and the meaning that the agent performing them has in living.[20] Moralities of denial make the life of the person living them *less* worthwhile for that person: in a morality of denial, the actions that are mandated by morality must be motivated by (and in turn tend to reinforce) feelings of guilt, shame, resentment, self-punishment and so on. (2) All moralities which make the equality of human beings their fundamental value are moralities of denial.

I agree that there is a useful distinction to be drawn between moralities of affirmation and moralities of denial. And I am also willing to admit that, other things being equal, we have good reason to choose moralities of affirmation, and shun moralities of denial. Hence *if* all moralities which make the equality of human beings their fundamental value are moralities of denial, then Nietzsche's critique of moral egalitarianism exposes a real problem.

I take it that it is true to claim that *some* moralities which have the equality of human beings as their fundamental value are moralities of denial. (If this were not the case then Nietzsche's criticisms in the first essay of the *Genealogy of Morality* would not hit home in the way they do.) But if it is only *some* and not *all* moralities which have the equality of human beings as their fundamental value that are moralities of denial, then Nietzsche's criticism will do nothing to show that moral egalitarianism *per se* is flawed.

In what follows I will argue that even Nietzsche must admit that it is false to claim that all moralities which have the equality of human beings as their fundamental value are moralities of denial. I shall attempt to do this by providing a counter-example: a conception of the moral equality of human beings which is also a morality of affirmation. I suspect that this account will not be equally acceptable to all those on the egalitarian plateau. But other egalitarians will, I hope concede two things: first that the egalitarian requires *some* sort of reply to Nietzsche's slave morality thesis;[21] and second that the account I shall give is at least a plausible candidate for such a reply.

An Affirmative Account of Moral Equality

I shall argue that Kant's conception of moral equality makes the equality of human beings a morality of affirmation, rather than denial; and so, given the availability of Kantian accounts of equality, it is plainly false to claim that *all* moralities which place the moral equality of human beings at their centre are moralities of denial.

The most obvious way to envisage the equality of human beings is by analogy to an equality of physical magnitude (as when we say two sticks are of equal length); that is, to imagine that the equality of human beings must consist in their possession of an *equal amount* of some feature. But Kant thinks about the equality of human beings differently. Human beings are said to be *equal*, rather, because *each* must be valued for his or her own sake: the equality lies in the *attitude* with which each must treat others and with which each may in turn expect to be treated by them. For Kant, this attitude is *respect*.

Kant suggests that the reason why we should treat one another with respect is that every human being has a particular type of value, namely a dignity, which we appropriately respond to by valuing that person for their own sake. And valuing the person for their own sake *is* respecting them.[22]

Nietzsche has two chief worries about moral equality: first, that moral equality must involve levelling-down 'higher types', and second, moral equality is based on a reactive morality of denial. Neither worry can gain any purchase on a conception of moral equality that takes the dignity of human beings as its centre.

First, if one adopts the dignity of human beings as the centre of one's system of valuation, then it is simply untrue to claim that this involves a levelling down of any potential 'higher types'. To accord someone a dignity is to value them *for their own sake*. To claim that every human being has a dignity is to claim that every human being should be valued for his or her own sake. Therefore, those whom Nietzsche considers to be higher types are also to be valued for their own sakes.[23]

Nor do the sorts of prohibitions and restrictions that are part and parcel of belief in the dignity of human beings do anything to show that what we have is a morality of denial, rather than affirmation. Rather such prohibitions, are merely the inevitable result of holding every human being to be valuable for his or her own sake. As Paul Ricoeur puts it:

> [Y]ou shall not take life, you shall not steal, you shall not kill, you shall not torture. In each case, morality replies to violence. And if the commandment cannot do otherwise than to take the form of a prohibition, this is precisely because of evil: to all the figures of evil responds the *no* of morality. On the level of the ethical aim, however, solicitude, as the mutual exchange of self-esteems, is affirmative through and through. This affirmation, which can well be termed original, is the hidden soul of the prohibition. It is what, ultimately, arms our indignation, that is, our rejection of *indignities* inflicted on others.[24]

So I take it that it is simply untrue that all conceptions of morality which place the moral equality of human beings at their centre are moralities of denial. But an important question remains, which I shall return to in the conclusion: to what extent is our belief in the moral equality of human beings *in fact* part of a morality of affirmation, and to what extent is it, perhaps despite our best intentions, part of a morality of denial?

The Pathos of Distance Thesis

The pathos of distance thesis looks weak unless it can call upon support from the slave morality thesis. For, suppose it were accepted that valuing other human beings as equals need not be a reactive and resentful mode of valuation, and can be the centre of a morality of affirmation. What reason would there remain to believe in the pathos of distance thesis? Any such reasons, obviously, could not depend on the claim that belief in moral egalitarianism is slavish; they would have to stem from some other positive virtue that non-egalitarian values are suppose to have.

Nietzsche's only reason in favour of the pathos of distance thesis which is independent of the slave morality thesis seems to be a claim about the structure of the self. Recall the following passage, which I quoted earlier:

> Without the *pathos of distance* such as develops from the incarnate differences of classes, from the ruling caste's constant looking out and looking down on subjects and instruments and from its equally constant exercise of obedience and command, its holding down and holding at a distance, that other, more mysterious pathos could not have developed either, that longing for an ever-increasing widening of distance within the soul itself, the formation of every higher, rarer, more remote, tenser, more comprehensive states, in short precisely the elevation of the type 'man', the continual self-overcoming of man. [BGE 257]

Here Nietzsche argues that depth and greatness of the soul comes from *looking down*. But even if we grant that that such an exalted contempt is *a* means of making one's soul deep and great, this does little to make the case for the stronger claim that exalted contempt is the *only* means of making one's soul deep and great.[25] Nietzsche's position requires this stronger claim. But this claim is false: leaving aside the question of greatness, it is obvious that human beings can become deeper, more individual through relationships of mutual respect and recognition.[26] And if we think in terms of 'greatness', what reason is there to think that love will be outshone by contempt in the creation of 'great' human beings?

Nietzsche might at this point object that it is *only* vertical relationships of contempt which are able to create the right sort of relationship to oneself. But I cannot see what reason he could have for saying this unless he wants to make the further claim that viewing other human beings with a lofty contempt *just is* an intrinsic part of the best human lives. But such a claim would beg the question: for there are a number of candidates for being 'great men' or 'higher types' who are quite able to lead their exemplary lives, and create new ways of looking at the world and of living in it without any touch of exalted contempt. Some examples might be Nelson Mandela, Socrates, William James, John Dewey.[27]

So it follows that the pathos of distance thesis has no separate plausibility.

Conclusion

We have seen that Nietzsche's criticisms of moral egalitarianism are unconvincing, in as much as there is at least one way of conceiving of moral equality according to which moral equality is a morality of affirmation. How should Nietzsche respond?

The first thing that Nietzsche would do is to point out that we should make a distinction between moralities that are affirmative in *theory* and those that are affirmative in *practice*. Someone could believe that their morality is one of affirmation, and even have a theory as to why their morality was indeed one of affirmation, but at the same time they could be wrong about this: indeed such self-deception is a hallmark of resentment. So it does not follow from anything that I have said that resentment-free moral egalitarianism is in fact possible.

This point is well taken, but if we descend to the level of individual psychology, then there do seem to be many people who are moral egalitarians, and whose moral egalitarianism is part of a morality of affirmation, rather than one of denial.[28] Nietzsche has two possible replies: first, he could simply bite the bullet and claim that, appearances to the contrary, even Nelson Mandela is secretly seething with resentment. But this seems desperate, absent some fairly powerful empirical evidence.

Second, and more promisingly, Nietzsche could concede that resentment-free egalitarianism is possible for some, but argue that this says something about the unusual physiology or psychological type of the resentment-free egalitarian, and it does nothing to show that resentment-free egalitarianism is possible, or even desirable for others.

The egalitarian will, I think, best reply to this claim by simply denying that resentment-free egalitarianism requires any special psychological or physiological type. But even leaving aside the doctrine of psychological types, we are each left with a number of searching questions: is *our* commitment to moral equality free of resentment and other negative emotions? And if it is not, is this because of something we could change (for example, by changing the way we think about our values), or is it something we are stuck with? And if our failure to be resentment-free egalitarians is something we are stuck with, does this undermine the plausibility of egalitarianism? Or should we simply admit that a large part of our moral consciousness is composed of a morality of denial, but argue it is nonetheless the best morality to have?[29]

References:
For a general bibliography of Nietzsche's works in German and English see end of volume.

Notes

1   From the speech he gave in court on his treason charge, April 20, 1964. He repeated the same words in his speech on his release after 27 years of incarceration.

2   See Philippa Foot 'Nietzsche's Immoralism' in Richard Schacht ed. *Nietzsche, Genealogy, Morality: Essays on Nietzsche's Genealogy of Morals*, Berkeley: University of California Press, 1994; Jonathan Glover, *Humanity: a Moral History of the Twentieth Century*, New Haven: Yale University Press 1999;

Martha Nussbaum 'Pity and Mercy: Nietzsche's Stoicism,' in Schacht, ed., *Nietzsche, Genealogy, Morality*; 'Is Nietzsche a Political Thinker', *International Journal of Philosophical Studies* 5, 1997, pp. 1–13.

3   See for example these characteristically pugnacious comments by Brian Leiter: 'Lack of 'scholarly caution' would be a charitable characterization of the work of those intent on excoriating Nietzsche's alleged 'political thought'... Nussbaum [in 'Is Nietzsche a Political Thinker?'] should remind us how readily Nietzsche inspires scholarly recklessness in the service of moral indignation.' *Nietzsche on Morality*, London: Routledge 2002, pp. 292–3.

4   I explain these terms of art later.

5   There are also some thinner principles of equality, for example, the principle of formal equality (namely the principle that like cases must be treated alike), and Aristotle's principle of proportional equality (namely that we should treat equals equally, and unequals unequally in proportion to their relevant differences). These do not entail the moral equality of all human beings (Aristotle's principle of proportional equality is compatible with his commitment to slavery for instance), and they are not incompatible with anything Nietzsche says. When I talk of equality and egalitarianism in this chapter I should be understood to be referring to the thicker principle of *moral* equality.

6   For this way of explaining the role of the concept/conception distinction and its relation to equality, see Dworkin, *Taking Rights Seriously*, Cambridge Mass: Harvard University Press, 1978, pp. 134–40, and Kymlicka, *Contemporary Political Philosophy*, (Oxford: Oxford University Press 2nd edition 2001, pp. 3–5. We can see claims such as Bentham's 'each person is to count for one, and no one for more than one' and Kant's 'Every man has a legitimate claim to respect from his fellow men and is *in turn* bound to respect every other' [*Metaphysics of Morals* p. 462, tr. Mary Gregor, Cambridge: Cambridge University Press 2nd edition 1996] as attempts to provide a conception of the concept of moral equality in the field of moral theory. Rawls's theory of justice as fairness, Nozick's entitlement theory and Dworkin's 'luck egalitarianism' provide leading conceptions of the concept of moral equality in political philosophy.

7   The idea of a considered judgement (and of course of reflective equilibrium) comes originally from Rawls: see the section 'Some remarks about Moral Theory', pp. 40–6 of *A Theory of Justice*, Oxford: Oxford University Press revised edition, 1999.

8   Will Kymlicka, *Contemporary Political Philosophy* 2nd ed. pp. 3–5.

9   A note on translations and abbreviations. Quotations from *Beyond Good and Evil* are from R.J. Hollingdale's translation (Harmondsworth: Penguin, 1973), except for one occasion (§30) where I preferred Kaufmann's translation (New York: Vintage, 1996), and are abbreviated as *BGE* plus the relevant section number. Quotations from *On the Genealogy of Morality* are from Carol Diethe's translation (ed. Keith Ansell-Pearson, Cambridge: Cambridge University Press, 1994), and are abbreviated as *GM* plus the relevant essay and section number.

Quotations from *The Gay Science* are from Josefine Nauckhoff's translation (ed. Bernard Williams, Cambridge: Cambridge University Press, 2001). Quotations from the *Will to Power* are from the R.J. Hollingdale and Walter Kaufmann edition (New York: Vintage, 1968), and are abbreviated as *WP* plus section number.

10   The non-aristocratic (egalitarian) society will, of course, agree that some human beings are better than others *in certain respects*, and that it can be morally legitimate to construct an order of rank for human beings in these particular respects. (For example, the golf handicapping system constructs an *order of rank*, according to which the better players are at the top and the worse players at the bottom.) But the egalitarian denies that it is possible or morally appropriate to attempt to rank people *as human beings*.

11   'The essential thing in a good and healthy aristocracy is, however, that it does *not* feel itself to be a function (of the monarchy or of the commonwealth) but as their *meaning* and supreme justification – that it therefore accepts with a good conscience the sacrifice of innumerable men who *for its sake* have to be suppressed and reduced to imperfect men, to slaves and instruments. Its fundamental faith must be that society should *not* exist for the sake of society but only as foundation and scaffolding upon which a select species of being is able to raise itself to its higher task and in general to a higher *existence*' [BGE 258].

12   As Nietzsche puts it, our belief in moral equality is one which says 'I am morality itself, and nothing is morality besides me!' [BGE 202].

13   This approach to conflicts between our moral values and others is influenced by Ronald Dworkin's 'Objectivity and Truth: You'd Better Believe It', *Philosophy and Public Affairs* 25, no. 2 (Spring 1996) pp. 87–139.

14   See for example the already quoted passage from *BGE* 259.

15   See for example, *Beyond Good and Evil* 30: 'Our highest insights must – and should – sound like follies and sometimes crimes when they are heard without permission by those who are not predisposed and predestined for them'. (Kaufmann's translation)

16   See for example, *WP* 287: 'The ideas of the herd should rule in the herd'. For this interpretation, see Leiter, *Nietzsche on Morality* pp. 296–7.

17   See Leiter: 'Nietzsche is not claiming that people are *actually* too altruistic and too egalitarian in their practice; he is worried that (as a consequence of the slave revolt in morals, etc.) they are now 'imprisoned among... concepts' of equality and altruism, and that the conceptual vocabulary of value is itself the obstacle to the realization of certain forms of human excellence. This is a very different charge, one that raises subtle psychological questions that no one, to date, has really explored.' [*Nietzsche on Morality*, p. 300].

18   'The noble type of man feels *himself* to be the determiner of values, he does not need to be approved of, he judges 'what harms me is harmful in itself', he knows himself to be that which in general first accords honour to things, he

creates values. Everything he knows to be part of himself, he honours: such a morality is self-glorification' [BGE 260].

19   'This reversal of the evaluating glance – this *inevitable* orientation to the outside instead of back onto itself – is a feature of *ressentiment*: in order to come about, slave morality first has to have an opposing, external world, it needs, physiologically speaking, external stimuli in order to act at all, – its action is basically a reaction' [GM I.10].

20   In Nietzsche's terms, 'In the foreground stands the feeling of plenitude, of power which seems to overflow, the happiness of high tension, the consciousness of a wealth which would like to give away and bestow' [BGE 260].

21   The person who has best argued this case, it seems to me, is Charles Taylor: see the final chapter of his monumental *Sources of the Self*: 'Nietzsche's challenge is based on a deep insight. If morality can only be powered negatively, where there can be no such thing as beneficence powered by an affirmation of the recipient as a being of value, then pity is destructive to the giver and degrading to the receiver, and the ethic of benevolence may indeed be indefensible. Nietzsche's challenge is on the deepest level, because he is looking precisely for what can release such an affirmation of being. His unsettling conclusion is that it is the ethic of benevolence which stands in the way of it. Only if there is such a thing as agape, or one of the secular claimants to its succession, is Nietzsche wrong.' [Cambridge: Cambridge University Press 1989, p. 516].

22   'The *respect* that I have for others or that another can require from me (*observantia aliis praestanda*) is therefore recognition of a *dignity* (*dignitas*) in other men, that is, of a worth that has no price, no equivalent for which the object evaluated (*aestimii*) could be exchanged. ... Every man has a legitimate claim to respect from his fellow men and is *in turn* bound to respect every other' [*Metaphysics of Morals* p. 462].

23   The only way in which belief in universal human dignity could be thought to involve levelling down would be if a potential higher type needs to treat others in ways incompatible with their dignity to ensure his flourishing.

24   Paul Ricoeur, *Oneself as Another*, tr. Katherine Blamey, Chicago: Chicago University Press, 1992, p. 221. One could also point out that there are many things (for example, regret and pity) that Nietzsche's preferred person must say 'no' to, even if he is tempted by them; so the mere fact of opposing things cannot make a system of valuation reactive.

25   Indeed elsewhere he himself suggests *any* form of protracted constraint is sufficient to expand and deepen the soul: see *BGE* 188.

26   Hegel of course was the first to philosophically theorize this point. Habermas helpfully glosses the point as follows: 'In a symmetrical relation the point of mutual recognition is that the two persons involved seem to sacrifice their independence; but in fact each gains a new kind of independence by coming to recognise, in the mirror of the eyes of the other person, who he or she is. Both become for themselves the kind of characters they mutually attribute to each

other. Both gain awareness of their individuality by seeing their own images reflected in the dense and deep exchange of an interpersonal relation.' ['From Kant to Hegel and Back Again: The Move Towards Detranscendentalization', *European Journal of Philosophy* vol. 7.2, 1999: pp. 129–57; p. 140]. For further discussion of the claim within a philosophical context, see Axel Honneth, *The Struggle for Recognition*, (tr. Joel Anderson, Cambridge: Polity Press 1995; and within a psychotherapeutic context see Jessica Benjamin, *The bonds of love: Psychoanalysis, feminism, and the problem of domination*, New York: Pantheon, 1988.

27   Perhaps Nietzsche's counterargument would be that great men have to be creative in a way that forces them to be solitary and not care about others. But this is just to express the deeply flawed (and self-serving) Romantic view of the creative genius. On Nietzsche's conception of 'greatness', in general see Leiter, *Nietzsche on Morality*, pp. 115–24.

28   Nelson Mandela or Desmond Tutu would be obvious examples here. (For example, the South African Truth and Reconciliation Committee, over which Tutu presided was remarkable for its *lack* of sentiments of revenge and recrimination.) But each of us, I would suggest, also encounters many less famous resentment free egalitarians.

29   Acknowledgements: thanks to the participants of the Friedrich Nietzsche Society Conference 2004, and to the Research Seminar at the University of Keele for helpful comments.

REBECCA BAMFORD

The Virtue of Shame:
Defending Nietzsche's Critique of *Mitleid*

Nietzsche's critique of *Mitleid* is notorious. It has given rise to the widespread and intuitively plausible view that Nietzsche (1) endorses practical cruelty, (2) rejects *Mitleid*, and (3) fails to accept that it is right to abhor all human suffering. This invites the conclusion that Nietzsche flirts dangerously with moral bankruptcy. How can we defend Nietzsche's critique from the kind of moral intuitionist who believes that it 'just is right' to abhor the kind of cruelty which endorses mass suffering, and to feel and to express *Mitleid* for all those unfortunates who suffer? One answer, which I shall develop here, is to target the effect of moral intuitionism upon our understanding of Nietzsche's critique.

Agreement on what cruelty is, let alone agreement on its moral status or on the moral value of suffering, is not so easy to achieve as might initially be supposed by a moral intuitionist. The intuitionist simply assumes the moral incompetence of Nietzsche's perspective on cruelty and suffering, as well as the moral incompetence of those who are prepared even to imagine this perspective as defensible. However, Nietzsche offers us good reason to think that *Mitleid* is genuinely dangerous, in a way that the pure phenomenon of human suffering simply is not. I argue that moral intuitions about Nietzsche as an exemplar of practical cruelty can be overturned. My argument is based upon the possibility of abandoning the notion of pure and unmediated passivity as intrinsic to the phenomena of human suffering and of *Mitleid*, as identified by Nietzsche. I claim that wrongly identifying intrinsic passivity in the phenomenology of *Mitleid* and of suffering generates the moral sceptical intuition. Once this case of mistaken identity is uncovered, I suggest, there is no reason to remain subject to the force of the intuition. I support my account with a fresh reading of

'The Ugliest Man', from Book IV of Nietzsche's *Thus Spoke Zara-thustra*.

Nietzsche on *Mitleid* and Human Suffering

We should begin by taking a brief look at how closely suffering and *Mitleid* are connected in Nietzsche. The phenomenological experience of suffering is interpreted specifically in terms of *Mitleid*, as for Nietzsche, this is the only means by which one individual can authentically appreciate the pain or suffering of another.[1] This holds even though access to each other's qualitative pain-experience remains impossible:

> Our personal and profoundest suffering is incomprehensible and inaccessible to almost everyone; here we remain hidden from our neighbour, even if we eat from one pot. But whenever people *notice* that we suffer, they interpret our suffering superficially. It is the very essence of the emotion of *Mitleid* that it strips away from the suffering of others whatever is distinctively personal [GS 338].

The inaccessibility of another's suffering prompts Nietzsche to consider two questions: first, whether or not it is good for us to be full of *Mitleid*, and, second, whether or not this is good for those unfortunate persons who suffer [GS 338]. Nietzsche asks, 'where are your greatest dangers?' and answers that they lie 'in *Mitleid*' [GS 271]. On the face of it, the claims that *Mitleid* is not in our best interests, and that it is dangerous, seems particularly counter-intuitive. But these are cast into the shade by what is perhaps Nietzsche's most provocative statement on *Mitleid*: 'of course one ought to *express* [*Mitleid*], but one ought to guard against *having* it' [HH 50].

At first glance, this remark seems to be made in curiously bad faith – in which case, we could accuse Nietzsche of cynicism, at the very least. However, note that Nietzsche does not claim that we do not experience *Mitleid*. Neither does he suggest directly that we should feign *Mitleid* – he limits himself to a warning against the having of *Mitleid*, in the possessive sense. In order to pre-empt the charge of cynicism, it is helpful to compare this warning remark to the following passage:

> We benefit and show benevolence to those who are already dependent on us in some way (which means that they are used to thinking of us as causes); we want to increase their power because in that way we increase ours [...] [GS 13].

Read in terms of power, the warning to express *Mitleid* but to guard against having it can be viewed not as a cynical remark, but as a practical one.[2] Nietzsche had already explained in *Human, All Too Human* that the unfortunate man wrongly counts *Mitleid* as the greatest good on earth. For Nietzsche, the stupidity of this notion is underlined by the guilty enjoyment of power by these unfortunates as they realize that, despite their overall weakness, they still have one form of power left to them: 'the power to hurt' [HH 50].

Developing this analysis further, Nietzsche compares the unfortunate man with 'children who weep and cry, *so that* they will be pitied', and argues that expressions of pain and misfortune are basically aimed at hurting the spectators of the misfortune, in order that the unfortunate might quench the thirst for *Mitleid* that is to be equated with the thirst for self-enjoyment [HH 50]. Nietzsche's complaint is that 'most people are too dishonest, and a few men are too good, to know anything about this source of shame' [HH 50]. Yet although he knows that the dishonest and the good may try to deny the pleasure of inflicting pain in such a way, Nietzsche concludes his analysis by siding with Prosper Mérimée:

> Know that nothing is more common than to do harm for the pleasure of doing it [HH 50].

This may be viewed productively alongside Nietzsche's comment that the slave revolt in morals begins when *ressentiment* itself becomes creative and ordains values [GM 1, 10]. The noble morality that affirms itself is contrasted with the slave morality that, in rejecting what Nietzsche calls 'an 'outside'', reveals its reversal of an evaluating gaze as a creative act characteristic of *ressentiment* [GM 1, 10]. What

is meant by the reversal of the evaluating gaze is demonstrated particularly clearly in *HH* 50, in which our natural intuition that the weak
and suffering unfortunate is powerless, is challenged by Nietzsche's
interpretation of the unfortunate man as reviving and nourishing his
self-image through the very receipt of *Mitleid*.

   This is an important point. We have seen that Nietzsche acknowledges pleasure in the infliction of pain and suffering. Nietzsche's
analysis certainly has a practical basis; cruelty is shown to be a good
investment in that it promises to preserve the being of the one who is
cruel.[3] As Danto suggests, this kind of practical cruelty merely affirms
that 'this is the way that the world is', insofar that, in Nietzsche, there
is a passive sense of suffering that means to be acted upon, rather than
being active oneself.[4] Drawing on this assumption of passivity, Danto's
claim here is that Nietzsche quite simply affirms cruelty as a part of
his critique of *Mitleid*. Resultantly, Danto concludes that Nietzsche's
view is that 'the wood must suffer if the table is to be built', but also
claims an element of *Schadenfreude* on Nietzsche's part in the sheer
spectacle of suffering. Hence on this account, the critique of *Mitleid* is
not only an exemplar of practical cruelty, but also leaves room for the
emergence of a voluptuously cruel Nietzsche, one who is engaged in a
polemic against 'moral sympathy theorists' such as Schopenhauer.[5]

   Nietzsche's Schopenhauerianism has generated substantial critical interest amongst Nietzsche scholars in recent years.[6] We need to
be clear here about the extent to which Nietzsche's critique is directed
towards Schopenhauer's views on *Mitleid*. It has been argued, for example, that *HH* 50 & 103, *D* 134, *GS* 99 *and BGE* 201 & 225 col-
lectively count as substantial textual evidence in favour of the view
that a problem of translation obscures the context of Nietzsche's critique of *Mitleid* understood as a moral ideal.[7] The claim is that
Nietzsche's polemics against *Mitleid* as a moral ideal are to be understood as clearly directed at Schopenhauer's ethics, but that reception
of this view is discouraged because this fact is obscured in English by
the fact that most translators of Schopenhauer render *Mitleid* as 'compassion', while most translators of Nietzsche render *Mitleid* as 'pity'.[8]
Hence on this account, there seems to be a real danger of missing
Nietzsche's intention, and thereby missing the real target, of his critique: for example, in the light of the translation problem, Nietzsche's

claim cited earlier, that the unfortunate man wrongly counts *Mitleid* as the greatest good on earth, is clearly targeted at Schopenhauer's view that compassion is the source of every moral action. If both are rendered in the original German as *Mitleid*, then the point is immediately obvious.

We certainly should be careful when reading Nietzsche in translation. However, at the same time, we should also be careful to keep in mind the broader intentions underlying Nietzsche's critique of *Mitleid*. While some of Nietzsche's remarks certainly do target Schopenhauer's affection for moral sympathising directly, constructing a response to Schopenhauer is not all that Nietzsche is doing here. The danger of interpreting Nietzsche's remarks on *Mitleid* purely in terms of his Schopenhauerianism is that we fail to appreciate the broader, cultural, significance of Nietzsche's worry about the effect of *Mitleid*. Reading Nietzsche's critique as a part of his broader cultural concern with the problem of nihilism underlines the active need which Nietzsche has to challenge our moral intuitions about the phenomenon of *Mitleid*. Hence we ought to balance the explanatory force of Nietzsche's Schopenhauerianism against that of Nietzsche's concern with the cultural problem of nihilism.

Nihilism, Culture, and Human Suffering

In a broad sense, nihilism should be seen as a crisis in values: Nietzsche's concern in his critique of culture was with the crisis of values affecting European culture at the end of the nineteenth century.[9] Nietzsche gives a lyrical account of the crisis in value in the prophet's speech heard by Zarathustra:

> And I saw a great sadness come over mankind. The best grew weary of their works. A teaching went forth, a belief ran beside it: Everything is empty, everything is one, everything is past! And from every hill it resounded: Everything is empty, everything is one, everything is past! We have harvested, it is true: but

why did all our fruits turn rotten and brown? What fell from the wicked moon last night?

All our work has been in vain, our wine has become poison, an evil eye has scorched our fields and our hearts.

We have all become dry; and if fire fell upon us we should scatter like ashes – yes, we have made weary fire itself.

All our wells have dried up, even the sea has receded. The earth wants to break open, but the depths will not devour us! Alas, where there is still a sea in which one could drown: thus our lament resounds – across shallow swamps. Truly, we have grown too weary even to die; now we are still awake and we live on – in sepulchres! [Z II, The Prophet].

The collapse of values is represented in the Prophet's speech by the themes of weariness and emptiness. Note that this passage is context-ualized in temporal terms by its situation as the words of the prophet who sees the future. It thus encapsulates both Nietzsche's fears for the future of modern culture and his acknowledgement of the extent to which these fears are already present in that culture. The notion of time is of particular significance here. In analyzing the moment in this passage, Nietzsche makes reference not only to time in a general sense, but also to the connection between time and human existence.[10] Specifically, in acknowledging the significance of the future and the present tenses of nihilism, it becomes necessary to acknowledge the past tense as well: the nihilistic attitude does not appear overnight, but rather develops from out of the past.

The state of having no today is a result of the effect of the past upon the individual, who finds him/herself aware of the problem of culture from a position within the crisis in values. Nietzsche describes this state as '*suffering from culture's past*', in a particular and signifi-cant sense: the sense of inheritance [HH 249]. Not only do such indivi-duals suffer from 'a feeling similar to that of a man who has inherited riches that were acquired through illegal means, or a prince who rules because of his forefathers' atrocities', namely from the past; such individuals also suffer from the future, in that they regard 'the future with melancholy', knowing that their 'descendants will suffer from the past' in the same way [HH 249]. It would therefore be short-sighted, I think, to claim that nihilism is represented by sadness in the Prophet's speech. The sadness to which the Prophet refers is the consequence of nihilism, rather than the cause. The tone that the Prophet describes as resounding from the hills is that of emptiness, and it is emptiness to which nihilism corresponds.[11] The universal belief of emptiness as representative of the collapse of Western values is symbolic of the emotive emptiness that is evoked by its summative claim that nothing is true and that everything is permitted.[12]

I shall briefly consider how this view of nihilism as part of culture is reflected in Nietzsche's genealogy of values. Genealogy as a method, applied to the genesis of morality, reveals how morality came into being and how it is sustained.[13] In *BGE*, for example, Nietzsche's genealogical reading shows that fear, taken as the determinant of the power relations within a community and between discrete communities, is the source or 'mother' of morality in as far as moral values are established in terms of how certain actions will affect the well-being of the herd [BGE 201].[14] This slave revolt of morality is successful on three counts: the slave, or weak type, is by nature more shrewd, calculating and prudent; the number of such types outweighs the number of strong types; and the weak type has erected a convincing set of myths in order to support the moral code.[15] Christianity is one such myth; as we see in *GM*, Christianity is the final expression of the ascetic ideal expressed by slave morality.[16]

Fear of the oppressor by the oppressed is the factor at work in what Nietzsche calls the *ressentiment* of the slave type.[17] His critique of morality thus applies this awareness of the significance of power to the principles of herd-morality, showing that rather than being reducible to a so-called 'pure' principle of moral rectitude (namely the concept of goodness), these principles are, like their logical opposites, reducible to power. As Nietzsche argues, the notion of moral intention as explanatory falls by the wayside when the significance of power is recognized:

> there is a world of difference between the reason for something coming into existence in the first place and the ultimate use to which it is put, its actual application and integration into a system of goals; that anything which exists, once it has somehow come into being, can be reinterpreted in the service of new intentions, repossessed, repeatedly modified to a new use by a power superior to it [...] [GM II, 12].

The underlying focus of Nietzsche's discussion here is not morality *per se*, but ontology. In opposition to Plato, whose ontology is founded on the Form of the Good, Nietzsche's critique of morality is founded upon the basic organic processes of 'reinterpretation and mastering' of everything in existence [GM II, 12].[18] The ontological significance of morality is thus displaced by Nietzsche's will to power, which is categorically beyond good and evil.[19]

Because Nietzsche views nihilism as congenital to culture, rather than as a transitory affliction, he prescribes the restoration of the tragic disposition as a conceptual version of 'gene therapy', a therapy which arises from out of his genealogical method.[20] Also congenital to culture in Nietzsche's opinion is the oscillation between on the one hand the drive towards an optimism of weakness, characterized by the rise of Socratic optimism and by the slave-revolt in morality that is driven by fear, and on the other hand the drive towards a pessimism of strength, characterized by the tragic. These two impulses balance each other, and the tension between them provides culture with its source of value. But it would be a mistake to view their relationship as antagonistic in a pure sense. Nietzsche invokes the analogy of dance in order to make this point clear:

> one might remember that *dancing* is not the same thing as staggering wearily back and forth between different impulses. High culture will resemble a daring dance, thus requiring, as we said, much strength and flexibility [HH 278].

As Nietzsche understands it, the tragic disposition characterizes an individual who can forget the 'terrible anxiety' caused by death and time by consecrating himself to something 'supra-personal' [UM IV, 4]. What Nietzsche prescribes is the reinforcement of the counterbalancing effect of the tragic pessimism of strength upon the Socratic optimism of weakness, which is increasingly dominant within modern culture. The optimism of weakness safeguards the weak individual for the sake of self-preservation, while the pessimism of strength is willing to sacrifice the strong individual for the sake of celebrating the unmediated power of life, whether life is individuated or not. The inverse relation between the optimism of weakness and the pessimism of strength that provokes the necessary tension to yield cultural values, is mediated by Nietzsche's awareness of their roots in the same thing: an interpretative ontology of the nature of existence. This interpretative ontology is of course Nietzsche's doctrine of the will to power.[21] Nietzsche is opposed to nihilism construed as a problem for culture; but he also acknowledges that nihilism is an ever-present element of culture, by virtue of the link between culture and power.[22]

Returning to the issue of Nietzsche's cruelty in the critique of *Mitleid*, then, I remain unconvinced that there is a necessary link between cruelty and practicality.[23] While the practicality that Nietzsche is advocating is conceived of in active terms, any account which trades in such a necessary connection has assumed an active/passive dynamic to be at work in the power-relationships between individuals, thereby insinuating into Nietzsche a morally dubious teleology of cruelty as guiding action. However, this kind of intuitionist account does not square with an account of Nietzsche as engaged in a critique of culture which aims to confront and counter the nihilistic imbalance caused by the imbalance of Socratic optimism and tragic pessimism in modern culture. To divorce cruelty from practicality, and thus to disrupt the effects of intuitionism in our understanding of Nietzsche's critique, we need to question the value accorded to this active/passive dynamic. In order to do so, I draw on work by Henry Staten, using the concept of innocence in Nietzsche to develop Staten's account into one which denies authentic intersubjective passivity.[24]

Defending Nietzsche's Critique: Abandoning Passivity

Staten's reading of Nietzsche's critique is deeply indebted to the active/ passive dynamic, which is hardly surprising given Staten's project of pursuing a psycho-dialectical reading of logic and libido in Nietzsche. Staten's reading certainly owes much to Freud, but is also authorized by Nietzsche's own interests in desires, drives and instincts, and in a 'real physio-psychology' [BGE 23].[25] Although he does not argue that will to power is sexual, or that it can be equated to the Freudian libido,

Staten highlights the complement between the aggression of the Freudian libido and the aggressive eroticism of the pleasure in excitation of
will to power.[26] For Staten, this is linked with Nietzsche's exploration
of sadomasochistic subjectivity, which includes the fluidity of sadomasochistic affect – the interchangeability of subject positions in the
relationship between the sadist and the masochist. For my purposes,
the notion of intersubjective fluidity is especially important in the
context of defending Nietzsche's critique of *Mitleid*.

Staten describes a model of suffering using the idea of a mirror,
which stands as an explanation of Nietzsche's attraction to cruelty in
its non-dialectical form.[27] We are asked to imagine two individuals,
one inflicting suffering, and one who suffers, in what we can call an
intersubjective power-relationship:

> The one who inflicts suffering forces the sufferer to turn towards him and grant
> him an absolute recognition; he thus appropriates the substance of the sufferer
> as mirror of his own being, the sufferer reflects him back to himself with an in-
> tensity and inevitability which belong only to the being of the inflicter of pain.[28]

Staten's reading centres on the intersubjective fluidity of sadomasochistic affect present in Nietzsche's remarks on the striving for distinction in *D* 113, in which Nietzsche challenges the constitution of
empathy as wholesome in terms of power. For Staten, the pathos of
distance and the distinction of rank order in Nietzsche are variants of
the 'striving to impress one's being violently on the substance of the
other'.[29] The sufferer can only echo; he cannot authentically experience or truly understand the inflicter of pain's feelings, or respond to
them, and thus he remains alienated from what I would want to call
his natural interpretative freedom. Recalling Nietzsche's point that we
cannot have access to one another's pain and suffering, Staten's idea
of the mirror also seems to reflect the distance, or alienation, that per-
sists between each individual in modern culture, even where individuals interact. Awareness of intersubjective alienation recalls an image
in which Nietzsche evokes the researcher's (perhaps all too familiar)
view of the universe as 'the infinitely refracted echo of an original
sound, that of humanity, and as the multiple copy of a single, original
image, that of humanity'.[30]

For Staten, Nietzsche 'recoils from the expansiveness of the Dionysian', his *Mitleid* turning to nausea at the fear of 'contamination and violation of his being' by the herd.[31] Staten is clearly aware of Nietzsche's deep feeling for the suffering of the 'masses of humanity'; however for him, Nietzsche's response to this feeling is to fortify himself against it by affirming the ascendant life, which he thinks incorporates a tendency to become a 'celebration of isolation, cruelty and appropriativeness'.[32] Thus, while acknowledging a dichotomy between passivity/negation and violently appropriative aggression, which might possibly be bridged by what he calls an 'active receptiveness', Staten concludes that recognition is cruelly forced upon the passive sufferer by the person who is actively inflicting pain.[33]

In Staten's sadomasochistic model, the sufferer is appropriated. She is granted no recognition on reflecting the substance of the (cruel) inflicter of pain's being. But consider the case of the unfortunate man from *HH* 50. There it is the spectator whose being is appropriated by the unfortunate sufferer. This unfortunate man inflicts the cruelty of his 'eloquent laments and whimpering' on the spectator, who responds with *Mitleid* [HH 50]. The tables are turned, and where the spectator becomes the unfortunate, the unfortunate becomes the spectator. Yet the original roles are also retained: being-appropriation continues as described in Staten's model even while the reversal takes place. In the light of this, we can see that there is no longer a clear 'passive' role to be ascribed to a spectator, an inflicter of pain or to an unfortunate sufferer. The power-relationship of mirroring is not, as in Staten's account, only the forced recognition of being-appropriation within an active/passive dynamic. Identifying the presence of the passive in the power-relation is misleading because, as we have seen, there is in fact no utterly passive role for either individual within the power-relation by virtue of the dialectical necessity of activity. Mirroring may thus be taken to describe the power-relationship in an active sense, as multidirectional rather than as unidirectional.

Hence what Staten acknowledges as 'active receptiveness', but which he rejects in favour of relying upon passivity, does a much better job of helping us to grasp Nietzsche's critique than the inherent violence of being-appropriation, conceived of as a symptom of power effected through cruelty. Violence is accurate only as a description of the level of energy and activity of will to power; Nietzschean power is intrinsic to activity, which can be taken as characteristic of Nietzsche's fundamental aestheticism in terms of the utter centrality of interpretation.[34] The activity of the sufferer, the observer, and the inflicter of pain are all power-dependent, on a Nietzschean account. It is therefore essential to understand the power-relationship as one of innocence, rather than one of cruelty or violence in an unmediated sense. I shall consider some of Nietzsche's remarks on innocence conceptualized in the terms of child's play in relation to his concept of the *Übermensch*, in order to bring the significance of innocence to Nietzsche's notion of being as an interpretative process of becoming into light.[35]

The free play of creation that is to be understood in the same breath as we discuss Nietzsche's will to power is not the same as the free play of the imagination of the knowing, mature, and above all, *serious* agent that a Kant or a Descartes might have envisaged. Rather, such free play of creation is that of a child, as Nietzsche's Zarathustra knows:

> The child is innocence and forgetfulness, a new beginning, a sport, a self-propelling wheel, a first motion, a sacred Yes.
>
>   Yes, a sacred Yes is needed, my brothers, for the sport of creation: the spirit now wills *its own* will, the spirit sundered from the world now wins *its own* world [Z I, Of The Three Metamorphoses].[36]

We ought not to overlook the sense in which the play of a child is not quite the same thing as, say, a play in a theatre, and this sense is that of representation.[37] The aestheticist will is not of the order of representation.[38] It is interpretative, never merely representative; after all, there can be no representations – no facts – which are uninterpreted.[39] The *Übermensch* and its corresponding ontological foundation of will to power are darkened within the popular conception by the lingering shadow of teleological relentlessness, which is signified by the question of the goal that is lacked by eternal recurrence. This is never more so than when we are asked to accept that the most terrifying and painful experiences are aesthetically justifiable.

It is through the redemption from revenge against time that it is therefore possible to read the *Übermensch* as a figure of nonteleological 'will-to-power': the innocent expression of existence by a force, within a necessarily indeterminate contingency of other forces.[40] This expression of existence can only be creative:

> Where is innocence? Where there is will to begetting. And for me, he who wants to create beyond himself has the purest will.
>   Where is beauty? Where I have to will with all my will; where I want to love and perish, that an image may not remain merely an image [*Z* II, Of Immaculate Perception].

It is not the quantification of development towards the *Übermensch*, where this is understood as an ideal of virtue, which is at stake for Nietzsche. To express a moral imperative, even towards the cultural defeat of nihilism, is precisely what he guards against. What Nietzsche looks to instead is the future qualitative phenomenology of the *Übermensch*, symbolised within the texts by the play and innocence of the child as a part of the affirmation of life.

What can change, through this account of the mirroring power-relationship as innocent, is our perception of the significance of power for intersubjectivity in the case of *Mitleid*. Taken together with the awareness of the power relationship, Nietzsche's argument is strong enough to overturn the preconception of *Mitleid* as a positive moral emotion within the wider context of his critique of value. Unless the spectator can overcome the drive to have *Mitleid*, to suffer from it rather than simply to express it, he/she loses the dynamism of his/her own power and risks having his/her being appropriated. Where *Mitleid* is held and expressed, without the possibility of appropriating the substance of the other, the individual cannot be recognized and thus has no power. But where *Mitleid* is merely expressed, rather than held, the individual retains power while still embodying the power-relationship. Within Nietzsche's imagination, the possibility exists of a situation where all higher individuals consciously restrict themselves to expressing *Mitleid* in a benevolent manner, rendering them immune to the attempts by the resentful herd to appropriate their beings, and yet doing so without authentic cruelty [GS 345].

With a sense of the benevolent expression of *Mitleid* in mind, recognition is no longer absolute in Staten's original sense, but is shared. The benevolent spectator is no longer appropriated but purposely grants recognition to the unfortunate sufferer, whose complaining is intended to force recognition. To put this into Staten's original language, sadomasochistic affect flows both ways; but as I see it, intersubjective fluidity not only allows for the interchange of subject positions, it also allows for an authentic intersubjective merger on the ground of power, which offers a challenge to an individuated conception of pure subjective awareness as well as to the classical subject positions of sadist and masochist. As such, embodiment of the power-relationship is clearly not a matter of pure, unmediated, passivity distinct from, and contrasted against, violent activity.

Confirmation: Intersubjectivity in 'The Ugliest Man' as Pure Activity

Here I conduct an exegetical reading of *Z* IV, The Ugliest Man, in order to provide a textual illustration of an intersubjective power-relationship which challenges the conception of pure passivity. The interaction begins when Zarathustra encounters an 'unutterable' character sitting on the path that he is following. Before Zarathustra is even aware of this character's identity, he is 'overcome by the great shame of having beheld such a thing'. The Ugliest Man is singular: 'shaped like a man, and yet hardly like a man'. Before Zarathustra can move forward, the Ugliest Man asks him a riddle: 'What is the *revenge on the witness?*' This riddle is, like that of the Sphinx, one of identity: the Ugliest Man is asking Zarathustra to proclaim his identity. Zarathustra is able to identify him as the murderer of God, and as such, is overcome once again: but this time, he is wounded by the axe of *Mitleid*. Translating this into the terms of my earlier discussion of the unfortunate man, Zarathustra is initially cast as the spectator in this section, while the Ugliest Man at first plays the role of the unfortunate man, the sufferer, who treads 'all roads to death and destruction'.

Some of the symbolism in this passage explains the reason why the mirroring power-relation has been classified as one of activity/

passivity. At the beginning of the passage Zarathustra's feet are running through forests and mountains, giving an impression of speed and urgency. But when he steps into the kingdom of death in which the Ugliest Man is lurking, he goes 'slowly and ever slower and at last stopped' when faced with the Ugliest Man himself. Even his mood changes, from a state of rejoicing, to a state of being 'plunged into dark recollections.' This descent is reflected by Zarathustra's being overcome first by shame, and then by *Mitleid* – in effect, a transition from activity to apparent passivity. The Ugliest Man appropriates Zarathustra's being through the positing of his riddle of identity – and it is no accident that this is conceived of specifically as a riddle of identity, which directly reflects the appropriative process of mirroring at work in their interaction. The Ugliest Man tells Zarathustra that he knows the axe that fells him, thus apparently confirming the analysis of the active/passive model of mirroring. Now, if this were the whole story, Zarathustra would be unable to overcome the test of *Mitleid.* Indeed, at the end of the passage Zarathustra goes on his way 'even more thoughtfully and slowly than before', which implies a lingering element of passivity.

However, after Zarathustra has guessed who he is, the Ugliest Man tells him that he is not fleeing from persecution – as might easily be assumed of the murderer of God – but from *Mitleid* [Z IV, The Ugliest Man]. It is little people, according to the Ugliest Man, who call *Mitleid* a virtue and who place it highly within a hierarchy of value. He thinks that this evaluation of *Mitleid* is a result of a lack of reverence for his 'great misfortune, great ugliness, great failure'. The Ugliest Man pleads with Zarathustra, his 'last refuge', to protect him, as Zarathustra is the only one who has understood 'how he feels who has killed God – how the murderer of God feels'. This constitutes the Ugliest Man's final attempt to appropriate Zarathustra's being: the Ugliest Man attempts to reinforce the turn of Zarathustra's initial shame to *Mitleid* by encouraging him to think of himself as benevolent. Anyone else would have given him 'alms, his *Mitleid,* in glance and speech'; but the Ugliest Man notes that Zarathustra's initial shame honoured his wealth in 'big things, in fearsome things, in the ugliest things, in the most unutterable things'. Zarathustra does not succumb to this tactic. In recommending his road to the Ugliest Man, and commanding that the Ugliest Man should speak with his animals, Zarathustra shows benevolence:

> My cave is big and deep and possesses many corners; there the best hidden man can find his hiding place. And close by it are a hundred secret and slippery ways for creeping, fluttering and jumping beasts.
>   You outcast who cast yourself out, do you not wish to live among men and the *Mitleid* of men? Very well, do as I do. Thus you will also learn from me; only the doer learns [Z IV, The Ugliest Man].

Benevolence points to the expression of *Mitleid* but not to the having of *Mitleid*, in as far as benevolence is linked here to the notion of fair trade: the Ugliest Man warns Zarathustra against his road, and it is in return for this that Zarathustra recommends the Ugliest Man his own path. The fact of benevolence attests to Zarathustra's activity, rather than to passivity.

Zarathustra's revulsion for God's murderer stems not from his understanding and experience of those feelings, but from the mutual alienation of himself and the Ugliest Man from one another. Zarathustra's being is saved from appropriation by his shame.[41] In his horror, 'chilled to his very marrow', Zarathustra reflects the substance of the Ugliest Man's being, but also finds that the substance of his own being is redeemed, and reproduced, through his expression of benevolence. Zarathustra's *Mitleid* for the Ugliest Man ultimately turns back to shame, which is symptomatic of this:

> How poor is man! (he thought in his heart) how ugly, how croaking, how full of secret shame!
>   They tell me that man loves himself: ah, how great must this self-love be! How much contempt is opposed to it! [Z IV, The Ugliest Man]. [42]

The shame that Zarathustra feels at the sight of the Ugliest Man and which is preferable to the *Mitleid* of the little people, is more fundamental than *Mitleid*.[43] Zarathustra is therefore able to resist the test of *Mitleid* by cultivating the sense of shame that he experiences in the face of such ugliness. The strength of Zarathustra's self-love allows him to cultivate shame, and to express *Mitleid*, without rendering himself a victim of pure passivity.

Conclusion

Zarathustra remarks that while he loves the great despisers, 'man, however, is something that must be overcome'. Critically, this is as true of Zarathustra himself as it is of the Ugliest Man. Zarathustra is a creature of the heights, just as the Ugliest Man, in despising himself so deeply, achieves comparable and deeply ironic 'height'.[44] Their interaction reveals Zarathustra's ability to develop, or rather, interpret, his shame into benevolence, and which thereby points the way to the future. This way forward is symbolized in the text by the value inversion of the exchange of directions, which also stands for intersubjective activity. But where the Ugliest Man warns Zarathustra against his road, which leads quite literally to 'nowhere', and which may be understood as nihilism, Zarathustra recommends his own path to the Ugliest Man.

Now this road, admittedly, also leads to nihilism. However, Zarathustra's road also points to the possibility of cultural therapy by demanding that in following the road, we not only arrive at the cultural position of nihilism but we confront it, and we confront it in its full horror and pain. It is therefore in the phenomenal vulnerability of this moment of confrontation that I think Nietzsche's analysis of modern culture, and his critique of *Mitleid*, can best be appreciated. We can challenge the intuitionist's suspicion of Nietzsche's critique of *Mitleid* by retaining a strong sense of virtue as important in all of his writings. This sense of virtue is particularly important in *Z*. Zarathustra's benevolence, his capacity for honesty, and most particularly his capacity for shame, allow us to admire him as a virtuous character.[45] Our admiration, and Zarathustra's virtue, both point towards the cultural rebirth at which Nietzsche's critique of *Mitleid* is aimed.

References

For a general bibliography of Nietzsche's work in German and English see end of volume.

Babich, Babette E., 'Against Analysis, Beyond Postmodernism', Babich, Debra B. Bergoffen & Simon V. Glynn, *Continental and Postmodern Perspectives in the Philosophy of Science*, Aldershot: Avebury, 1995.

Clark, Maudemarie, 'On Knowledge, Truth, and Value: Nietzsche's debt to Schopenhauer and the Development of His Empiricism', Christopher Janaway (ed.), *Willing and Nothingness: Schopenhauer as Nietzsche's Educator*, Oxford: Clarendon Press, 1998.

Cooper, David E., *Authenticity and Learning*, London: Routledge & Kegan Paul, 1983. 'Self and Morality in Schopenhauer and Nietzsche', Christopher Janaway (ed.), *Willing and Nothingness: Schopenhauer as Nietzsche's educator*, Oxford: Oxford University Press, 1998.

Danto, Arthur C., *Nietzsche as Philosopher*, New York: Columbia University Press, 1965.

Gadamer, Hans-Georg, *Truth and Method*, Garrett Barden & John Cumming (eds.), New York: Seabury Press, 1975.

Lampert, Laurence, *Nietzsche's Teaching: An Interpretation of Thus Spoke Zarathustra*, New Haven: Yale University Press, 1986.

Leiter, Brian, *Nietzsche on Morality*, London: Routledge, 2002.

Lingis, Alphonso, 'The Will to Power', David B. Allison (ed.), *The New Nietzsche*, Cambridge, MA: MIT Press, 1985.

Loeb, Paul S., 'Time, Power and Superhumanity', *Journal of Nietzsche Studies*, 21, Spring 2001.

Magnus, Bernd, Stanley Stewart and Jean-Pierre Mileur, *Nietzsche's Case: Philosophy as/and Literature*, London: Routledge, 1993.

Megill, Allan, *Prophets of Extremity: Nietzsche, Heidegger, Foucault, Derrida*, Berkeley: University of California Press, 1985.

Miller, Elaine P., 'Harnessing Dionysos: Nietzsche on Rhythm, Time, and Restraint', *Journal of Nietzsche Studies*, 17, Spring 1999.

Nehamas, Alexander, *Nietzsche: Life as Literature*, Cambridge: Harvard University Press, 1985.

O'Murchadha, Felix, 'Nature as Other: A Hermeneutical Approach to Science', Babette E. Babich, Debra B. Bergoffen & Simon V. Glynn, *Continental and Postmodern Perspectives in the Philosophy of Science*, Aldershot: Avebury, 1995.

Rogers, Peter, 'Simmel's Mistake: The Eternal Recurrence as a Riddle About the Intelligible Form of Time as a Whole', *Journal of Nietzsche Studies*, 21, Spring 2001.

Stanley Rosen, *The Mask of Enlightenment: Nietzsche's Zarathustra*, Cambridge: Cambridge University Press, 1995.

Schrift, Alan D., *Nietzsche and the Question of Interpretation: Between Hermeneutics and Deconstruction*, New York & London: Routledge, 1990.

Schutte, Ofelia, *Beyond Nihilism: Nietzsche without masks*, Chicago & London: The University of Chicago Press, 1984.

Solomon, Robert, *Living With Nietzsche: What the Great "Immoralist" Has to Teach Us*, Oxford: Oxford University Press, 2003.

Staten, Henry, *Nietzsche's Voice*, New York: Cornell University Press, 1990.

Notes

1   Leiter [2002, p. 57].
2   See Danto [1965, pp. 173–4].
3   Staten [1990, p. 102].
4   Danto [1965, pp. 173–4].
5   Danto [1965, pp. 184–5].
6   See for example Clark [1998], and Cooper [1998].
7   Leiter [2002, p. 57].
8   Leiter [2002, p. 57].
9   Kaufmann [1974, p. 121] counts the theme of value as the 'thread of Ariadne' by which we can be guided through the 'labyrinth' of Nietzsche's thought. See

also *WP* 2, in which Nietzsche claims that nihilism means '*That the highest values devalue themselves.* The aim is lacking: 'why'? finds no answer.'

10   See Miller [1999, p. 15]. On Nietzsche's philosophy of time, see also Loeb [2001] and Rogers [2001].

11   Though it might seem paradoxical to represent a tone by using the notion of emptiness, this embellishes the picture that Nietzsche is drawing of nihilism in relation to philosophy.

12   Schutte [1984, p. 2].

13   Cooper [1983, p. 93].

14   See Cooper [1983, p. 93]. Cooper shows convincingly that the initial fear held by the community, which provokes it into committing its energies to defending its members, yields an initial non-moral judgement in which the warrior type, at the forefront of such defence, is classified as good in the sense of noble. However, when the safety of the community is ensured, and its collective energies are directed inwards rather than outwards, it is precisely this warrior type who poses the greatest threat to the weaker community members. Thus the fear of the community changes, and provokes the establishment of a system of rules that work to emasculate the strong type. As he argues, 'the values codified by the system of rules will be ones like pity, charity, humility, meekness, equal rights and turning the other cheek'.

15   Cooper [1983, p. 93].

16   Leiter [2002, p. 190].

17   Leiter [2002, p. 194]. For an example of Nietzsche's argument that renders the power relation between the weak and strong types clear, see *D* 189.

18   There is an obvious link here to Kant's grounding of his ontology within the notion of morality, to which Nietzsche objects.

19   For the purpose of providing a simple definition, the will to power may be considered as Nietzsche's most fundamental view of being, resulting from his perspectival conclusion that there are only interpretations of moral (and other) phenomena: 'we need a new, more definite conception of the concept 'life.' My formula for it is: Life is will to power' [WP 254]. See Richardson [1996], for a discussion of the relationship between the psychological and ontological aspects of will to power. However, we should note that an authentic definition of the doctrine of will to power is more complex: any answer to the question of what will to power is depends upon the descriptive approach taken. On this point see Lingis [1985].

20   Leiter distinguishes between the ordinary sense of genealogy as the history of family pedigree and Nietzsche's critical genealogy of morality. See Leiter [2002, pp. 167–8].

21   As Nietzsche points out, nihilism represents a 'pathological transitional stage' where what is pathological is the 'tremendous generalization' of inferring that there is no meaning at all [WP 15].

22   See *A* 55–7.

23   Such as that advocated by Danto [1965].
24   Staten [1990].
25   Staten [1990, p. 9].
26   Staten [1990, p. 100].
27   Staten [1990, pp. 102–3].
28   Staten [1990, pp. 102–3].
29   Staten [1990, pp. 102–3).
30   *TL:* 148. In the same passage, the researcher's project is directly linked to human suffering and happiness by analogy to the astrologer.
31   Staten [1990, p. 103].
32   Staten [1990, p. 103].
33   Staten [1990, p. 147].
34   On power as intrinsic to activity, see Cooper [1983, pp. 82–3].
35   The notion of the innocence of becoming also provides evidence of continuity between Nietzsche's 'early' and 'later' works.
36   The image of the child is deeply significant within Nietzsche; it is rare that he uses this image in negative terms. On innocence and the child in Nietzsche, see Babich [1995, pp. 31–51]. Babich draws on Nietzsche's reference to the seriousness of a child at play to illustrate the inadequacy of many interpretations of Nietzsche's dictum of will to power that read into it a doctrine of will to cruelty, which complements my rejection of a unity between practicality and cruelty in the critique of pity. See also Kaufmann's note 38 to *GS* 310 in which, citing *WP* 797, he remarks that the *pais paizon*, or child playing, is one of the central images in Nietzsche's thinking and is derived (by way of Friedrich Schiller's play theory of art) from Heraclitus.
37   Gadamer attempts to free the concept of play from the subjective meaning that he thinks it has within modern aesthetics. In his view, play refers specifically to the 'mode of being of the work of art itself', although play is limited in terms of representation to representing itself. Gadamer [1975, pp. 91 & 97]. On Gadamer's notion of play, see also O'Murchadha [1995, pp. 189–203].
38   Lingis [1985, p. 41].
39   Schrift [1990, p. 151].
40   Lingis [1985, p. 50].
41   Rosen [1995, pp. 219–20].
42   Lampert [1986, p. 297].
43   Rosen [1995, pp. 219–20].
44   Rosen therefore holds that the Ugliest Man is an expression of the ironic 'height' of a decaying European culture [1995, p. 222].
45   See Solomon [2003] for a discussion of Nietzschean virtues.

GUDRUN VON TEVENAR

Nietzsche's Objections to Pity and Compassion

[1]

Most of us are aware that there is a difference of some sort between pity and compassion, though we usually find it difficult to describe this difference with any precision. This is not surprising as these two attitudes overlap extensively due to the fact that both are based on our capacity for empathy which can, in appropriate circumstances, give rise to sympathy with the misfortunes and suffering of others. Sympathy can be expressed in varying ways depending on circumstances and the personalities and attitudes of agents, and it is here, I suggest, that most of the differences separating pity from compassion are to be found. As I have examined this topic at length elsewhere,[1] I will give here just a brief and much simplified summary.

It is generally agreed that both pitying and compassionate agents have sympathy with the suffering of others and are distressed by it. But while pity concentrates mainly on the suffered condition, say, famine or homelessness, compassion shows in addition also attentive and benevolent concern for the way persons endure their suffering. In other words, compassion focuses on persons who suffer while pity focuses on the condition suffered. But focusing just on the suffered condition tends to make persons suffering the condition feel unaddressed and thus alienated and this, in turn, allows a gap of distance, of separation, of otherness, to develop in the relation of pitying agents and the pitied which can easily lead to feelings of superiority and contempt on the part of pitying agents and to feelings of alienation, shame, and inferiority on the part of the pitied. Compassion, by contrast, with its attentive and benevolent concern for persons who suffer, is based on awareness of our common humanity[2] and thus, at its best, is able to bridge the damaging gap of separation and otherness with its associated negative feelings.

Yet, while it is indeed difficult to distinguish precisely pity from compassion in theory, in practice most people most of the time display a sensitive awareness of that distinction in their everyday use of these terms. They might, for instance, describe the patience, attentiveness, and kindness shown to someone in need as compassionate, while using the term pity to convey the unstable mixture of distress and unease which leads agents to the impulsive doing of something of help so as to be able to leave it behind. But practical awareness of a difference between pity and compassion is found most tellingly in the fact that the ascription of pity allows an extension utterly inappropriate in the ascription of compassion, inasmuch as we can use the term pity not just to describe an attitude of sympathy and distress at the suffering of others but also to convey superiority and even contempt. Consider here the ambiguity of a simple statement such as 'I pity you'. Without further details of context, these three words can with equal plausibility express sympathy as well as contempt for a person – they can even express disgust. Such ambiguity is not found in the ascription of compassion. Or consider whatever it is a person rejects when she exclaims 'I don't want your pity!' Does she reject the genuine sympathy available in compassion, or the superficiality of some sentimental gesture or phrase possible in pity?

So, while it is generally agreed that both pity and compassion are expressions of sympathy with the misfortunes and suffering of others, pity can do so in ways which permits also the expression of non-sympathetic attitudes of condescension and contempt. Hence it follows that only pity, and not compassion, is open to the much voiced objection of allowing, and perhaps even fostering, feelings of superiority and contempt and thus of shaming and humiliating its recipients.[3]

[2]
Due to the fact that there is only one German word, namely *Mitleid*, for pity and compassion, it is frequently not immediately obvious from an original text whether the author is talking about pity or compassion without careful consideration of context. Yet in the case of Nietzsche, context alone is often not conclusive, hence the variations

in translation, and close scrutiny of the kinds of objections voiced by Nietzsche against *Mitleid* is necessary. And here one can distinguish three different kinds of objections. These are (1) psychological objections; (2) detrimental to recipients objections; and (3) detrimental to givers objections.

(1) Psychological Objections:
Schopenhauer, famously, celebrated *Mitleid* as the greatest of all virtues and as the sole basis of genuine morality. He argued that *Mitleid* alone is able to overcome our naturally selfish inclinations and thus to motivate agents to act solely for the well-being of others, this being *the* characteristic of morally worthy actions. Nietzsche vehemently rejected this elevation of what he considered to be one of the more regrettable outcomes of slave morality. And while objections against Schopenhauer's promotion of *Mitleid* are voiced throughout Nietzsche's work, *Daybreak* 133 is notable for its strong polemic against Schopenhauer's psychological explanations of it. In *D* 133 Nietzsche alleges that Schopenhauer could not possibly have had much relevant experience of *Mitleid* because 'he had observed [it] so imperfectly and described [it] so badly'. And Nietzsche utterly dismisses as 'mere inventions' Schopenhauer's psychological foundations of *Mitleid* such as its supposed motivational purity of selflessness. Nietzsche derides the superficial evidence of selflessness and claims in opposition that subconsciously we are always and throughout concerned solely with our own selves. He tells us that:

> In truth: in *Mitleid* [...] we do no longer think consciously of our selves, but are doing so *very strongly unconsciously:* as when, if our foot slips [...] we perform the most purposive counter movements [...] [D 133].[4]

Initially, this example is quite puzzling as the analogy of a slipped foot does not seem to hold when used for *Mitleid,* since it describes the restoration of lost balance without reference to an external cause, which in the case of *Mitleid* would be the perception of someone suffering. However, I believe this is precisely Nietzsche's rather subtle point: he claims that consciously *Mitleid* may be selflessly concerned with external facts – the suffering of others – unconsciously, however, acting on the impulse of *Mitleid* is nothing but an intricate, purposive manoeuvre to restore our own internal balance. So the selflessness of *Mitleid* is only pretence; *Mitleid* is just part of our effort to recover psychological balance. Nietzsche further claims that we harbour a whole clutch of motives for *Mitleid*, which includes 'hoping to present ourselves as the more powerful and as a helper, being certain of applause, wanting to feel how fortunate we are by contrast, or to relieve boredom'. And he even goes as far as claiming that *Mitleid* can be just a case of 'subtle self-defence or even a piece of revenge' [D 133].

(2) The detrimental to recipients objections:
Nietzsche gives the title *Being Pitied* to *Daybreak* 135 and there provides us with a particularly flamboyant detrimental to recipients objection. He states that the mere idea of being pitied 'evokes a moral shudder' in savages, because to savages, being still, we are meant to assume, uncorrupted by conventional morality, 'to offer pity is as good as to offer contempt'. Indeed, should a defeated enemy weep and plead then savages will, out of *Mitleid* and contempt, let him live, humiliated like a dog, while those who endure suffering with defiant pride repulse *Mitleid* and thus earn their admiration and praise. There are two points here: note that mere pleading for *Mitleid* already exposes one as weak and contemptible, and this is compounded with humiliation should these pleas be successful and one is actually shown *Mitleid* in response. For now one is no longer a defeated enemy who can retain some dignity and add to the glory of the victor when killed, now one is just a wretched dog – not worthy of such a death. For the next example of a detrimental to recipients objection let us turn to *Daybreak* 138, which, because of its deep insights and impressive psychological observations, deserves to be quoted (almost) in full.

> Becoming *more tender [Das Zärtlicherwerden]*
> If we love, honour, admire someone, and then afterwards discover that he is *suffering* [...] our feeling of love, reverence and admiration changes in *an essential way:* it becomes more *tender [zärtlicher]* [...] Only now does it seem possible that we might be able to *give something back* to him, while previously he lived in our imagination as too elevated *[erhaben]* for our gratitude. This capacity to give back something gives us great joy and exultation *[Erhebung]*. We seek to find out what will ease his pain, and give this to him; should he

want consoling words and looks, attentions, services, presents – we give them; – above all however, should he want us *to suffer* at his suffering, we will give ourselves out as suffering, but have in all this *the enjoyment of active gratitude:* which is, in short, *benevolent revenge* [...]. From all this it follows that even in the most favourable case, there is something degrading in suffering and something elevating *[Erhöhendes]* and conducive to superiority in pitying *[Mitleiden]* [D 138].

Here Nietzsche invites us to retrace the steps, each seemingly easy and harmless, by which the slow and degrading reversal of status of a sufferer is accomplished. The key words are 'tender' *[zärtlich]* and variations on 'elevation' *[Erhebung, erhaben etc]*. Remember that outside of the domain of romantic love, we are tender or become more tender to those perceived as vulnerable either because of neediness or suffering or because they are fragile or very young. And we show our tenderness by being gentle, considerate, protective. Yet note how this can all too readily slide, according to Nietzsche, into a somewhat different attitude where vulnerability is now seen as making the other more accessible, nearer, smaller than before, so that, in an insidiously erosive way, it becomes tempting and easy to invade his space and undermine his dignity. In this way, Nietzsche claims, the 'tenderness' of *Mitleid* can belittle recipients and diminish their status.

As a further consequence of the pitying relation we have reversal of the respective positions of participants. Prior to being pitied, the sufferer was admired and revered, now, however, he is belittled and made dependent, while the pitier, who previously looked up to him, now occupies the elevated position of superiority. Thus, when looking at the process of *Mitleid* in the way Nietzsche suggests here, one cannot but concede some plausibility to his claim that what actually goes on is a kind of revenge.

(3) The detrimental to givers objections:
The most widely known detrimental to givers objection is the claim that in the 'suffering-with' of *Mitleid* two now suffer and one of them needlessly and uselessly. Regardless of the dubious validity of this claim because of the phenomenological distinctness of the two kinds of suffering, Nietzsche goes into rhetorical overdrive and predicts that if *Mitleid* were to rule for just one day, humanity would perish im-

mediately.[5] But Nietzsche has other arguments too. Thus Zarathustra
declares, in the by now familiar detrimental-to-recipients tone, that he
badly wronged a sufferer's pride when he helped him. But, importantly, Zarathustra also declares that he washes his hand and also wipes
clean his soul because he has helped a sufferer, and he admits, furthermore, that he feels ashamed because of the sufferer's shame.[6] These
latter statements show quite conclusively that Nietzsche believed
agents pollute and degrade themselves when they show *Mitleid* and
that *Mitleid* is therefore detrimental to its givers. The claim that *Mitleid* is shaming and thus degrading to givers as well as receivers seems
surprising given that Nietzsche held, as in *D* 138 discussed above, that
the giving of *Mitleid* actually fosters feelings of superiority. This apparent contradiction can be dissolved by noting that it is Zarathustra
who speaks here: because Zarathustra, being the exemplar and teacher
of a noble kind of morality, has no need for the supposedly devious
and underhand methods of *Mitleid* inherited from, and still reeking
with the stench of, their origin in slave morality's resentment[7] in order
to feel superior. Zarathustra, as portrayed by Nietzsche, *is* superior and
hence is supposed to feel shame when having recourse to the paradigm virtue of slave morality – namely *Mitleid.*

   Variations of the psychological and detrimental to recipients objections described above are widely known and much used even in our
ordinary, everyday reactions to instances of pity. But the detrimental
to givers objection is, I believe, distinctly Nietzschean and we will see
later on how this kind of objection is informed by distinctly Nietzschean views of the role and significance of suffering.

[3]
On examining the three kinds of objections with the pity/compassion
distinction as briefly outlined at the beginning of this essay in mind,
we find that Nietzsche's objections are almost exclusively concerned
with *Mitleid* understood as pity and not as compassion. Notice that
Mitleid as described by Nietzsche is either contaminated from the beginning with contempt and shame as in the examples of the savages
and Zarathustra, or *Mitleid* seems preoccupied mainly with the mental
state of the agent and not with the sufferer. But understanding *Mitleid*
merely as pity is, I suggest, the main reason why Nietzsche's objec-

tions, though highly sophisticated and eminently plausible, nonetheless somehow miss their target as far as Schopenhauer is concerned. Because Schopenhauer, when elevating *Mitleid* as the highest virtue, emphasizes different aspects from those singled out by Nietzsche. Thus Schopenhauer claims that agents with *Mitleid* can act selflessly and solely for the weal of sufferers precisely because they see in sufferers someone like themselves. In other words, *Mitleid* for Schopenhauer cannot be other than compassion because, as described by him, there is no gap of distance and otherness between agents and sufferers and hence no associated negative feelings of alienation and shame. This is not to say, of course, that Schopenhauer had no idea of *Mitleid* understood as pity. Indeed, he takes great pains to distinguish his kind of *Mitleid*, i.e. compassion, from various deviations and aberrations such as those that Nietzsche later concentrates on. Thus Schopenhauer admits that we do at times 'benefit' others from motives other than genuine *Mitleid*, for instance from the motive of malice, as

> when I do good to one man in order to annoy another whom I do not benefit, or to make the other man's sufferings more acute, or even to put to shame a third who does not benefit the first, or, finally, by my action to humiliate the man whom I benefit.[8]

Naturally, Schopenhauer refused to grant these kinds of actions any moral value whatsoever, since he regards the moral value of compassion as entirely dependent on the motive to act purely for the weal of others. We can see, then, that Schopenhauer could willingly and wholeheartedly agree with most of Nietzsche's objections and yet keep his own theory intact, since he elevates compassion while Nietzsche denigrates pity.

This conclusion, though interesting, is also quite puzzling and leads to two closely related questions: first, did Nietzsche truly believe that mere pity is all there is to *Mitleid*? Second, if so, was that because he lacked 'inner understanding' of the misery and contingency of suffering as Nussbaum claims?[9] I suggest the answer to both these questions is 'no'.

[4]
Yet before we can answer these questions in detail, we must gain an understanding of Nietzsche's attitude towards suffering, one's own and the suffering of others. Nietzsche was highly critical of the attitude towards suffering prevalent at his time, and indeed now, where suffering, particularly the suffering of others, of the multitude of others, mattered and mattered greatly. He blamed Christianity for this and also, more narrowly because applying only to the educated, Schopenhauer. Nietzsche observed how both Christianity and Schopenhauer ascribe to our suffering empirical as well as metaphysical significance. Christian dogma links empirical suffering here on earth to both original and personal sin and promises release via purification and atonement as well as salvation via Christ; while Schopenhauer states that our empirical suffering is but the inevitable outcome of a metaphysical reality governed by a blind, relentless drive to life – the Will. Thus both theories offer an explanation why suffering is so pervasive and the seemingly inescapable lot of each and everyone. Indeed, considering the nature of these explanations, one can readily come to see why both theories value and promote *Mitleid* as they see in it an appropriate because somewhat soothing and consoling response to suffering. Yet Nietzsche utterly rejects this response, particularly because of its openness to passivity and its easy slide to resignation. Nor is that all. Even more abhorrent, because more threatening to Nietzsche's revaluation project, are the wider consequences of the Christian and Schopenhauerian views, inasmuch as both drain value out of this our earthly lives. Christianity postulates life on earth as a mere testing station and hence just preliminary to the real life to come in the beyond; and Schopenhauer, with his well-known pessimism, goes even further by claiming that it would be better for us not to be born, thus rejecting life altogether. Given that one of Nietzsche's most urgent aims was the affirmation and, indeed, re-affirmation of life, it is not surprising that the combination of *Mitleid* and negative significance of suffering should be seen by him as a threat and odious obstacle to this aim.

Against *Mitleid* and against the negative significance of suffering Nietzsche puts forward his own proposals. He argues in *On the Genealogy of Morals*[10] that suffering and particularly the suffering of others, i.e. the suffering of the sick, weak, and misshapen multitude of the herd, must not be allowed to obstruct the life of the strong – those lucky, talented, healthy few who must be promoted because needed as blueprint for future men. He therefore warns us against what he calls 'the conspiracy of the sufferers against the well-formed and victorious'[11] and makes his famous, or perhaps infamous, claim that the weak pose the greatest danger to the strong, and that the strong and healthy have to be shielded from polluting contact with the sick with their secret resentment and veiled pleas for *Mitleid*. On a more positive note, Nietzsche urges us to accept our suffering as an integral part of a worthwhile life, to actively and purposefully master it and not just passively 'suffer' it. Active acceptance and mastering are not just better ways of coping with suffering, they function at the same time as an affirmation of life. Hence Nietzsche despised the feeble resignation and impotent resentment with which member of the herd fail to accept their suffering, thus fail to cope, thus fail to affirm.

But while Nietzsche despised wretched suffering, he greatly admired the 'noble' suffering of those who were able to overcome their suffering, even their very severe suffering, and thereby turn suffering into a heightened sense of power, creativity, and distinction. Endured like this, suffering can become a merit of such magnitude as to lift the sufferer high above those not so distinguished. Listen to Nietzsche in *BGE* 270:

> [...] this spiritual and silent arrogance of sufferers, this pride of the selected in knowledge, of the 'initiated', of the almost sacrificed, needs all forms of disguise to protect itself from the touch of intrusive and pitying hands and of everything else that is not like itself in pain. Profound suffering makes noble, it separates [BGE 270].

[5]
With the above in mind, let us now turn to the second of our two questions and Nussbaum's claim that Nietzsche lacked 'inner understanding' of the misery and contingency of suffering. Nussbaum accuses Nietzsche of insensitivity for the way suffering can be erosive of human well-being. She argues that Nietzsche had no grasp of the simple truth that one functions badly when one is hungry and that stoic

self-command is just not possible when suffering from what she terms 'basic vulnerability'. Nussbaum contrasts 'basic vulnerability', which comprises deprivations of resources utterly central to human mental, physical, and intellectual functioning, from 'bourgeois vulnerability' with its relatively comfortable pains of loneliness, ill health, bad reputation, and so on. These latter pains, Nussbaum argues, are indeed painful enough but not such as to impair human functioning altogether. She insists that Nietzsche simply ignored 'basic vulnerability' since he apparently believed that even a beggar could be a stoic hero so long as socialism and *Mitleid* did not keep him weak. Thus Nussbaum concludes that despite all his famous unhappiness Nietzsche was without 'inner understanding of the ways contingency matters for virtue'.[12]

These are powerful and thought provoking objections. However, I suggest that they somewhat miss their point because Nietzsche was not interested in virtue, did not address himself to the multitude, and did not, therefore, envisage the possibility of members of the herd growing into stoic heroes. Moreover, there is ample evidence throughout his writings as well as in his letters that he was not insensitive to the fact that deprivation – mental and physical – stunts growth and that severe pain and misery not only hurts but also harms people. Yet Nietzsche nonetheless, and here lies the novel and controversial nature of his thought, refused to grant suffering, even severe suffering, the kind of significance assigned to it through the influence of Christianity and Schopenhauer. For this leads, almost inevitably, to *Mitleid* and hence, Nietzsche feared, to erosion of the will to power of those precious, privileged few by undermining their confidence in themselves and in their lives. The truly objectionable feature of suffering, Nietzsche holds, is not the well-acknowledged fact that it hurts and harms people, but the non-acknowledged and deeply deplorable fact that so many sufferers simply fail to respond appropriately to their suffering and thus allow themselves to become feeble, impaired, wretched; in other words, they allow themselves to 'suffer' hurt and harm. One can conclude, then, that Nietzsche was not insensitive to the misery and contingency of suffering but simply refused to accept its alleged wider significance.

[6]

Regarding the question whether Nietzsche truly believed that mere pity is all there is to *Mitleid*, one must concede that much speaks for such a conclusion since, as we have seen, most of the objections put forward by Nietzsche against *Mitleid* apply to *Mitleid* understood merely as pity and not as compassion. Because of this some commentators[13] as well as translators[14] believe that pity is all there is to Nietzsche's *Mitleid* and thus to doubt that Nietzsche had any inkling of the existence and power of compassion. In what follows I will argue that Nietzsche was aware of the existence of compassion and, indeed, feared its power.

To see why this is so, let us focus again on the difference between pity and compassion with the help of Nietzsche's own words. Zarathustra declares:

> But I am a giver: gladly give I as a friend to friends. But strangers and the poor may help themselves to the fruit of my trees: it shames less that way.[15]

Let us leave aside the question of shame and concentrate solely on the attitude of the speaker who describes himself as a giver. He gladly gives to friends – presumably out of friendship, and also gives to strangers and the poor – presumably out of *Mitleid*. So Zarathustra gives to both, but note the difference in his attitude towards them! With the first group Zarathustra identifies because of the bond of friendship, he is attentive to them as someone like himself – as a friend to friends. But the second group, the strangers and poor, he keeps at a distance, a distance defined by their condition of strangeness and poverty. This is precisely the distance we have earlier defined as characteristic of the attitude of pity. It separates the needy by defining them – as with a label – by their condition of strangeness and poverty thus failing to attend to them as persons, as someone like oneself. One consequence of keeping strangers and the poor in this way separate and at a distance is that, after opening the gates to one's orchard, nothing stops one now from happily continuing one's own pursuits such as, perhaps, feasting with one's friends while the needy are away in the orchard.

Contrast this with what Nietzsche writes in *On the Genealogy of Morals*[16] where he speaks of the danger the weak pose for the strong as well as of the danger of 'great *Mitleid*'. Nietzsche informs us that 'the failed, downcast, and broken' are the ones 'who most dangerously poison and call into question our confidence in life, in man, in ourselves'. Thus he warns us against what he calls 'the conspiracy of the sufferers' and against a time when the weakest

> [...] might succeed in *shoving* their own misery, all misery generally *into the conscience* of the happy: so that they would one day begin to be ashamed of their happiness and perhaps say to each other: 'it is a disgrace to be happy! there *is too much misery!*' [GM III, 14].

But how do the weak manage to *shove* their misery into the conscience of the happy? They do it by inducing in them 'great *Mitleid*'. It begins, according to Nietzsche, with the 'veiled look' in the eyes of the wretched which produces in the strong a 'deep sadness'. Nietzsche eloquently describes that 'veiled look' as a dangerous mixture of pain and secret resentment: dangerous, because the resultant 'deep sadness' in the strong is just the beginning. For Nietzsche predicts that this sadness will eventually grow into guilt and shame until, in the end, the happy begin to doubt their very right to happiness in face of '*too much misery*'. In other words, the misery and wretchedness of the weak has potentially serious consequences for the strong inasmuch as it undermines their hitherto unquestioned confidence in the superior value of themselves and their lives.

Please note that the objection to *Mitleid* in *GM* III, 14 is also of the detrimental-to-givers kind, but, unlike Zarathustra earlier, the agent now experiences and succumbs to 'great *Mitleid*', and is thus not able to simply cleanse herself of its effects by 'washing her hands and wiping her soul'. Why not? The reason why she cannot simply cleanse herself of the effects of 'great *Mitleid*' is, I suggest, because the difference between great and ordinary *Mitleid* is precisely the difference between compassion and pity. Pity is usually episodic; it arises in response to a distressing incident and once the psychological balance is restored again, things return to normal. Not so with compassion or great *Mitleid*. Compassion has the capacity, eloquently described by Nietzsche, to permanently alter one's outlook to life. So, while the effects of pity can be wiped away, the effects of compassion cannot.

Lets go into this in more detail. We defined general *Mitleid* as distress at the suffering of others. There is ample everyday evidence that in the case of pity this distress usually leads to action that can relieve, at one and the same time, both the suffering of others and the distress of agents. This is precisely the case with Zarathustra: feeling pity for the hungry, he opens the gates of his orchard (or makes a credit card donation) thus relieving the hungry (or contributing to the relief of the hungry) and his own distress. And now he can switch off, as it were, and continue untroubled with his previous lifestyle. Not so, however, with the agent Nietzsche describes in *GM*! Having looked deeply into the eyes of the wretched, that agent now experiences a 'deep sadness'; a sadness, moreover, which Nietzsche believes will eventually undermine her previous enjoyment and affirmation of life. In other words, after looking deep in the eyes of pain, even if they also harbour secret resentment, things no longer remain the same as the agent is now troubled by doubt about her previously unquestioned right to happiness, unsettled by the thought that 'it is a disgrace to be happy! *there is too much misery!*' So, unlike Zarathustra, this agent will not be able to merrily feast with her friends while the hungry are away in the orchard.

So what is the difference? The difference is, firstly, that Zarathustra feels *Mitleid* merely as pity while the deeply sad agent feels what Nietzsche calls 'great *Mitleid*', which we can now confidently translate as compassion. By allowing the pain of others to move her in such a way as to feel solidarity with them, the compassionate agent bridges the gap of separation and otherness by acknowledging them as persons with whom she has a common bond. And that very acknowledgement prevents her now from continuing to enjoy the kind of self-affirming outlook that Nietzsche believes is – and wants to maintain as – the birthright of the strong. So that, unlike mere pity, great *Mitleid* or compassion tends to have long lasting consequences for one's outlook on life. We have seen that merely pitying agents can move on once they have relieved, or seemed to have relieved, the distress of the sufferer and thereby also their own distress. This is not the case with compassionate agents. As Nietzsche clearly grasped, their 'great sadness' results in uncertainty towards their right to happiness in face of the suffering of others and thus leaves an indelible mark on their future attitude to life. Secondly, acknowledging solidarity with sufferers also initiates the dreaded slide into 'degeneration', since Nietzsche believed that once tempted by compassion to succumb to sadness and feelings of guilt, the agent has forfeited, as it were, her right to membership of the strong since she now identifies with miserable members of the herd.

It is this very power to tempt the strong to identify with the weak, thus subverting confidence in their own superiority, that, I suggest, Nietzsche most fears about 'great *Mitleid*' or compassion. Hence the polemic, hence the passionate rhetoric of his objections. For Nietzsche certainly has no objections to feeding the hungry! Indeed, it would be a great mistake to conclude, as Nussbaum seems to have done, that Nietzsche rejects feeding the hungry when he rejects *Mitleid.* Feeding the hungry is perfectly all right as long as it is done from an overflow of strength, from an abundance of power,[17] and not from *Mitleid*, especially not from 'great *Mitleid*' – that's simply too dangerous!

Thus we can give an unequivocal 'no' in answer to the question whether Nietzsche believed that pity is all there is to *Mitleid*, since, quite obviously, Nietzsche was well aware of at least some of the distinctive features of compassion. As we have seen, the distinctive feature Nietzsche gives particular attention to is the effect compassion can have on its givers when it tempts them to succumb to 'deep sadness'. This particular feature Nietzsche believed to be extremely dangerous. Indeed, he considered its danger so great that he devotes much of *GM* III, 14 to illustrate and warn against it. Such as:

> But there could not be a greater or more disastrous misunderstanding than that the happy, the well made, the powerful of body and soul should thus start to doubt their *right to happiness* [...] away with this disgraceful softening of feelings! That the sick *do not* make the healthy sick [...] should surely be the highest viewpoint on earth [...] but that requires above all else that the healthy remain *separated* from the sick, protected even from the sight of the sick so that they do not misidentify themselves with the sick [...] the higher *must* not degrade itself into a tool of the lower, the pathos of distance *must* in all eternity also keep their tasks apart.

[7]
Now, commonsense intuition, saturated as it is, according to Nietzsche, with values of slave morality, generally gives a positive gloss to *Mitleid* despite its occasional misgivings over pity. Nietzsche, however, dismisses compassion even more vehemently than he dismisses pity. This is, of course, not surprising given that pity is, for Nietzsche, a useless, misdirected, and, seen from the perspective of the strong, quite inconsequential outcome of slave morality, while compassion, by contrast, is much more dangerous, as we have just seen. And in order to bring home his dismissal of 'great *Mitleid*' or compassion most forcefully, the only two times Nietzsche mentions 'great *Mitleid*' in *GM* III, 14 is in conjunction with 'great disgust' or 'great nausea' *[Ekel]*. Thus, fairly near the beginning he states:

> What is to be feared, what has a disastrous effect like no other disaster, that would not be the great fear of but the great *disgust [Ekel]* at man, likewise the great *compassion [Mitleid]* with man. Suppose, that these two should mate one day, then unavoidably something most sinister and uncanny would immediately come into this world, the 'last will' of man, his will to nothingness, nihilism.

And right at the end of *GM* III, 14 Nietzsche urges in a conspiratorial tone:

> So that we may, my friends, defend ourselves at least a while longer against the two worst plagues that may have been kept just for us – against the *great disgust at man!* against the *great compassion with man!*...

The great potential for danger and doom built by Nietzsche into this weird and unsettling combination of disgust and compassion is, I suggest, targeted directly against two of Schopenhauer's most distinctive legacies: his doctrine of compassion and his pessimism. On substituting disgust for pessimism (not a difficult thing to do), it becomes apparent why the combination of compassion with disgust-cum-pessimism can so readily lead to similar results in the philosophy of both Schopenhauer and Nietzsche. Giving due regard to their respective metaphysical assumptions, it can be seen without too much difficulty how easily the attitudes of compassion and disgust can combine to form a broad road leading directly to nihilism. Yet note how divergent are the interpretations accompanying this broad road to nihilism! Schopenhauer endorses compassion, denies this world, and sees in nothingness bliss and release; while Nietzsche negates compassion, affirms this world, and dreads the very prospect of nothingness. So, while the function and potential of compassion is acknowledged by both Schopenhauer and Nietzsche, they disagree, profoundly, about the desirability of what they both see as one of compassion's most distinctive results.

We can conclude, then, that unlike the case of pity which Schopenhauer could reject because not an instance of genuine *Mitleid*, both Schopenhauer and Nietzsche talk about the same thing when they talk about compassion. Obviously this does not prevent them from giving it opposing value. According to Schopenhauer, compassion is a right attitude because it reflects a true state of affairs, namely, the merely phenomenal distinctness of individuals. So that, if I give alms to a beggar, I do so, in a way, because I recognize, however vaguely, that here in front of me is someone like myself.[18] But according to Nietzsche, compassion is mistaken because it leads to a weakening of the strong and thus to a levelling of distinctions by narrowing 'the pathos of distance'. And this levelling, in turn, leads to decadence and rejection of life; all of which Nietzsche deeply abhors, hence his vociferous protests in *GM* III, 14.

[8]
We have set out to answer two questions: 1) is Nietzsche's utter rejection of any form of *Mitleid* due to the fact that he is unaware of, or insensitive to, the suffering of others? and 2) does he believe that there is no more to *Mitleid* than mere pity? We have answered both questions negatively. Firstly, Nietzsche was not insensitive to the suffering of others but dreaded what he believed to be highly deplorable consequences of giving suffering a wide significance. Not, to be sure, because he was unmindful of the fact that hurt and harm are painful and damaging, but because he feared that excessive emphasis on suffering, pervasive as that is to life itself, might lead to disgust *[Ekel]*, pessimism, and nihilism. Secondly, Nietzsche showed by his use of the three different kinds of objections that he was aware that there is a difference between *Mitleid* understood merely as pity and *Mitleid*

understood as compassion. And his most distinctive objection, the detrimental to givers objection, is aimed particularly at compassion as described by Schopenhauer and endeavours to prevent what Nietzsche believed to be compassion's most regrettable effect: the temptation to give in to 'deep sadness' by identifying with suffering members of the herd.

Naturally, while admiring the subtlety and initial persuasiveness of Nietzsche's objections, this is not the same as admitting that one cannot doubt the correctness of some of Nietzsche's conclusions. Critics of Nietzsche could note, for instance, the absence of any consideration whether compassion might not at times actually benefit its recipients; or critics could ask whether 'deep sadness' is the only possible lasting effect of compassion; or, indeed, critics might wonder whether 'great disgust' and 'great compassion' do invariably go hand-in-hand. Yet, while one might rightly disagree with some of Nietzsche's conclusions, there can be no doubt that he was extraordinarily astute and profound in his observations and displayed great psychological skill in pointing out some of the less desirable consequences of pity and compassion. He well observed, for instance, that pity can be detrimental to its recipients while nonetheless being relatively safe to its givers, since nothing detrimental or demanding usually accrues to givers when the needy are kept safely at a distance. Nietzsche also noted that compassion, by contrast, can be very demanding on its givers – and thus might be deemed detrimental to them – since allowing oneself to acknowledge a common bond with sufferers might seriously undermine one's previous, and perhaps happy and self-affirmative, outlook on life.

References

For a general bibliography of Nietzsche's works in German and English see end of this volume.

Arendt, Hannah: *On Revolution*, 1965, Penguin Books.

Blum, Lawrence: 'Compassion' in *Explaining Emotions*, A.O. Rorty (ed.), University of California Press, 1980.

Cartwright, D.E.: 'Schopenhauer's Compassion and Nietzsche's Pity' in *Schopenhauer Jahrbuch 69*, 1988, p. 557–67.

Clarke, Maudemarie: 'Friedrich Nietzsche *On the Genealogy of Morality*', translated, with Notes by Maudemarie Clark and Alan J. Swensen, Introduction by Maudemarie Clark, Hackett, Indianapolis/Cambridge, 1988.

Nussbaum, M.: 'Pity and Mercy: Nietzsche's Stoicism' in *Nietzsche, Genealogy, Morality*, Richard Schacht (ed.), University of California Press, 1994.

Schacht, Richard: (ed.), *Nietzsche, Genealogy, Morality*, Essays on Nietzsche's *Genealogy of Morals*, University of California Press, 1994.

Schopenhauer, Arthur: *On the Basis of Morality*, with an Introduction by D.E. Cartwright, Berghahn Books, Providence/Oxford, 1995.

Notes

1   Gudrun von Tevenar: *Pity and Compassion*, University of London, 2001.

2   To stress the feeling for 'common humanity' in compassion is not to say that compassion cannot also be felt for other sentient beings. It can, and is indeed endorsed and promoted as such by most advocates for compassion.

3   On the difference between pity and compassion with regard to Schopenhauer and Nietzsche see also Cartwright [1988]. Blum [1980] has also done very insightful work on this topic. Blum states that 'compassion involves a sense of shared humanity, of regarding the other as a fellow human being. This means that the other person's suffering [...] is seen as the kind of thing that could happen to anyone, including oneself'. And Blum distinguishes this from pity where 'one holds oneself apart from the afflicted person and from their suffering, thinking of it as something that defines that person as fundamentally different from oneself. In this way the other person's condition is taken as given, whereas in compassion the person's affliction is seen as deviating from the general conditions of human flourishing. That is why pity (unlike compassion) involves a kind of condescension, and why compassion is morally superior to

pity' [pp. 511–12]. See also Arendt [1965]. Arendt's account is particularly interesting, in as much as she describes various differences between pity and compassion and relates these to public (political) and private spheres. Arendt claims, moreover, that these differences are such as to raise doubt whether pity and compassion are indeed related. 'For compassion, to be stricken with the suffering of someone else as though it were contagious, and pity, to be sorry without being touched in the flesh, are not only not the same, they may not even be related'. One of the reason this may be so is that, according to Arendt, compassion is a passion, while pity is a mere sentiment [pp. 85–9].

4   All quotations from Nietzsche are my own translations.

5   *Daybreak* 134.

6   *Zarathustra* II, Of Pitiers.

7   *GM* I, 14.

8   Schopenhauer: *On the Basis of Morality*, introduction by D.E. Cartwright; Berghahn Books; Providence & Oxford, 1995; p. 164.

9   See Nussbaum in Schacht (ed), p. 161.

10   *GM* III, 14.

11   *GM* III, 14.

12   see Nussbaum in Schacht (ed) 1994.

13   For instance Cartwright in *Schopenhauer Jahrbuch 69*, 1988, pp. 557–67.

14   For an exception to always translating Nietzsche's *Mitleid* as pity, see reference above to Maudemarie Clarke where it is translated as compassion. Yet, this too has problems, as not all the instances of *Mitleid* cited in *GM* are, on my reading, instances of compassion. The majority are instances of pity. It might be useful, therefore, to consider using *Mitleid* as a technical term and not to translate it.

15   *Zarathustra* II, Of Pitiers.

16   *GM* III, 14.

17   *BGE* 260.

18   see Schopenhauer's metaphysical explanation of compassion in the appendix to his *On the Basis of Morality.*

THOMAS BROBJER

The Development of Nietzsche's Ethical Thinking

One way to better understand Nietzsche's ethics, and his many statements relating to morality, is to follow his ethical development. This seems to be an approach taken by few, if any, commentators on Nietzsche. This is unfortunate, for, as we will see, many of Nietzsche's statements are arguments against positions he himself earlier held (for example, Christian and Kantian morality, a Schopenhauerian emphasis on *Mitleid* or pity, utilitarianism and Stoic morality). Many of his statements, viewed according to this developmental perspective, become more comprehensible.

Nietzsche's ethical development can, in my view, be divided into five principle periods:

1. A religious period in his childhood, not well defined, but lasting to about 1865 (or a few years longer), consisting of a relatively conventional morality, with an emphasis on conscience and duty. This can be regarded as a form of Kantian or deontological morality.

2. A second period, consisting of two main tendencies, and covering the period ca 1865–75. The first tendency is an affirmation of Schopenhauerian pity. The second is an emphasis on aesthetic morality (placing aesthetic values above those of ethical values), coloured by amoralism.

3. A vaguely utilitarian period, ca 1875–80, in which Nietzsche emphasizes naturalism, and an historical approach as a principle method of analysis. This period is characterized by an emphasis on utility, biology and survival, and of pleasure and pain as important categories. Parallel to this, there is also a tendency to amoralism.

4. A period of amoralism, characterized by a severe critique of morality, especially utilitarianism and deontology (Kant), ca 1880–84. During the period 1880–82 Nietzsche seems also to have been fairly strongly influenced by Stoic moral thinking with their emphasis of

self-control and an ascetic way of life (and thus his severe critique of them later). Especially during this period Nietzsche read a large number of relevant works about historical and theoretical aspects of ethics. 5. A period of immoralism. This is a further radicalization of the previous period, ca 1885–88. Among others, morality is seen merely as a symptom.

I will concentrate my discussion on the first three periods since they are least well known. In fact, my approach here differs from that of almost all earlier studies and discussions of Nietzsche's ethics, which have ignored his development and almost without exception have concentrated on the late Nietzsche's views, and especially on the content of *On the Genealogy of Morals* (1887).

This division of Nietzsche's ethical development follows fairly closely the general divisions and changes in Nietzsche's thinking into three periods (the early, middle and late Nietzsche). Since this refers to Nietzsche's published writings, it does not include the young Nietzsche (before 1869 or 1872), but few would object to describing the young Nietzsche as religious. The first three of these conventional periods (the young, the early and the middle Nietzsche) corresponds well to the first three divisions that I have made of his ethical development. The conventional period of the late Nietzsche, ca 1882/83–89 has here been divided into two periods, to emphasize Nietzsche's reading and development, and the breaks between these last periods are slightly shifted.

For the period up to the end of the 1870s, this development is perhaps best described by Nietzsche himself in section 272 of *Human, All Too Human*, called 'Annual rings of individual culture', where he describes the first three stages of both a general and his own intellectual development:

> Men at present begin by entering the realm of culture as children affected religiously, and these sensations are at their liveliest in perhaps their tenth year [corresponding to Nietzsche's first religious ethical period], then pass over into feebler forms (pantheism) while at the same time drawing closer to science; they put God, immortality and the like quite behind them but fall prey to the charms of a metaphysical philosophy. At last they find this, too, unbelievable; art, on the other hand, seems to promise them more and more, so that for a time

metaphysics continues just to survive transformed into art or as a mood of artistic transfiguration. [Corresponding to Nietzsche's second ethical period, characterized by Schopenhauer and aesthetic ethics]. But the scientific sense grows more and more imperious and leads the man away to natural science and history and especially to the most rigourous methods of acquiring knowledge, while art is accorded an ever gentler and more modest significance. All this nowadays usually takes place within a man's first thirty years. It is the recapitulation of a curriculum at which mankind has been labouring for perhaps thirty thousand years.[1] [Corresponding to Nietzsche's third, more naturalistic and historical ethical period].

This ethical division also corresponds well with Nietzsche's religious development which can be divided into five similar periods:[2]

1. The pious and devote Christian childhood, 1844–61.
2. The period of loss of faith, 1861–65.
3. Passive atheism: Nietzsche as non-believer. Almost no critique of Christianity, 1866–74.
4. Critique of Christianity is expressed, but not yet a major theme, 1875/6–79
5. Antichrist: Nietzsche's atheism is radicalized and made more explicit, 1880–88.[3]

Here the first two religious periods correspond to the first ethical period, while the last two ethical periods correspond to the last atheist period.

The division made above about Nietzsche's ethical development is based on my reading of Nietzsche's philosophy and statements about morality, but it is also partly confirmed by Nietzsche himself, who briefly discusses his ethical development in the preface to *On the Genealogy of Morals* (1887).[4] He there writes:

> Because of a scruple peculiar to me [...] my curiosity as well as my suspicions were bound to halt quite soon at the question of where our good and evil really *originated*. In fact, the problem of the origin of evil pursued me even as a boy of thirteen: at an age in which you have 'half childish trifles, half God in your heart', I devoted to it my first childish literary trifle, my first philosophical effort – and as for the 'solution' of the problem I posed at that time, well, I gave the honour to God, as was only fair, and made him the *father* of evil.[5]

A note, from between October 1858 and March 1859, seems to con-
firm Nietzsche's words; in it he lists 'freedom', 'freedom of will' (in
Latin), 'predestination', 'unlimited power of God?', 'the freedom of
God' and states in the only sentence in the note: 'God not good, not
evil, beyond human concepts'.[6] Compare also Nietzsche's letter to
Pinder from the end of March/early April 1859 where he suggests the
theme 'About godly and human freedom' to think and write about. He
continues: 'Just toss the question around. What is freedom? Who is
free? What is freedom of the will? etc.' It seems likely that we in this
note and letter see a sign of Nietzsche's beginning loss of faith, and of
his thinking which in 1862 lead to his two important *Germania* essays
'*Fatum und Geschichte*' ('Fate and History') and '*Willensfreiheit und
Fatum*' ('Freedom of the Will and Fate').[7]

This description corresponds well to the first period of his ethical
development. He continues in the preface of *On the Genealogy of
Morals* to describe how and why he was able to change approach –
and that he with this new approach at first gave different answers
(though, these are not specified).

> Fortunately, I have since learnt to separate theology from morality and ceased
> looking for the origin of evil *behind* the world. Some schooling in history and
> philology, together with an innate sense of discrimination with respect to
> questions of psychology, quickly transformed my problem into another one:
> under what conditions did man devise these value judgements good and evil?
> *and what value do they themselves possess?* Have they hitherto hindered or
> furthered human prosperity? [...] Thereupon I discovered and ventured divers
> answers [...] out of my answers there grew new questions, inquiries, con-
> jectures, probabilities – until at length I had a country of my own.[8]

These 'divers answers' included for a while pity and later utility.
However, Nietzsche does not emphasize the views he has left behind,
but instead those which he still believes valuable and correct in 1887.
In section four of the preface to *GM* Nietzsche then lists a number of
sections from the three volumes of *Human, All Too Human* for which
he argues this is true, i.e. that he already then held the views he argues
for in 1887. This may sometimes be correct, but I will show below
that in many respects the late Nietzsche's view on morality had
changed significantly since 1878.

An alternative and valuable way to view Nietzsche's relation to and discussion of ethics is to argue that he really began to be interested in ethics and morality at the time of writing *Daybreak* (1880/81), and from then on he basically has one and the same overall view, even if it was radicalized (periods 4 and 5). This is supported by Nietzsche's own statements in the preface to *D*: 'At that time [at the time of writing *D*] [...] I commenced to undermine our *faith in morality*',[9] and in *Ecce Homo:* 'With this book begins my campaign against *morality* [...] With 'Daybreak' I first took up the struggle against the morality of unselfing'.[10]

However, this view needs at least to be refined. Nietzsche's view of ethics did in some ways develop also after 1880. Furthermore, his interest clearly began before *D*. He has a full book on morality in *HH*, book 2: 'On the History of the Moral Sensations.' That Nietzsche was already in *HH* concerned about ethics, is, apart from his discussions in that work, also admitted by Nietzsche himself, as we have seen above, who wrote in *GM*:

> My ideas on the *origin* of our moral prejudices [...] received their first, brief, and provisional expression in the collection of aphorism that bears the title *Human, All Too Human: A Book for Free Spirits.* [...] They were already in essentials the same ideas that I take up again in the present treatises.[11]

That Nietzsche's interest in and concern about ethics increased first in 1876/77 and then dramatically in 1880/81 can be seen simply in how often he uses words like *Moral, Sittlichkeit* and *Tugend* (virtue). The occurence of these three words increase almost three-fold in 1876/77, and in 1880/81 yet again almost five-fold. However, this does not apply to the word *Ethik* and words based on that 'root'. Such words are relatively frequent during his first two periods (until 1875), but thereafter become less and less frequent. I suggest that this is due both to that when the young Nietzsche discusses ancient morality, as a philologist, he mostly uses the word ethics, and to the fact that Schopenhauer uses the word *Ethik* more frequently than *Moral*.

Before discussing and characterizing each of Nietzsche's five ethical periods – treating in most detail the first three periods since they are least well known – four general points need to be clarified:

1. Nietzsche says so little about ethics before ca 1878 that his views in the first two periods are not well defined.
2. One aspect of Nietzsche's relation to ethics which is not clearly visible when it is divided into periods is consistent and constant tendencies and aspects. For example, an emphasis on the heroic. Even more important, as a red thread though his ethical thinking, is his 'amoralism' (which I have tried to emphasize). It is there already in the first period, visible e.g. in his rejection of free will in his early fatum essay. In the second period it become more pronounced, and is part of his aesthetic morality. It is also present in his third period, for example visible in his naturalism: 'The complete unaccountability of man for his actions and his nature is the bitterest draught the man of knowledge has to swallow'.[12] That it is present in the last two periods, that is during the 1880s, is obvious and already emphasized above.
3. Another important constant is the role of antiquity, and especially Greek antiquity, in Nietzsche's ethical thinking.[13] In this essay this will be greatly *underestimated*. This is due to the fact that I am discussing and relating Nietzsche's ethical development to the nineteenth century conventional discussions and classifications of ethics. My own view is that Nietzsche essentially along all five periods was strongly influenced by ancient Greek ethical thinking, and thus had a close kinship to virtue ethics, as I have argued earlier.[14]
4. A constant theme of this essay is the importance of self-overcoming for Nietzsche's views of ethics and for his ethical development. That Nietzsche himself had held many of the ethical views he later attacks and criticizes is a question of some importance, since, apart from historical analysis (which he also uses extensively in his dissection of ethics), psychological speculation and introspection is his main approach and 'method' when it comes to moral analysis and ethical discussion.

Nietzsche continually emphasizes self-overcoming, *Selbstüberwindung*, generally and he discusses his own (ethical) development in terms of *Selbstüberwindung*. For example, in *Beyond Good and Evil*, 32 he writes:

> The overcoming of morality, in a certain sense even the self-overcoming of morality: let this be the name for that protracted secret labour which has been

reserved for the subtlest, most honest and also most malicious consciences as living touchstones of the soul.[15]

In the poem at the end of the text, he emphasizes how he continually develops and practices self-overcoming:

> Am I another? A stranger to myself? Sprung from myself? A wrestler who subdued himself too often? Turned his own strength against himself too often, checked and wounded by his own victory? [...] only he who changes remains akin to me.

In notes from the 1880s he writes: 'My strongest quality [*Eigenschaft*] is self-overcoming' and 'Practice self-overcoming'.[16] And directly related to ethics he states:

> The self-overcoming which the researcher in the fields of ethics has to demand of himself is not to be prejudiced against positions and deeds which he earlier had learnt to respect; he must, as researcher 'have crushed his honouring heart'.[17]

Nietzsche's Ethical Periods

1. A Religious Period

This period belongs to Nietzsche's childhood; it is not well defined, but lasts to about 1865 (or a few years longer), consisting of a relatively conventional morality, with an emphasis on conscience (*Gewissen*) and duty.

There is almost no discussion of ethics or morality in Nietzsche's early letters, but in one to his mother and sister, 20 August 1861, he writes: 'what God does, is well done', reflecting both an acceptance of Christian views and a certain sense of fatalism which could be a good breeding-ground for amoralism. (We can note that this statement is surprisingly closely related to his later concept of *amor fati*.) In another letter, to Granier, 28 July 1862, he writes that he has been spending the summer with 'refuting materialism'. We are not told how he did this or from what position this was done, but it seems likely that it was done from a religious and conventional moral perspective. There is also very little discussion of ethics or morality in Nietzsche's papers before 1865. However, in November 1862 he makes a few reflections on ethics. The first is a more personal note:

> That night I wanted to do some Latin [school]work, but met with Stöckert and conversed with him about the influence of art on morality, or rather on the relation between art and morality. We spoke until 2 a.m.[18]

This is immediately followed by a more theoretical discussion – in line with his two essays on 'Fate and History' from earlier in the spring (which were strongly influenced by Emerson) – connecting morality to what is necessary (fate):

> Every necessary act is justified, every useful act is necessary. Immoral is every act which is not necessary and brings suffering to others; we become very dependent on public opinion when we feel regret and feel doubt about ourselves. If an immoral action is necessary, then we regard it as moral.[19]

This statement, with its fatalism or emphasis on acceptance of what is necessary, can possibly, like the statement in the letter above, be seen as foreshadowing Nietzsche's later amoralism and concept of *amor fati*.

During the summer of 1863, he excerpts from and discusses Emerson's essays '*Schönheit*' and '*Naturphysiognomie*' in *The Conduct of Life*, touching on the relationship of beauty, nature and ethics.[20] Apart from the Bible and religion, Emerson seems to have been the most important intellectual influence on the young Nietzsche's view of ethics.

In 1864 he emphasizes the difference between ancient and modern ethics,[21] and he briefly touches on ethical themes in his school-essay on Oedipus and Theognis. In both he expresses scepticism about emphasizing or interpreting them as primarily ethical, instead he argues that they reflect a tragic and aristocratic attitude.[22] He even explicitly states that it was not ethical questions which attracted him to Theognis, but the confusing fragmentary nature of his extant writings.

There exists such limited information about Nietzsche's views of ethics during his first twenty years that this period is difficult to characterize. Nonetheless, it is reasonable to refer to his ethical views at this time as Christian and conventional. We ought also to note the similarity to Kantian ethics, which also emphasizes conscience and duty.[23]

Important for ending this period is that Nietzsche lost his faith between 1862–65. This in itself did not obviously change his views on ethics, which is more clearly related to his discovery of Schopenhauer, but it created the precondition for such a change. The most important direct philosophical influences on this development are likely to have been his reading of Ralph Waldo Emerson and Ludwig Feuerbach's *Das Wesen des Christenthum* and David Friedrich Strauss' *Das Leben Jesu* in 1865 and the closely allied Daniel Schenkel's *Das Charakterbild Jesu* (third edition, 1864),[24] which seems finally to have confirmed and reinforced his loss of faith in the Christian God and religion.[25] His scepticism regarding Christianity is fairly obvious in writings from the spring of 1862, most clearly so in the essay *Fatum und Geschichte* and in a draft to a letter to Krug and Pinder, 27 April 1862.[26] An important, but non-philosophical, probable additional cause for Nietzsche's increasing scepticism towards Christianity was the teaching of historical criticism at Pforta, i.e. the approach or method of regarding religious texts not as holy but as historical documents to be interpreted by means of their historical content and context.

One anecdote from his schooldays, told by Elisabeth, probably well describes his generally serious, dutiful and somewhat stubborn character as a child. It also illustrates his strong belief in duty, conscience and self-control. One day as the young pupils were leaving school it began to rain heavily. The other boys ran as fast as they could while Franziska from the flat-window saw Nietzsche walking unhurriedly and bareheaded, using his cap and his handkerchief to protect his slate from the rain. She signalled him to run, but he continued solemnly walking. When he arrived home completely soaked, Franziska scolded him for not running home and trying to avoid becoming completely wet. Nietzsche, however, answered earnestly: 'But mother, in the school-statues it is written: The boys, when leaving the school, shall not run and rump but walk calmly and well-behaved to their homes.'[27]

2. A second Period characterized by Pity and Aesthetic Morality

This period, ca 1865–75, contains some relevant philological work and consists of two main tendencies. During this time, Nietzsche did much philological work, including some with references to ethics, especially in his discussions of Democritus. The first tendency is involved with Schopenhauerian pity. The second has an emphasis on aesthetic morality (placing aesthetic values above those of ethical values), also coloured by amoralism.

As in the previous period, there is little explicit discussion of morality. Nietzsche certainly was less interested in ethics during this period than he would be later, and he read almost no work which specifically dealt with it, although ethics was discussed in a number of books he read. Before discussing the two ethical tendencies Nietzsche adopted during this period, let us first examine his discussion of morality in relation to his philological work.

In late 1865 he excerpts several pages from a theological journal, and thereafter seems to be discussing or elaborating on this, criticizing Christianity and priests for two pages. Among others, he denies, in good Enlightenment tradition, that morality is dependent on what concept of God one has.[28]

Nietzsche discusses ethics much more extensively in 1867/68, but then almost exclusively from a philological perspective, mostly in relation to his work on Democritus. He frequently mentions, and sometimes briefly discusses Democritus' ethical works and fragments – but these discussions have almost only philological relevance and almost no philosophical content. He frequently discusses whether Democritus' ethical works (fragments) are genuine or have been falsely attributed to him. He discusses influences on him, such as from Pythagoras, and Democritus' possible influence on later thinkers, including Aristotle. A few notes seem to imply that he intended to work more directly with Democritus' ethical writings, but he seems to have done little of this. Occasionally, Nietzsche's notes include ethical evaluations.[29]

Although he mostly shows appreciation of Democritus, he occasionally also expresses mild critique.[30] Frequently one can notice an influence from Schopenhauer and Lange on his writings, both on these more philological ones and on the few more general reflections which can be found among them.[31] We can further see a scepticism towards ethics, and an emphasis on the unconscious, both aspects probably influenced by Schopenhauer.[32] Other ethical statements are based on F.A. Lange's book *History of Materialism* (1866).[33]

Among these mainly philological notes one can also find a three page working through Aristotle's ethics.[34] On another occasion he writes down topics for future essays to write, including '*Schopenhauer als Schriftsteller*', '*Pessimismus im Alterthum*' and '*Goethes Ethik*'. One can find a few notes which are related to the first two, but unfortunately none for the last one.

After he became professor in Basel in early 1869, his notes become more extensive, and include more non-philological reflections. Two tendencies related to ethics are then visible during this period.

The first tendency is a Schopenhauerian emphasis on *Mitleid*, pity. Pity or compassion, *Mitleid*, is a central concept in Nietzsche's view of ethics. During this period he approved of it, but after his break with Schopenhauer in 1876 he would severely criticize it. This later critique is well known, but his appropriation of pity during this time is less well known. Already immediately after his discovery of Schopenhauer, he writes an important letter to his mother and sister, 5 Nov. 1865, which expresses his new more pessimistic *Weltanschauung* and partly new view of ethics. His new view gives less emphasis to duty and more to pity and compassion:

'Perform your duty!' Good, my dear ones, I am performing them or strive to perform them, but where do they end? How do I know that everything I should do is duty? And let us assume that I live sufficiently according to duty, is the animal of burden more than the human, when it better fulfills what is expected of it [...] Or: one knows that life is suffering [...] one practices moderation, one

is meagre towards oneself and loving towards others – simply because we feel
pity with our comrades in suffering.[35]

To Deussen he writes, Feb. 1870, 'Pity will for us become a truly
intimate feeling',[36] and to Gersdorff, 18 September 1871: 'Always
emphasize through your deeds your inner agreement with the dogma
of love and pity'.[37] He frequently refers to pity in letters from this
time, and in 1875, in a letter to Gersdorff, 13 December, he for the
first time speaks of '*Mitfreude*', the feeling of joy with someone else
(still affirming *Mitleid*): 'You have the wonderful ability to feel *Mitfreude*, to me, that is even more rare and noble than that of pity'.
Later, he will play out *Mitfreude* against *Mitleid*.

After he has intellectually and philosophically rejected pity, he
will speak of his own too great ability to feel it, with statements such
as 'Pity is my weakness', 'Is pity not a feeling out of hell?' and the
whole fourth part of *Also sprach Zarathustra* deals with the danger of
pity.[38] In several letters after 1876 he emphasizes that he easily feels
pity, and that he therefore recognizes and suffers from its consequences.

With regard to the second tendency, in Nietzsche's first and most important book from this period, *The Birth of Tragedy* (1872), morality
plays a very subordinate and minor role. In the preface to the second
edition of that book from 1886 he exaggerates somewhat by emphasizing its '*antimoral* propensity' where amoral would be more true.[39]
He further justifies this claim by stating in *Ecce Homo* that: '*aesthetic*
values [are] the only values the *Birth of Tragedy* recognizes'.[40]
Expressed differently, at the time of writing *BT*, Nietzsche regarded
aesthetical values as more important and fundamental than moral
values. He states himself: 'Already in the preface addressed to
Richard Wagner, art, and *not* morality, is presented as the truly *metaphysical* activity of man. [...] Indeed, the whole book knows only an
artistic meaning and crypto meaning behind all events'.[41] This is a
position that he will return to, at least in the experimental sense, in the
notes from 1881 while writing *The Gay Science*: 'The aesthetic
judgements (taste, discomfort, revulsion etc) are the basis of our valu-
ations. These are then the basis of our moral values' and 'The beau-

tiful, the revolting etc is the older judgement [...] Reduction of the moral to the aesthetic!!!'[42]

Nietzsche's *affirmative* ethics of this period can be characterized as being constituted of essentially three strands: an aesthetic morality, an ethics of character, and a tragic ethics. These three strands are not separate but to a large extent integrated into one another. To this should be added, as discussed above, a strong Schopenhauerian influence.[43] We can note that the first of these three alternatives lies, more or less, outside the most common conventional definitions of ethics in the late 19th century. Aesthetic morality is clearly expressed in such statements as: 'for it is only as an *aesthetic phenomenon* that existence and the world are eternally *justified*'.[44] The tragic W*eltanschauung* which Nietzsche favours also implies an ethical stance: a heroic, fate accepting, partly unconscious ethics. Apart from the many descriptions of this in *BT*, this view can be exemplified by his more personal statement: 'I know of no better aim of life than that of perishing, *animae magnae prodigus*, in pursuit of the great and the impossible.'[45] Nietzsche expresses in *BT* critical views, including, though not primarily, ethical, against Socrates and Euripides for emphasizing consciousness and thereby to destroy the old tragic W*eltanschauung*.

3. A vaguely Utilitarian Period

In this period, ca 1875–80, Nietzsche emphasizes naturalism, utility, biology and survival, and pleasure and pain as important categories. He also regarded history as the principle method for understanding morality. This period is also coloured by a streak of amoralism.

Nietzsche's relation to utilitarianism changes in important ways during his life. During the early 1870s Nietzsche's ethics consists mainly of an ethics of character and an aesthetic ethics. During the middle period (1875–82) his ethics is a mixture of ethics of character, utilitarianism and immoralism. By the end of the middle period Nietzsche distances himself from utilitarianism and during the 1880s his ethics consists mainly of ethics of character and immoralism. With immoralism I primarily refer not to any affirmative ethics but to his critique of modern ethics which is prominent during both the middle and late period and not inconsistent with his ethics of character. Nietzsche's change of attitude towards utilitarianism appears not to have been noticed in the secondary literature.[46]

The early Nietzsche (ca 1869 to 1875) expresses strong critique of utilitarianism, explicitly, implicitly, and against many of its major and minor assumptions. There is only one explicit reference to utilitarianism in the published (and unpublished) writings of the early Nietzsche, but this is harshly critical:

> If, on the other hand, the doctrines of sovereign becoming, of the fluidity of all concepts, types and species, of the lack of any cardinal distinction between man and animal – doctrines which I consider true but deadly – are trust upon the people for another generation with the rage for instruction that has by now become normal, no one should be surprised if the people perish of petty egoism, ossification and greed, fall apart and cease to be a people; in its place systems of individualist egoism, brotherhoods for the rapacious exploitation of the non-brothers, and similar creations of utilitarian vulgarity may perhaps appear in the arena of the future.[47]

More implicit critique without naming utilitarianism is occasionally voiced, with critical references to the present age which is supposed to be one which continually labours for the purpose of the greatest possible common utility,[48] and to 'one theory' which holds that 'the ultimate goal is to be found in the happiness of all or of the greatest number'.[49]

The early Nietzsche strongly rejects the importance and ethical relevance of happiness. He rejects it outright, he contemptuously connects it with comfort and contentedness, and he emphasizes the importance of suffering for human development, especially for the genius and the hero. Closely related to this, the early Nietzsche also denies that there is any clear-cut distinction between pleasure and pain. He also denies that values can be determined by numbers and majority decisions. He also objects to the utilitarian emphasis on conscious rather than unconscious motives and aspects, and the closely associated theoretical and optimistic approach to culture and morality which believes in the importance of reform and its consequences. Nietzsche also rejects both the vulgar egoism which he sees in utilitarianism and altruism. Finally, he denies that it is consequences of actions which determine moral values.

Nietzsche's development in going from the early to the middle period is often characterized by a change from a somewhat idealistic and romantic stance to a more positivistic and Enlightenment-inspired position. Another, and probably better, way to describe this is to stress that Nietzsche's main concern continues to be culture, but his earlier emphasis on its aesthetical aspects is now exchanged for a greater interest in morality and a more scientific approach. Essentially unaffected by the change is Nietzsche's ethics of character and his relation to antiquity, but as we shall see below, he now combines it with an utilitarian approach instead of an aesthetic one. This utilitarian tendency is prevalent in the first three books of *HH* (1878–80). In *D* (1881), after having read Mill and Spencer, Nietzsche moves away from utilitarianism and by the *GS* (1882) he has again become as hard a critic of utilitarianism as he was in the early period, if not harsher. This change is also reflected in Nietzsche's views of utilitarian thinkers. His praise of the earliest utilitarian thinker, Helvétius, is noteworthy:

> What is the whole of German moral philosophy from Kant onwards, with all its French, English and Italian branches and parallels? A semi-theological assault on Helvetius and a rejection of the open views or signposts to the right path which, gained by long and wearisome struggle, he at least assembled and gave adequate expression to. Helvetius is in Germany to the present day the most reviled of all good moralists and good men.[50]

This view is echoed as late as in 1885, when he claims in two notes that Helvétius and utilitarianism is 'the *last great event in morals*,' better than the German alternatives à la Kant and Schopenhauer with their 'duty' and 'pity', but he is nonetheless critical of this approach stating that an emphasis on pleasure is fundamentally typical of a herd morality.[51] Nietzsche also had high positive expectations of Mill and Spencer *before* he read them in 1880.

One fundamental strand of utilitarianism which Nietzsche accepts in *HH* is the belief that the sole ground for human actions, motives and values is pleasure and pain. This can be exemplified by Nietzsche's statement: 'All 'evil' acts are motivated by the drive to preservation or, more exactly, by the individual's intention of procuring pleasure and avoiding displeasure'[52] and 'without pleasure no life; the struggle for pleasure is the struggle for life'.[53] Nietzsche will leave this view when he discovers and elaborates on 'will to power' between 1880 and 1883. The other major utilitarian strand which Nietzsche accepts at this time is that of the ultimate importance of utility. This can be exemplified by: 'Knowledge can allow as motives only pleasure and pain, utility and injury'[54] and 'it is only from the standpoint of *utility*, narrower and wider, that work can be evaluated'.[55] Nietzsche's affirmation of some important utilitarian traits seems thus to be both descriptive and normative. At this time Nietzsche also seems to accept the idea of progress, both generally and for the case of morality. 'To us, however, the very *existence* of the temperate zone of culture counts as progress.'[56] The idea of progress is, of course, something which the later Nietzsche strongly attacks.

Of special interest is Nietzsche's view on the genealogy and origin of morality. He begins to discuss this in the first volume of *HH* and the discussion reaches a crescendo in *GM*. In *HH* Nietzsche sees the origin of ethics in social utility: 'Such actions, whose basic motive, that of utility, has been *forgotten*, are then called *moral* actions [...] Thus it comes to appear that morality has *not* grown out of utility; while it is originally social utility'.[57] However, simultaneously he holds the view that good and evil has a twofold prehistory, in that of the rulers and in that of the ruled. This latter view is the view he will retain and it will be known as his concept of master and slave morality. The former view he begins to question in *D* and outright rejects in the *GS* and even more so in *GM*.[58]

Nietzsche makes no explicit references to utilitarianism (nor to eudaemonism or hedonism which often are used as synonyms to utilitarianism by Nietzsche) in the three separate volumes of *HH* and hence we do not have any explicit approval of utilitarianism by him. There is also no mention of these concepts in his notebooks of this period. Furthermore, he makes no references in *HH* 'the greatest numbers' and '*laissez-faire*' which he often associates with utilitarianism. This is probably the reason that his utilitarian tendency during these years has been observed by so few commentators. When he refers to utilitarianism in *D* his first reference is neutral and his second slightly critical.[59] His references to utilitarianism in his notebooks from 1880 and onwards are critical.[60] From the *GS* and onwards his references become clearly critical.[61]

I have not found any explicit references to utilitarianism, eudaemonism, and hedonism in the letters written at this time. What we can note for this period, 1875–80, is the absence of explicit critique of utilitarianism, in contrast to earlier and later, and an acceptance of some of its fundamental assumptions (naturalism, the primacy of pleasure and pain, utility, the idea of progress and the belief that the origin of morality was social utility).

The fact that Nietzsche does not explicitly express his at least partial allegiance to utilitarianism at this time can be a reflection of his earlier harsh critique which would make such a step more difficult to take, but it can also be a reflection of the fact that he also still affirms an ethics of character and heroic morality which to a large extent is incompatible with utilitarianism, and because there are many strands of utilitarianism which Nietzsche does not accept even at this time. He never accepts happiness as of ultimate importance and in a critical spirit, he often associates it with comfort and contentment.[62] Although Nietzsche regards utility as of outmost importance at this time, he explicitly denies that what is useful is also necessarily true.[63] Furthermore, Nietzsche rejects altruism and sympathy, accountability, punishment, equality, the belief that numbers can determine value, and more generally abstractions and generalizations.

One circumstantial way which points to Nietzsche's more positive valuation of utilitarianism during this period is his close friendship with Paul Rée, who was positive towards utilitarianism. Another is Nietzsche's generally favourable view of the 'English' and of 'English thinking' at this time. It has not generally been noticed that in the period 1875 to 1879/80 Nietzsche had such a positive view of English thinking. This is relevant for his view of ethics, for he, and many others during the nineteenth century, regarded utilitarianism as typically 'English'. Nietzsche's reading of British–American texts then became wide and affected his general attitude towards the British. He also began to read British–American fictional literature, e.g. Walter Scott, Fielding, Swift, Sterne, Longfellow's poetry and American humorous authors (especially Mark Twain).

It is possible that this sympathy and reading of British–American texts influenced his break with Schopenhauer, Wagner, Kant and his earlier idealistic thinking. Nietzsche continued to read a fairly large number of British–American books with interest and sympathy in the following years and it seems likely that the British–American influence was important not only for the breach (or during the breach) but also for reinforcing Nietzsche's positivistic thinking throughout his middle period, at least until 1880/81.[64]

Under the influence of Paul Rée, Nietzsche was during 1876 pushed further in his affiliation to naturalism, positivism and Darwinism. For a while he seems even to have adopted a view closely related to positivism. In several notes from 1877 he writes: 'Positivism completely necessary',[65] 'Not to shy away from a temporary coarsening (through the supremacy of natural science, mechanics)',[66] and 'Necessary, to take in me the whole of positivism, and yet to remain a carrier of idealism (preface)'.[67] At this time he begins to express increasingly pro-British sympathies.

> The most favourable time for a people to become leaders in scientific matters, is that, in which enough power, toughness, firmness, has been inherited by the individual to enable him a victorious and happy isolation from public opinion: This time has now again arrived in England, which is at present undeniably ahead of all other peoples in philosophy, natural science, history, in the fields of discovery and of cultural dissemination. The great scientific minds negotiate with one another as kings, who all regard themselves as related, but recognize each other's independence.[68]

In 1877, Nietzsche, in a letter to Rée from early August, referred to British philosophers and thinkers as 'the only philosophically good company which exist at present'. In the same positive spirit he writes another letter to Rée two years later, at the end of July 1879, saying: 'Could you send me an informative book, if possible of English origin, but translated into German and with clear and large print?' A year earlier, Nietzsche had ordered the *Brockhaus* book-catalogue especially for the purpose of finding German translations of French and English books. In *Assorted Opinions and Maxims* (1879), section 184, entitled 'How natural history should be narrated' Nietzsche praises the British for being the best at discussing science:

> Up to now it [natural history] has not yet discovered its proper language [...]
> Nonetheless, it must be allowed that the English have taken admirable steps in
> the direction of that ideal with their natural science textbooks for the lower
> strata of the people: the reason is that they are written by their most dis-
> tinguished scholars – whole, complete and fulfilling natures – and not, as is the
> case with us, by mediocrities.

Nietzsche seems also to have begun to read Mill, Spencer and
Lecky in 1880/1881 with positive expectations, but these expectations,
partly under the influence of French thinkers and literary critics, were
quickly disappointed and Nietzsche turned strongly against the British.

Nietzsche's naturalism and historical relativism during this period
leads to a sense of amoralism. He rejects the importance, or even the
relevance, of motives and intentions for morality. We have no free
will and hence we have no moral responsibility. 'The complete unaccountability of man for his actions and his nature is the bitterest
draught the man of knowledge has to swallow'.[69] He also argues that
man is an animal and part of the natural world in which there is no
morality: 'the modern age [...] has for the first time demolished the
ancient walls between nature and spirit, man and animal, morality and
the physical world'.[70]

Moral principles, even relativistic moral principles, assume or
presuppose moral opposites, presuppose good and evil things, thoughts
and deeds. Nietzsche, however, rejects the belief in moral opposites.
'Between good and evil actions there is no difference in kind, but at
the most one of degree. Good actions are sublimated evil ones; evil
actions are coarsened, brutalized good ones.'[71]

4. A Period of Amoralism

The period of amoralism is characterized by a severe critique of
morality, especially utilitarianism and deontology (Kant), ca 1880–84.
During the period 1880–82 Nietzsche seems to have read and been
fairly strongly influenced by Stoic moral thinking (and, in line with

his approach of self-overcoming, he later expresses severe critique of it).

There is in Nietzsche's critique of morality a sense of fatalism – things could not be different. He writes: 'let us beware of saying that there are laws in nature. There are only necessities: there is nobody who commands, nobody who obeys, nobody who trespasses.'[72] To this aspect of Nietzsche's rejection of morality can be included his attempt to reduce morality to physiology, which is a common theme in his writings from this time onwards. For example, his references to 'the *physiological* phenomena behind the moral predispositions and prejudices'.[73] One consequence of Nietzsche's belief that the universe is all connected and determined by laws (necessities) is that to want anything different is to want everything different (cf. Nietzsche's *amor fati* and the idea of the eternal recurrence).

At least by the time of writing *D* he also rejects an emphasis on consequences of acts as the motive of acts, by now he also begins to regard utilitarianism as an echo of Christianity and he begins more or less explicitly to criticize utilitarianism again. By the *GS* such critique, both general and specific, becomes frequent and harsh,[74] and there-after it will increase further.

5. A Period of Immoralism

Here we have a further radicalization of the previous period, ca 1885–88. During this period, Nietzsche argues that we cannot know the con-sequences of actions, nor the motives behind those actions, he denies free will, he denies moral opposites and he believes that man is part of nature, and that in the natural world there is no morality. Nietzsche does not only reject specific presuppositions of morality, but fre-quently also rejects the whole concept of morality as being an error, a fatal error. 'Thus I deny morality as I deny alchemy, that is, I deny their premises'[75] and Nietzsche calls Zarathustra 'the annihilator of morality.'[76] In *Twilight of the Idols* Nietzsche summarizes much of what he has stated previously about morality:

> One knows my demand of philosophers that they place themselves *beyond* good
> and evil – that they have the illusion of moral judgement *beneath* them. This
> demand follows from an insight first formulated by me: *that there are no moral
> facts whatever.* Moral judgement has this in common with religious judgement
> that it believes in realities which do not exist. Morality is only an interpretation
> of certain phenomena, more precisely a *mis*interpretation.[77]

In *Ecce Homo* Nietzsche shows his contempt of morality by stating:
'*Definition of morality*: morality – the idiosyncrasy of *décadents* with
the hidden intention of *revenging themselves on life – and* successfully. I set store by *this* definition. – '[78] In the next, and penultimate
section of the book Nietzsche writes 'all this was believed in *as
morality! – Ecrasez l'infâme! – '*, that is, destroy morality. Typical of
the late Nietzsche is also his severe critique of Christian morality.

One of the most interesting aspects of the late Nietzsche's immoralism is his claim that our moral evaluations should not be
regarded as true, but as symptoms of our values and character ('moralities too are only a *sign-language of the emotions*'),[79] really only
symptoms of the underlying character. In still more general language,
Nietzsche states that he attempts 'to understand moral judgements as
symptoms and sign language which betray the processes of physiological prosperity or failure.'[80] A consequence of this is that morality
and virtue are for Nietzsche not so much questions of normative statements as of interest as signs of character, as sympto-matology.[81] When
other moral philosophers discuss a particular morality or moral problem they typically emphasize the intentions of acts or the results of
acts. Nietzsche's immediate instinct is to treat the morality as a symptom and use it to make a diagnosis of the creator or supporter of that
morality.

The concept and word immoralism characterizes much of the late
Nietzsche's view of ethics. He began using it extensively in 1885, and
it signifies a clearly positive concept for him: 'we good Europeans'
are 'atheists and immoralists'.[82] Thereafter he would frequently refers
to himself, and those like him, as immoralists. In *EH* Nietzsche explains what he means by this:

> At bottom my expression *immoralist* involves two denials. I deny first a type of
> man who has hitherto counted as the highest, the *good*, the *benevolent,*

beneficient; I deny secondly a kind of morality which has come to be accepted and to dominate as morality in itself – *décadence* morality, in more palpable terms *Christian* morality. The second contradiction might be seen as the decisive one, since the over-valuation of goodness and benevolence by and large already counts with me as a consequence of *décadence*, as a symptom of weakness, as incompatible with an ascending and affirmative life: denial *and destruction* is a condition of affirmation. [...] No one has yet felt *Christian* morality as *beneath* him.[83]

Closely related to immoralism is the concept and expression 'beyond good and evil', which, after all, is almost a synonym to it. Nietzsche writes down this expression for the first time when he read Emerson's *Essays* during the autumn 1881 (in the margin of the book), and begins to use it in 1882 and 1883, to later use it as the title of his most philosophical book (1886).

References:
For a general bibliography of Nietzsche's work in German and English see end of volume.

Notes

1   That this relates to Nietzsche's own development is still more clear in an early draft, KSA 14, 140f. In this earlier draft Nietzsche writes in the form of 'we' instead of 'they', i.e. the note then began: 'We at present begin [...] our [...] [etc.]'. He even went so far as to write a note in 1877, intended to be included in his next book, where he rejects his earlier writings: 'I want expressly to inform the readers of my earlier writings [i.e. *The Birth of Tragedy* and the *Untimely Meditations*] that I have abandoned the metaphysical-artistic views which fundamentally govern them: they are pleasant but untenable. He who speaks publicly early is usually quickly forced to publicly retract his statements'. KSA 8, 23[159], written between the end of 1876 and the summer of 1877.) KSA is the conventional abbreviation for *Friedrich Nietzsche: Kritische Studienausgabe*, 15 volumes, edited by G. Colli and M. Montinari, 1967–80. Volume 14 is a commentary volume. KSB is the abbreviation for the corresponding eight volumes of Nietzsche's letters, by the same editors. These letters have not been translated into English (except a small selection by

Middleton, see below). I refer to Nietzsche's letter by recipient and date, which means that they can easily be identified since they are published in chronological order in KSB.

KSA does not contain Nietzsche's writings before he became a professor in Basel in 1869. This material has been published in: *Friedrich Nietzsche: Frühe Schriften*, München, C.E. Beck'sche Verlag, 1933–40, reprinted 1994, 5 vols, abbreviated BAW (followed by volume and page numbers).

2   I use the terms morality and ethics as essentially equivalent.

3   I have discussed the first four periods in 'Nietzsche's Changing Relation to Christianity: Nietzsche as Christian, Atheist and Antichrist', in *Nietzsche and the Gods* edited by Weaver Santaniello, New York, 2001, pp. 137–57 and the last period in 'Nietzsche's Atheism' in *Nietzsche and the Divine*, edited by James Urpeth and John Lippitt, Manchester, 2000, pp. 1–13.

4   In fact, I had constructed the division before I realized Nietzsche's discussion in the preface of *On the Genealogy of Morals*.

5   *GM*, Preface, 3.

6   KGW I.2, 5[16]: '*De libertate / Freiheit? / Heiden. Sklaven / Gott nicht gut nicht böse / erhaben über menschliche Begriffe / De voluntatis libertate / Vorherbestimmung? / Unbeschränkte Macht Gottes? / De dei libertate.*'

7   KGW I.2, 13[6+7]. See also KGW I.2, 12[27+30] and the previously unpublished KGW I.2, 13[5].

8   *GM*, Preface, 3.

9   *D*, Preface, 2.

10   *EH*, Dawn, 1 and 2.

11   *GM*, Preface, 2.

12   *HH* I, 107.

13   For example, Nietzsche writes: '*Indem ich über die Mittel nachsann, den Menschen stärker und tiefer zu machen als er bisher war […] Drittens ehrte ich die Philologen und Historiker, welche die Entdeckung des Alterthums fortsetzten, weil in der alten Welt eine andere Moral geherrscht hat als heute und in der That der Mensch damals unter dem Banne seiner Moral stärker böser und tiefer war: die Verführung, welche vom Alterthum her auf stärkere Seelen ausgeübt wird, ist wahrscheinlich die feinste und unmerklichste aller Verführungen.*' KSA 11, 34[176]

14   I have previously argued this case in my book *Nietzsche's Ethics of Character: A Study of Nietzsche's Ethics and its Place in the History of Moral Thinking*, Uppsala, 1995, and in the article 'Nietzsche's Affirmative Morality: An Ethics of Virtue', *Journal of Nietzsche Studies* 26 (2003), pp. 64–78.

15   Compare also his discussion of self-overcoming in *Jenseits von Gut und Böse*, 61 and 224. See also KSA 9, 7[219] and *Der Fall Wagner*, Vorrede, 1.

16   KSA 10, 4[13] and KSA 11, 25[178], '*Selbstüberwindung üben*'.

17   KSA 11, 27[4], summer–autumn 1884. '*Die Selbstüberwindung, welche der Forscher auf dem Gebiete der Moral von sich fordert, ist die, nicht vorein-*

genommen gegen Zustände und Handlungen zu sein, die er zu verehren
angelernt ist; er muß, solange er Forscher ist "sein verehrendes Herz zer-
brochen haben".'

18   BAW 2, 142f., Nov. 1862: *'Nachts wollte ich lateinische Arbeit machen, kam*
aber mit Stöckert in ein Gespräch über den moralischen Einfluß der Kunst oder
mehr über das Verhältniß von Kunst und Moral. Sprachen bis 2 Nachts. Zuletzt
noch Einiges über unsre Herzenssituationen'.

19   The relevant German text in full is: *Nichts ist verkehrter als alle Reue über*
Vergangenes, nehme man es wie es ist, ziehe man sich Lehren daraus, aber lebe
man ruhig weiter, betrachte man sich als ein Phänomen, dessen einzelne Züge
ein Ganzes bilden. Gegen die andern sei man nachsichtig, bedaure sie
höchstens, lasse sich nie ärgern über sie, man sei nie begeistert für jemand, alle
sind nur für uns selbst da, unsern Zwecken zu dienen. Wer am besten zu
herrschen 'versteht', der wird auch immer der beste Manschenkenner sein.
Jede That der Notwendigkeit ist gerechtfertigt, jede That notwendig, die
nützlich ist. Unmoralisch ist jede That, die nicht notwendig dem Andern Not
bereitet; wir sind selber sehr abhängig von der öffentlichen Meinung, sobald
wir Reue empfinden und an uns selbst verzweifeln. Wenn eine unmoralische
Handlung notwendig ist, so ist sie moralisch für uns. Alle Handlungen können
nur Folgen unsrer Triebe ohne Vernunft, unsrer Vernunft ohne Triebe und
unsrer Vernunft und Triebe zugleich sein. BAW 2, 143.

20   BAW 2, 257–61, July 1863.

21   BAW 2, 221, July 1863. This may well have been part of his plan to write his
final essay on comparing ancient and modern literature.

22   BAW 2, 369, April–May 1864 and BAW 3, 15 and 69.

23   The importance of conscience and duty for the young Nietzsche's ethics is
perhaps more visible in the next period, when we see what views he leaves. For
duty, see his letter to mother and sister immediately after having discovered
Schopenhauer in early November 1865 (quoted below). For the importance of
conscience, see his statement in 1868, when he already had gone beyond it, that
an act is not necessary, already the thought (even the character) is enough to be
regarded philosophically as a murderer (briefly discussed below).

24   In a letter from 1865, Elisabeth complains to Nietzsche that he had told her so
much about 'that unfortunate Strauss' during the Easter holiday.

25   Already before Christmas 1861 Nietzsche planned to wish for, or wanted to
acquire, an unidentified book which Gustav Krug refers to in a letter to
Nietzsche as 'that dangerous book'. This may have been Feuerbach's *Das*
Wesen des Christenthum.

26   The essay 'Fatum und Geschichte' begins with the words: *'Wenn wir mit*
freiem, unbefangenem Blick die christliche Lehre und Kirchengeschichte an-
schauen könnten, so würden wir manche den allgemeinen Ideen widerstrebende
Ansichten aussprechen müssen.' Later he writes: *'es stehen noch grosse*
Umwälzungen bevor, wenn die Menge erst begriffen hat, dass das ganze

Christenthum sich auf Annahmen gründet; die Existenz Gottes, Unsterblichkeit, Bibelautorität, Inspiration and anderes werden immer Probleme bleiben. Ich habe alles zu leugnen versucht: o, niederreissen ist leicht, aber aufbauen! [...] der Zweifel, ob nicht zweitausend Jahre schon die Menschheit durch ein Trugbild irre geleitet.' BAW 2, p. 54f.

In the letter, Nietzsche writes: 'First when we recognize that we are only responsible to ourselves, that a reproach over a failed direction in life only relates to us, not to any higher power [...] Christianity is essentially a question of the heart [...] The main teachings of Christianity only relate the fundamental truths of the human heart; they are symbols [...] To become blessed through faith means nothing other than the old truth, that only the heart, not knowledge, can make one happy. That God became human only shows that humans should not seek their blessedness in eternity, but instead found their paradise on the earth; the delusion of an otherworldly world has brought the human spirit into a false relation to this world: it was the product of a peoples childhood. [...] It [humanity] recognizes in it "the beginning, the middle, the end of religion".'

27 Elisabeth Förster-Nietzsche, *Der junge Nietzsche*, p. 28f.

28 Nietzsche among others writes: '*Zu Grunde liegt der ungeheure Denkfehler Theismus und Moralität zu identificiren oder überhaupt die Moral abhängig zu machen von der Anschauung, die man von Gott hat.*' KGW I.4, 35[1] and 36[1]. See my forthcoming article '*Beiträge zur Quellenforschung*', Nietzsche-Studien 34 (2005) where I have shown that 35[1] is an excerpt from *Zeitstimmen aus der reformirten Kirche der Schweiz, herausgegeben unter Mitwirkung schweizerischer Theologen von H. Lang, evangelischer Pfarrer in Wartau*, Zweiter Jahrgang, Winterthur, 1860.

29 KGW I.4, 57[18].

30 KGW I.4, 57[48].

31 KGW I.4, 56[2].

32 KGW I.4, 56[3]. 'The drive to act morally is there: one should, however, not make it conscious.'

33 KGW I.4, 57[26].

34 KGW I.4, 61[13+14].

35 The relevant German text in full is: '*Thue Deine Pflicht!' Gut, meine Verehrten, ich thue sie oder strebe danach sie zu thun, aber wo endet sie? Woher weiss ich denn das alles, was mir zu erfüllen Pflicht ist? Und setzen wir den Fall, ich lebte nach der Pflicht zur Genüge, ist denn das Lastthier mehr als der Mensch, wenn es genauer als dieser das erfüllt, was man von ihm fordert? Hat man damit seiner Menschheit genug gethan, wenn man die Forderungen der Verhältnisse, in die hinein wir geboren sind, befriedigt? Wer heisst uns denn uns von den Verhaeltnissen bestimmen zu lassen? Aber wenn wir dies nun nicht wollten, wenn wir uns entschlössen, nur auf uns zu achten und die Menschen zu zwingen uns wie wir nun sind anzuerkennen, was dann? Was wollen wir denn dann? Gilt es, ein möglichst erträgliches Dasein sich zu*

*zimmern? Zwei Wege, meine Lieben: man bemüht sich und gewöhnt sich daran
so beschränkt wie möglich zu sein und hat man dann seines Geistes Docht so
niedrig wir möglich geschraubt, so sucht man sich Reichthümer und lebt mit
den Vergnügungen der Welt. Oder: man weiss dass das Leben elend ist, man
weiss, dass wir die Sklaven des Lebens sind, je mehr wir es geniessen wollen,
also man entäussert sich der Güter des Lebens, man übt sich in der
Enthaltsamkeit, man ist karg gegen sich und liebevoll gegen all Anderen –
deshalb weil wir mitleidig gegen die Genossen des Elends sind – kurz, man lebt
nach den strengen Forderungen des ursprünglichen Christenthums, nicht des
jetzigen, süsslichen, verschwommenen. Das Christenthum lässt sich nicht
'mitmachen' so en passant oder weil es Mode ist.*

36   '*Mitleid wird uns eine wahrhaft vertraute Empfindung [...] dem einzelnen
        Menschen gegenüber seien wir mitleidig und nachgebend*'.

37   '*der großen Dunkelheit des Daseins, hier das eigentliche Bereich des Mit-
        leidens ist. Betone nur immer durch die That Deine innerste Übereinstimmung
        mit dem Dogma der Liebe und des Mitleidens – das ist die feste Brücke, die
        auch über solche Klüfte geschlagen werden kann*'.

38   Draft of letter to unknown recipient, possibly Salome, end of Nov. 1882:
        '*Mitleid meine schwache Partie*'. Letter to Rée and Salome, near 20 Dec. 1882:
        '*Ist nicht Mitleid ein Gefühl aus der Hölle?*'.

39   Compare also: 'It was *against* morality that my instinct turned with this
        questionable book, long ago; it was an instinct that aligned itself with life and
        that discovered for itself a fundamentally opposite doctrine and valuation of life
        – purely artistic and *anti-Christian*.' *The Birth of Tragedy*, Preface to second
        edition, section 5, (Aug. 1886).

40   *EH* TI, 1.

41   *BT*, Attempt at a Self-Criticism, 5. Compare also his discussion of *The Birth of
        Tragedy* in KSA 9, 12[220]: '*Geburt der Tragödie 1) gegen Wagner's Satz'die
        Musik ist Mittel zum Zweck' und zugleich Apologie meines Geschmacks an
        Wagner, 2. gegen Schopenhauer und die moralische Deutung des Daseins – ich
        stelle darüber die aesthetische, ohne die moralische zu leugnen oder zu ändern*'.

42   KSA 9, 11[78+79].

43   In a short two-page text entitles 'About Ethics' from 1868 Nietzsche describes
        his and Schopenhauer's ethics as not very normative. He also makes the anti-
        utilitarian statement that: 'From a philosophical point of view it is indifferent if
        a character expresses itself or if this expression is suppressed; it is not first the
        thought, no, already the constitution makes a murderer, he is guilty without
        deed. On the other hand, there exists an ethical aristocracy, just as there exists a
        spiritual one.' Friedrich Nietzsche, *Gesammelte Werke*, Musarion edition. Vol.
        1, p. 404.

44   *BT* 5. This remark is repeated in section 24.

45   *UM* II, 9. The words in Latin means 'careless of life'.

46 Surprisingly, there seems to be no full-length study of Nietzsche's relation to utilitarianism. However, in general works on Nietzsche's philosophy, his critique of utilitarianism is often mentioned without noticing that he for a time was closely affiliated to it himself. This is true for, for example, Kaufmann, Detwiler, Strong and Nehamas.

47 *UM* II, 9.

48 *UM* II, 7.

49 'According to one theory, the ultimate goal is to be found in the happiness of all or of the greatest number. [...] (Nietzsche descriptively states that men find it easier to sacrifice themselves for a community or the greatest number than for an individual.) As though it were more reasonable to let numbers decide when matters of value and meaning are the issue! The real question is surely this: In what way is your life least wasted? Surely only by your living for the benefit of the rarest and most valuable specimens, not for that majority which, considered as individuals, is the least valuable.' *UM* III, 6.

50 *HH* III, 216. Compare also KSA 8, 30[188] and 34[10] from 1878, where Nietzsche also approves of Helvetius as an ethical thinker.

51 KSA 11, 34[39] and 34[239], April–June 1885.

52 *HH* I, 99. This is repeated in similar words in *HH* I, 102: 'But these two points of view *suffice* to explain all evil acts perpetrated by men against men: one desires pleasure or to ward off displeasure; it is always in some sense a matter of self-preservation.'

53 *HH* I, 104. Compare *HH* I, 18: 'At the bottom of all belief there lies the *sensation of the pleasurable or painful* in respect to the subject experiencing the sensation [...] In our primary condition, all that interests us organic beings in any thing is its relationship to us in respect of pleasure and pain'. Other examples can be found in *HH* I, 34, 97 & 98; *HH* III, 12, 23 and *D* 104.

54 *HH* I, 34.

55 *HH* III, 286. Other examples can be found in *HH* I, 93, 95 and 97; *HH* II, 26, 101 and 364; *HH* III, 40, 190, 212 and 292 and KSA 8, 29[7].

56 *HH*, I, 236. Compare also: '*Wrath and punishment has had its time.* – Wrath and punishment is a present to us from the animal world. Man will have come of age only when he returns this birthday gift to the animals. – Here there lies buried one of the greatest ideas mankind can have, the idea of progress to excel all progress. – Let us go forward a few thousand years together, my friends! There is a *great deal* of joy still reserved for mankind of which men of the present day have not had so much as a scent! And we may promise ourselves this joy, indeed testify that it must necessarily come to us, only provided that the evolution of human reason *does not stand still!*' *HH* III, 183. Other examples can be found in *HH* I, 24 and 107; *HH* II, 184 and 185.

57 *HH*, III, 40. Other examples can be found in *HH* I, 39 and *HH* III, 44 and 57.

58 *D* 37 and *GS* 4.

59 *D* 230 and *D* 360 (The Greeks preferred power to utility).

60 I have found four references to utilitarianism in the notebooks covering the period 1880–82 (KSA 9). These are all critical; KSA 9, 11[50+106] and 15[15+69]. I have found no reference to *eudaemonism* in these notes.

61 *GS* 84: '[...] the utilitarians. After all, they are right so rarely that it is really pitiful.'

62 *HH* I, 235, 277 and 471. *D* 106, 108 and 429. See also KSA 14, p. 210 (5 clear points). However, for a time Nietzsche associates happiness with power and with his 'discovery' of will to power. Slowly he begins to clearly distinguish between happiness and will to power. But for a time this means that happiness can appear as an ultimate value. For a discussion of this, see W. Kaufmann, *Nietzsche: Philosopher, Psychologist, Antichrist*, Part III, Nietzsche's Philosophy of Power, p. 9. Power versus Pleasure, pp. 257–83.

63 *HH* I, 227.

64 I discuss Nietzsche's knowledge, reading and attitude towards British and American thinking and culture in a forthcoming monograph, *Nietzsche and the 'English'*.

65 KSA 8, 20[19], winter 1876/77: '*Positivismus ganz nothwendig*'.

66 KSA 8, 22[14].

67 KSA 8, 22[37].

68 KSA 8, 23[170], from the end of 1876 to the summer of 1877.

69 *HH* I, 107.

70 *HH* II, 185.

71 *HH* I, 107 and *WP*, 47+351

72 *GS* 109.

73 *D* 542.

74 The critique is visible from *GS* 4, 12, 21, 84 and onwards.

75 *D* 103. See also, for example; *D*, 3, 9, 14, 563. Much of the first part of *D* deals with the problem of morality.

76 *EH*, Why I Write Such Excellent Books, 1.

77 *TI*, The 'Improvers' of Mankind, 1.

78 *EH*, Why I am a Destiny, 7.

79 *BGE* 187.

80 *WP*, 258.

81 *TI*, The 'Improvers' of Mankind, 1 and *WP* 257: morality is: 'a fruit by which I recognize the *soil* from which it sprang'.

82 KSA 11, 34[205].

83 *EH*, Why I am a Destiny, 4 and 6.

Notes on Contributors

REBECCA BAMFORD is Post-Doctoral Fellow at the Center for Humanistic Inquiry at Emory University, Atlanta. In addition to Nietzsche, her research interests include the Philosophy of Mind and Psychology, African Philosophy and Post-colonialism.

THOMAS BROBJER is Associate Professor of Intellectual History at the University of Uppsala. He has published widely on various aspects of Nietzsche, including the study *Nietzsche's Ethics of Character* (1995).

CAROL DIETHE, formerly Reader in History of Ideas at Middlesex University, is translator of Nietzsche's *On the Genealogy of Morality*, (1994/2006). She is author of *Historical Dictionary of Nietzscheanism* (1999/2007); *Nietzsche's Women: Beyond the Whip* (1996); and *Nietzsche's Sister and the Will to Power* (2003). Her publications on feminist issues include *Towards Emancipation: German Women Writers in the Nineteenth Century* (1998) and a biography of Germany's founding feminist, Louise Otto-Peters (2002). Diethe is a founding member of the Friedrich Nietzsche Society and is also very interested in environmental issues.

KEN GEMES is Lecturer in Philosophy at Birkbeck College, University of London. His many publications are in the field of Philosophy of Science as well as Nietzsche, and he also has research interests in Freud and 19th century Degeneration Theory.

ROBERT GUAY is Assistant Professor of Philosophy at Binghamton University. He has published on Nietzsche and also does research work on Value Theory and the History of 19th century Philosophy.

EDWARD HARCOURT is Lecturer in Philosophy at the University of Oxford and Fellow of Keble College, Oxford. Currently his main research interests are in Ethics, particularly Meta-ethics, Moral Psychology, and connections between Aristotelian ethical thinking and psychoanalysis. He has also published on the Philosophy of Logic and Language and on Wittgenstein.

HERMAN SIEMENS is Assistant Professor in Modern Philosophy at the University of Leiden. He has published on Nietzsche and, together with other leading Nietzsche scholars, has been working since 1998 on the ongoing Nietzsche Dictionary project, the first volume of which appeared in 2004.

ROBIN SMALL is Associate Professor of Philosophy at the University of Auckland. He is author of *Nietzsche in Context* (2001), *Nietzsche and Paul Rée: A Star Friendship* (2005), and is editor and translator of *Paul Rée, Basic Writings* (2003).

HENRY STATEN is Professor of English and Comparative Literature and Adjunct Professor of Philosophy at the University of Washington. He is author of *Wittgenstein and Derrida* (1984), *Nietzsche's Voice* (1990), and *Eros in Mourning: Homer to Lacan* (1995).

GUDRUN VON TEVENAR is Hon Fellow and Tutor in Philosophy at Birkbeck College, University of London. She has published on Kantian Ethics. Her philosophical interests are the moral philosophies of Kant, Schopenhauer and Nietzsche.

JAMES WILSON is Lecturer in Ethics at the University of Keele. His work crosses moral theory and practical ethics and focuses on the theory and practice of equality.

General Bibliography

Friedrich Nietzsche in German:

Werke in drei Bänden, Karl Schlechta (ed.), Carl Hanser Verlag, Muenchen, 1966.

Kritische Gesamtausgabe, Giorgio Colli and Mazzino Montinari (eds.), Walter de Gruyter, Berlin, 2nd edition 1988.

Kritische Studienausgabe in 15 Bänden, Giorgio Colli and Mazzino Montinari (eds.), de Gruyter and Deutscher Taschenbuch Verlag, 1999.

Sämtliche Briefe: Kritische Studienausgabe in 8 Bänden, Giorgio Colli and Mazzino Montinari (eds.), de Gruyter and Deutscher Taschenbuch Verlag, 1986.

Friedrich Nietzsche in English:

The Antichrist, trans. W. Kaufmann, in 'The Portable Nietzsche' W. Kaufmann (ed.), Viking Penguin, New York, 1982.

Beyond Good and Evil, trans. W. Kaufmann, Vintage, New York, 1966.

The Birth of Tragedy (with *The Case of Wagner*), trans. W. Kaufmann, New York, 1967.

The Birth of Tragedy out of the Spirit of Music, trans. Shaun Whiteside, Michael Tanner (ed.), Penguin Books, 1993.

The Case of Wagner (with *The Birth of Tragedy*), trans. W, Kaufmann, New York, 1967.

Daybreak, Thoughts on the Prejudices of Morality, trans. R.J. Hollingdale, Maudemarie Clark and Brian Leiter (eds.), Cambridge Texts in the History of Philosophy, Cambridge University Press 1997.

Ecce Homo, trans. W. Kaufmann (with *On the Genealogy of Morals*, trans. W. Kaufmann and R.J. Hollingdale). New York, Vintage, 1967.

The Gay Science, trans. W. Kaufmann, New York, Vintage, 1974.

The Gay Science, trans. J. Nauckhoff, B. Willimas (ed.), Cambridge Texts in the History of Philosophy, Cambridge University Press, 2001.

Human, All Too Human, trans. R.J. Hollingdale, introduction by R. Schacht, Cambridge Texts in the History of Philosophy, Cambridge University Press, 1986.

Nietzsche contra Wagner, trans. W. Kaufmann, in the *Portable Nietzsche*, Kaufmann (ed.), New York, Viking, 1982.

On the Genealogy of Morals, trans. W. Kaufmann and R.J. Hollingdale (with *Ecce Homo*, trans. W. Kaufmann), New York, Vintage, 1967.

On the Genealogy of Morality, trans. Maudemarie Clark & Alan J. Swensen, introduction by Maudemarie Clark, Hackett, Indianapolis, 1998.

On Truth and Lying in a Nonmoral Sense, trans. Ronald Speirs (with *The Birth of Tragedy and Other Writings*) Raymond Geuss & Ronald Speirs (eds.), Cambridge University Press 1999.

Thus Spoke Zarathustra, trans. W. Kaufmann, in *The Portable Nietzsche*, W. Kaufmann (ed.), New York, Viking, 1982.

Thus Spoke Zarathustra, trans. A.D. Caro, A.D. Caro and R.B. Pippin (eds.), Cambridge Texts in the History of Philosophy, Cambridge University Press, 2006.

Twilight of the Idols, trans. W. Kaufmann, in 'The Portable Nietzsche', W. Kaufmann (ed.), Viking Penguin, New York, 1982.

Untimely Meditations, trans. R.J. Hollingdale, Daniel Breazeale (ed.), Cambridge Texts in the History of Philosophy, Cambridge University Press, 1983.

The Will to Power, trans. W. Kaufmann and R.J. Hollingdale, Vintage, New York, 1968.

Index